ENGLISH WITNESSES
OF THE
FRENCH REVOLUTION

English Witnesses
of the
French Revolution

Edited by

J. M. THOMPSON

KENNIKAT PRESS, INC./PORT WASHINGTON, N. Y.

ENGLISH WITNESSES OF THE FRENCH REVOLUTION

First published in 1938
Reissued in 1970 by Kennikat Press
Library of Congress Catalog Card No: 71-110925
SBN 8046-0907-1

Manufactured in the United States of America

PREFACE

Let me say a word as to the aim of this book.   It is not so
well known as it should be what a crowd of *English Witnesses*
was in France, at this time or that, in the course of the
French Revolution. Some had made a home there in the old
days, and stayed on through the new, in the hope that there
might be no need to move: nor was there, till, in the fifth
year of the *Revolution*, the course of the war, and a vain fear
of 'Pitt's plot,' gave rise to a change in the law. Some, when
they heard the news of the fall of an old world, and the rise
of a new, came post haste to share in the good work, or (it
might be no more) just to see and hear all that they could.
Not all of them, when they came to France, wrote down
what they found there. But a few did so—if not at the time,
at least when their friends asked them, 'What was it all
like?' or when, in old age, they wished to put down, while
their hand was not too weak, or their sight too dim, the
scenes which were still in their mind's eye—the deeds of a
brave old world which had had its day and ceased to be.

The *English Witnesses* whose tales will be found in this
book range from such great folk as the Duke of Dorset and
Earl Gower to young men, of no great note at the time, who
lived to make a name in the world—William Cobbett,
Francis Burdett, or William Wordsworth; from Young,
Moore, and Miles, who were quite at home in France, to
Owen or Nares, Wollaston or Weston, who knew no more
of it than could be learnt in a stay of a few weeks or a few
days. Some of those whom I have thought it worth while to
quote came to France with a mind to praise all they saw
there—though they might stay to curse what they had come
to bless; such were William Taylor, William Wordsworth,
and Tom Paine.   Some few lived in close touch with the
men of the time: Mrs. Swinburne and Quintin Craufurd were

v

two of the last friends of the Queen; the Abbé Edgeworth sat in the coach which took the King to his death, and stood close by when his head fell on the block. There will be found here, as well, a group of men such as Thomas Blaikie, George Monro, and Major Trench, who might not have been known to us, had not some call of work or stroke of chance put them in a front seat at that strange show of life and death.

I could not, of course, print all that I should have liked to print. I have been forced to pick out from the mass what seemed to me the best bits—those that had the most life or worth in them, and those that best told a tale of which, it is to be hoped, the world will not grow tired. Nor do I claim that there are no *English Witnesses* for whom I have not found room in this book. Far from it. There must be books that I have missed; nor have I searched the files of the press—seams that might well yield fresh ore. More than that, it is my hope that some of those who read this book may be led to look round at home for more tales of the same kind. For I am sure that, here and there, put by in an old room, or locked up in an old desk, may be found some rare book, or scrap of print, or (it may be), a page or two done by hand, thin and crisp with age, whose grey ink can still give new life to that old world. And it is my hope that, if such finds be made, I may come to hear of them, and have the chance, some day, to add them to this book.

J.M.T.

CONTENTS

PART I. PROLOGUE, 1785–1789

page

1. Approach to Paris   *Mrs. Piozzi*   1
2. The Neckers at home   *Sir John Sinclair*   2
3. The King   *Sir James Smith*   3
4. Royal extravagance   *Daniel Hailes*   4
5. Anglomania   *Sir James Smith*   7
6. Calonne's 'Notables'   *Lord Dorset*   8
7. A visit to Versailles   *Arthur Young*   9
8. Country house life   *Arthur Young*   11
9. Life in Paris   *Arthur Young*   12
10. Coming troubles   *Daniel Hailes*   13
11. 'A very critical time'   *Edward Nares*   18
12. 'Ripe for a revolution'   *Lord Clarendon*   19
13. Revolution foreseen   *Arthur Young*   20
14. 'Notables' and States-General   *Lord Dorset*   21
15. Shrove Tuesday   *Lord Dorset*   24
16. General Election   *Lord Dorset*   24
17. Paris described   *Sir Francis Burdett*   26
18. The Réveillon affair   *Lord Dorset*   26

PART II. CONSTITUENT ASSEMBLY, 1789–1791

19. The States-General   (1) *Lord Dorset*   29
    (2) *Thomas Blaikie*   31
20. The Queen sad   *Mrs. Swinburne*   32
21. Deadlock   *Lord Dorset*   33
22. Pamphleteering   *Arthur Young*   34
23. Parliamentary procedure   *Arthur Young*   36
24. 'National Assembly'   *Lord Dorset*   37
25. The Tennis Court oath   *Arthur Young*   39
26. The Royal session   *Arthur Young*   41

			page
27.	The King gives way	*Lord Dorset*	42
28.	Appeal to arms	*Lord Dorset*	45
29.	Crisis at Versailles	*Edward Rigby*	47
30.	The fall of the Bastille	(1) *Lord Dorset*	49
		(2) *Edward Rigby*	53
31.	A bloodless revolution	*Anon.*	60
32.	Lafayette and the National Guard	*J. G. Millingen*	62
33.	Provincial ignorance	*Arthur Young*	63
34.	Beggars	*Samuel Ireland*	64
35.	Chaos	*William Eden*	65
36.	The October days	(1) *Mr. Garlike*	66
		(2) *Lord R. Fitz-gerald*	68
		(3) *Mrs. Swinburne*	72
		(4) *Thomas Blaikie*	73
37.	The move to Paris	*Lord R. Fitzgerald*	74
38.	The royal family at the Tuileries	*Arthur Young*	77 .
39.	The Jacobin club	*Arthur Young*	78
40.	'A citadel besieged'	*William Taylor*	78
41.	'Thurst for war'	*Lord R. Fitzgerald*	79
42.	Growing pains	*William Taylor*	81
43.	The Champ de Mars	*Thomas Blaikie*	82
44.	Fédérés at the Tuileries	*Mrs. Walpole's sister*	82
45.	Federation (1) at Rheims	*C. B. Wollaston*	83
	(2) in Paris	*Helen Maria Williams*	84
	(3) in the country	*Helen Maria Williams*	85
46.	French journey	*William Wordsworth*	86
47.	News from Paris	*C. B. Wollaston*	88
48.	Paris changed	*W. A. Miles*	89
49.	The Queen at Saint-Cloud	*C. B. Wollaston*	90
50.	The Nancy Mutiny	*Lord Gower*	91
51.	'Paris governing'	*Lord Mornington*	93
52.	Paris and the Assembly	*Mary Berry*	96
53.	Mirabeau and Lafayette	*W. A. Miles*	98
54.	The King and Queen	*W. A. Miles*	99
55.	Paris diary	*Samuel Rogers*	100

CONTENTS

		page
56. Paris finance	*Lord Gower*	103
57. 'Two considerable mobs'		
(1) at the Luxembourg	*Lord Gower*	104
(2) at the Tuileries	*W. A. Miles*	105
58. Robespierre	*W. A. Miles*	106
59. 'Dagger Day'	(1) *Lord Gower*	107
	(2) *H. R. Yorke*	108
60. The King's health	*Lord Gower*	109
61. The political situation	*George Hammond*	110
62. The death of Mirabeau	(1) *J. G. Millingen*	113
	(2) *W. A. Miles*	113
63. The Saint-Cloud affair	*Lord Gower*	114
64. The Pope	*Lord Gower*	116
65. A beggar	*Miss Miles*	116
66. The Queen and the Gardener	*Thomas Blaikie*	117
67. The Revolution in Alsace	*John Owen*	118
68. The Flight to Varennes		
(1) in Paris	*Lord Gower*	119
(2) in the Provinces	*Stephen Weston*	122
(3) the return	*Miss Miles*	123
(4) public feeling	*J. G. Millingen*	124
(5) Secret history	*Quintin Craufurd*	125
69. 'Private truths'	*Lord Gower*	127
70. Tom Paine and his friends	*J. G. Millingen*	128
71. Republican manifesto	*Thomas Paine*	129
72. 'Matters coming to a crisis'	*Lord Sheffield*	131
73. Army allegiance	*Lieut.-Colonel Keating*	132
74. Voltaire's funeral	(1) *Lord Palmerston*	133
	(2) *J. G. Millingen*	133
	(3) *Stephen Weston*	134
75. Federation, 1791	*Lord Palmerston*	135
76. Since Varennes	*Francis Moore*	137
77. Champ de Mars massacre	(1) *Lord Palmerston*	138
	(2) *Lord Gower*	141
78. The Luxembourg gardens	*Stephen Weston*	143
79. King and Constitution	*W. Windham*	143

ix

Contents

PART III. THE LEGISLATIVE ASSEMBLY
1791–1792

			page
80.	The new Assembly	Lord Gower	144
81.	The King's position	C. B. Wollaston	145
82.	Paris pilgrimage	William Wordsworth	147
83.	Goodbye to the Queen	Mrs. Swinburne	148
84.	Beckford in Paris	William Beckford	148
85.	The Garde and the mob	Edward Jerningham	149
86.	A letter to Robespierre	Mrs. Shepherd	150
87.	Sight-seeing in Paris	William Hunter	151
88.	'The accursed revolution'	William Cobbett	152
89.	An English friend of the Queen	Quintin Craufurd	153
90.	Defeat	Lord Gower	155
91.	The mob in the Tuileries	Lord Gower	157
92.	The Queen at the Opera	Grace Elliott	158
93.	'The eve of a great crisis'	Lord Gower	159
94.	Travelling to Paris	John Moore	162
95.	'A trip to Paris'	Richard Twiss	163
96.	The fall of the throne	(1) John Moore	167
		(2) Lord Gower	170
		(3) Thomas Blaikie	172
		(4) John Moore	174
97.	Paris scenes (1) Jacobin Club	John Moore	180
	(2) Champs Elysées	John Moore	181
	(3) Temple	John Moore	182
98.	Insurrectional Commune	W. Lindsay	184
99.	Protestant patriotism	John Moore	187
100.	The prison massacres	(1) W. Lindsay	189
		(2) George Monro	190
101.	Invasion and Elections	George Monro	195
102.	A republican Bonfire	John Owen	201

PART IV. THE CONVENTION, 1792–1796

| 103. | 'To the people of France' | Thomas Paine | 202 |

CONTENTS

			page
104.	Political characters		
	(1) Dumouriez	*John Moore*	203
	(2) Marat	*John Moore*	205
	(3) Robespierre	*John Moore*	206
	(4) Roland and Danton	*John Moore*	206
105.	Will the King be tried?	*John Moore*	207
106.	Louvet and Robespierre	(1) *John Moore*	210
		(2) *William Words-worth*	212
107.	Republican manners	*John Moore*	213
108.	Scenes from the front		
	(1) Picardy volunteers	*Anon.*	215
	(2) A young Belgian patriot	*Anon.*	217
	(3) Dumouriez's army	*Anon.*	218
109.	The King's trial	(1) *George Monro*	220
		(2) *H. R. Yorke*	223
		(3) *Thomas Paine*	224
		(4) *George Monro*	225
110.	The King's execution	(1) *J. G. Millingen*	227
		(2) *The Abbé Edgeworth*	228
111.	The Emigration (1) Rome	*Lady Knight*	231
	(2) Brussels	*F. Daniel*	232
112.	Passports	*William Beckford*	233
113.	An English family in France	*Anon.*	234
114.	Dumouriez's treachery	*Thomas Paine*	235
115.	A letter to Danton	*Thomas Paine*	236
116.	The fall of the Girondins	*Anon.*	239
117.	Madame Roland in prison	*Helen Maria Williams*	239
118.	The executioner	*Thomas Paine*	240
119.	Life under the Terror	*Thomas Paine*	241
120.	National defence	*J. G. Millingen*	242
121.	English negotiations	*Sampson Perry*	243
122.	Paris during the Terror	(1) *Thomas Eldred*	245
		(2) *A. H. Rowan*	246
123.	Tribunal and Guillotine	*J. G. Millingen*	250

xi

Contents

		page
124. English advice to Robespierre	*N. S. J. Patterson*	252
125. Robespierre at home	*J. G. Millingen*	253
126. Danton and Barère	*J. G. Millingen*	255
127. Thermidor	*Major Trench*	256
128. The Revolution in Brittany		
(1) Quimper Cathedral	*Major Trench*	257
(2) A Temple of Reason	*Major Trench*	258
(3) A Vigilance Committee	*Major Trench*	259
(4) Revolutionary religion	*Major Trench*	260
129. Revolutionary plenty	*T. Wolfe Tone*	262
130. Young soldiers	*T. Wolfe Tone*	263
131. Farewell to Paris	*Henry Swinburne*	264

1. APPROACH TO PARIS

In the year in which her old friend Samuel Johnson died, Mrs. Thrale married Gabriel Piozzi, and travelled with him through France to Italy. Her impressions of Paris are much like those of other English visitors who crossed the Channel after the treaty of Versailles; but her view of the French character is an unusual frontispiece to the history of 1789.

THE fine paved road to this town has many inconveniences, and jars the nerves terribly with its perpetual rattle; the approach however always strikes one as very fine, I think, and the boulevards and guingettes look always pretty too; as wine, beer, and spirits are not permitted to be sold there, one sees what England does not even pretend to exhibit, which is gaiety without noise, and a crowd without a riot. . . . In the evening we looked at the new square called the Palais Royal, whence the Duc de Chartres has removed a vast number of noble trees, which it was a sin and shame to profane with an axe, after they had adorned that spot for so many centuries. The people were accordingly as angry, I believe, as Frenchmen can be, when the folly was first committed: the court, however, had wit enough to convert the place into a sort of Vauxhall, with tents, fountains, shops, full of frippery, brilliant at once and worthless, to attract them; with coffee-houses surrounding it on every side; and now they are all again merry and happy, synonymous terms at Paris, though often disunited in London; and *Vive le Duc de Chartres!*

The French are really a contented race of mortals; precluded almost from possibility of adventure, the low Parisian leads a gentle humble life, nor envies that greatness he can never obtain; but either wonders delightedly, or diverts himself philosophically with the sight of splendours which seldom fail to excite serious envy in an Englishman, and sometimes occasion even suicide, from disappointed hopes, which never could take root in the heart of these unaspiring people . . . .

I

Reflections must now give way to facts for a moment, though few English people want to be told that every hotel here, belonging to people of condition, is shut out from the street like our Burlington–house, which gives a general gloom to the look of this city so famed for its gaiety: the streets are narrow too, and ill-paved; and very noisy, from the echo made by stone buildings drawn up to a prodigious height, many of the houses having seven, and some of them even eight stories from the bottom. The contradictions one meets with every moment likewise strike even a cursory observer—a countess in the morning, her hair dressed, with diamonds too perhaps, a dirty black handkerchief about her neck; and a flat silver ring on her finger, like our ale-wives; a *femme publique*, dressed avowedly for the purpose of alluring the men, with not a very small crucifix hanging at her bosom; and the Virgin Mary's sign at an ale-house door, with these words:

The mother of my God am I,
And keep this house right carefully.

Hester Lynch Piozzi [September, 1785].

2. THE NECKERS AT HOME

The Comte de Vergennes was Minister of Foreign Affairs for Louis XVI. Jacques Necker, Protestant banker from Geneva, and Director General of Finance (1777–81), spent his retirement in attacking his successor, de Calonne (1783–7), and was soon recalled to office (1788–90). His wife, Suzanne Curchod, had been a friend of Gibbon; his daughter, aged 20, married the Baron de Stael-Holstein this year. Sir John Sinclair, Scotch agriculturalist, and M.P. for Lostwithiel, had published a History of the Public Revenue *two years before he visited Paris.*

IN January 1786 I took an excursion to Paris, and in the employment of my time there endeavoured to combine useful and agreeable occupations. With that view, I was accustomed to spend my mornings with the learned; to dine with the Count de Vergennes, M. Necker, and the other distinguished statesmen which France then possessed; and to dedicate the evening to the society of the gay. Being a

Member of the British Parliament, and known from my History of the Revenue as an author, I everywhere met with a most friendly reception. Having received an invitation to a family dinner with Monsieur Necker, I went early, and had the pleasure of finding the ladies occupied in a manner peculiarly gratifying to the national feelings of a Scotchman; for Madame Necker was reading Blair's sermons, and Mademoiselle Necker playing " Lochaber no more " on the piano. Monsieur Necker, overwhelmed by the pressure of public business, did not appear till immediately before dinner; and even before the cloth was removed, he received two or three letters, which he seemed to peruse with considerable interest. Madame Necker said that they probably related to the great political contest which he was then carrying on with Monsieur de Calonne, and which ultimately terminated in the removal of that minister from the helm. . . . At that time Monsieur Necker was so much occupied with political intrigues, that he devolved on the female part of his family the task of entertaining any strangers. He had contrived to inflame the too volatile spirits of the Parisians; but, being more of a financier than a statesman, he was quite unfit 'to ride in the whirlwind and direct the storm.' Hence he became unintentionally the source of all the mischiefs and horrors of the French Revolution.

John Sinclair.

3. THE KING

Sir James Edward Smith, botanist, afterwards founder of the Linnaean Society, pays a youthful visit to Paris (aet. 27), and is taken to see one of the usual sights—the King.

AUG. 6. Sunday being the best day in the week for seeing Versailles, Mr. Broussonet accompanied me thither. The road was crowded with all kinds of carriages, and those carriages with Chevaliers de St. Louis. We saw the royal family go to chapel, with young maids of honour painted of a rose colour, and old ones crimson. We saw the crowd adoring their grand monarque, little thinking how soon that adoration would cease. The King's countenance seemed agreeable and benignant, by no means vacant: his ears, which his hair never covered, were remarkably large and ugly, and he walked ill. He had some very fine diamonds in his hat. The Queen received company in her chamber, not having been out of it since her lying-in. The King's brothers had nothing striking about them.

Aug. 7. After dinner we were entertained with a shooting party of the Grand Monarque in the forest of St. Germain, about a mile from the town. The Maréchal attended the King on horseback. His Majesty arrived about half-past three in a coach, and having taken off his coat and blue riband, appeared in brown linen dress, with leather spatter-dashes. He proceeded on foot, immediately followed by eight pages in blue and white dresses made like his own. Each of them carried a fowling-piece ready loaded, and as soon as the King had fired off that in his hand, he took another from the page next him. . . . The greater part of the spectators were kept at a considerable distance, by guards forming a spacious ring. On the right and left of the King were persons with dogs, to raise the game of all kinds, which had been previously driven to the spot as much as possible. His Majesty killed almost everything he aimed at, so that the destruction on the whole must have been very great.

James Edward Smith [1786].

4. ROYAL EXTRAVAGANCE

Daniel Hailes, who acted as British Chargé d'Affaires for Lord Dorset during 1787–1788, was 'one of the most competent and far-sighted diplomats of the eighteenth century, one of the few men who realized the importance and predicted the results of the momentous events which preceded the Revolution.' [Preface to Despatches from Paris, 1784–1790, *Vol.] II. He here describes the 'derangement of the Finances' due (among other causes) to royal extravagance. A. R. J. Turgot was Louis XVI's Minister of Finance, 1774–81.*

4

ALTHOUGH I have always been in the perfect persuasion that the systems of reform proposed, and begun indeed, in this reign, by Mons. Turgot and Mons. Necker are as impracticable as they are inapplicable to the government of this Monarchy, and although it be evidently necessary that that powerful class which stands between the throne and the people should be supported by a part of the revenues of the country, yet (if I may be allowed the expression) the wise management of venality, and the economy of corruption and favour, by not heaping, as is the case in the present day, too many honours and emoluments on the same persons, offer such great resources as to constitute, perhaps, the only essential and practicable superiority of a good over a bad administration of the finances. It is to the Court, my Lord, that you must look for the sources of the present evil. The Queen, not only during the latter years of the reign of the late King, but even till after the birth of the Dauphin, by which event the succession seemed in some measure secured, was very far from enjoying that degree of power and influence which she is possessed of at present. But that event decided all the courtiers, and they hastened with precipitation to the standard of favor; while those who before had constituted Her Majesty's intimate and circumscribed society, were soon consolidated into a formidable party in the State. The strong propensity of this Princess to every kind of pleasure and expence has been improved into great advantage by all those who have considered only their own elevation and advancement. Her pretended friends, by administering to her pleasures, are become the intimate participators of her secrets, and, having once got possession of them, they may, in fact, be said to be masters of their own mistress, and to have secured by that means to themselves the permanence of that power, which otherwise the changeableness of her disposition rendered extremely precarious. . . . . .

The voice of the people is now and then, indeed, faintly heard indeed in their remonstrances, but as the avenues to the throne are all secured by the profusion of the Minister

to all who are in credit and power, it has little or no effect
and dies away for want of being seconded. I know it has
been said that the extent of the influence of the Queen's
party goes no farther than to the disposal of certain places
and pensions without interfering with the great line of
public business, and particularly that of foreign affairs,
but it ought surely to be observed, that, when any set of
them can command the person who holds the purse of the
State, they must necessarily have the greatest direct influence
in all internal, and a considerable indirect share in all Foreign
Affairs.

Your Lordship might expect with reason some particular
proofs in support of these general assertions of the prodig-
ality of the Department of Finance, were I not to repeat
what I have already had the honour of observing to you,
and which is that at the moment that this Country is in the
profoundest state of tranquillity that it can at any period
expect to enjoy, it is obliged every year to have recourse to
new loans. I know that the pretext for borrowing is the
paying off the debt contracted during the war, but Government borrows this year near two millions of livres, and the
amount of the reimbursement is no more than seventy-five,
and that too when the Sovereign is in possession of an
annual income of upwards of six hundred millions. . . . .

But, as if the derangement of the Finances were not
yet great enough, and as if Cherbourg were not sufficient to
swallow up all the unemployed treasure of France, immense
works are carrying on, or intend to be carried on in all the
Royal Houses. The additions to St. Cloud are estimated at
eleven millions; fifteen hundred workmen have been
employed for some months past at Fontainebleau. Compiègne, Rambouillet, and other places have been improved
in the greatest style of magnificence, and it is said the
Versailles is very shortly to undergo a thorough repair, the
expence of which can hardly be calculated. I will not trouble
your Lordship with the detail of the establishments of His
Majesty's brothers, which are equal, perhaps, to those of
some of the most independent Princes in Europe. The

inconsiderate people of the Capital are, however, constantly boasting the immense resources of the Kingdom, without reflecting that those resources are found in the most wretched and oppressed class in mankind. If it be a wise maxim that every Government should endeavour to preserve its customs and manners as distinct as possible from those of its neighbours, and keep alive those patriotic prejudices which are the source of persevering courage in war, and a steady attachment to internal produce and manufactures in time of peace, none has so much to re-proach itself with for an opposite conduct as that of France, the strong characteristic features that formerly marked the subjects of this monarchy are so much altered, that the French appear to be a different people to what they were before the beginning of the late war. Different circumstances have concurred to produce this effect, and men of a specu-lative turn of mind do not fail to discern in it, tho' at a distance, the most important revolutions. The intercourse of the French with the Americans whose manners and opinions could not but have influence, have brought them nearer to the English than they had ever been before. The almost unrestrained introduction of our daily publications (tolerated indeed by the Government from the conviction of the impossibility of preventing it) having attracted the attention of the people more towards the freedom and advantages of our constitution, has also infused into them a spirit of discussion of public matters which did not exist before. But amongst the most disadvantageous effects of this intercourse, may certainly be reckoned an almost universal taste for the elegancies and luxuries of British manufacture, a taste, which, since the war, has turned the scale of trade entirely against this nation. . . .

Daniel Hailes to Lord Carmarthen [October 25, 1786].

5. ANGLOMANIA

The treaty of Versailles (1783) intensified Anglo-French intercourse.

I was surprised, on being introduced into various Parisian circles in 1786, to hear much unreserved political talk, and

7

that of a nature which I had supposed would infallibly lead to the Bastile. Its prevailing tenour was, that neither the finances nor the authority of the government could long be supported; that the people would not long bear the excessive taxes and excessive oppression under which they groaned; and that the French in general were ardently desirous, and strongly flattered themselves with the hopes of being, in a very few years, governed as we are. This was the conversation of people of consideration and property, even connected with the court, and shining in the elevated walks of life. The prevailing sentiments of most ranks were much in favour of the English, as the wonderful adoption of our tastes and fashions of late years, and the avidity with which our publications were read, abundantly evince.

James Edward Smith [Paris, 1787].

6. CALONNE'S "NOTABLES"

On Feb. 22, 1787, Calonne, Controller-general of Finance, 1783–7 (cp. No. 2) convened 144 'Notables' at Versailles, in an attempt to find a way out of his financial embarrassments. John Frederick Sackville, third Duke of Dorset, an old Westminster, and a patron of cricket, was ambassador extraordinary to France, 1783–9, His Despatches from Paris, 1784–1790 (ed. Oscar Browning) are in the Camden Third Series, Vol. XIX.

HOWEVER difficult it may be to foretell the result of this Meeting, it is nevertheless obviously the consequence of embarrassment in the Finances to which the Comptrolleur Général finds himself alone unequal and which he has not the courage to face. The good effects of this measure are already conspicuous: the paternal goodness of His Majesty in thus calling together a meeting of His Subjects of different ranks in order to concert means of general relief and benefit to the community at large is talk'd of in terms of the highest praise and satisfaction.

The friends and well-wishers of Monsr. de Calonne are warm in their encomiums upon him, while others less prejudic'd are persuaded that little real advantage is to be expected, and consider the measure rather as a proof of a pressing emergency, and that, unless some at present unforeseen expedient shall be hit upon, some new system of economy adopted for diminishing the civil establishment of the Royal Family, the arrears of debt must ever continue to be enormous.

It is imagin'd that something will be agitated at the Assemblée for the relief of the Protestants, but as that Body is by no means affluent little advantage is to be hoped for from any offers they can have it in their power to make.

It is said that the subject of the alienation of the Crown Lands (Les Domaines du Roi), by which no doubt a large sum of money might be rais'd for the exigencies of Government, will also be discuss'd: but whether such a Meeting will be thought competent to decide upon so important and delicate a business is as yet quite problematical, and indeed it is believ'd that nothing less than an Assembly des États du Royaume can give ample security to such as might become purchasers, and even then it is apprehended that few would be found to venture, since it is understood to be a fundamental law of the land that the King cannot alienate his patrimony and that no act, how comprehensive soever it might be design'd, can give to purchasers of Crown lands full and secure possession.

Lord Dorset to Lord Carmarthen [January 4, 1787].

7. A VISIT TO VERSAILLES

Arthur Young, the famous agriculturalist, made his first journey across France with Lazowski, Polish tutor to the sons of the Duc de Liancourt, in 1787. He went again, travelling alone on horseback, in 1788; and again, in a hired post-chaise, in 1789. His Travels in France and Italy *were first published in 1792; new material was added in 1794. In the many later reprints, Part II ('General Observations,') has too often been omitted. The recent translation of the whole work into French, edited by Henri Sée [Colin, 1931], shows how highly Young's evidence is thought of by French historians of the Revolution. The Comte d'Artois is Louis XVI's second brother, afterwards Charles X; the Duc d'Orléans his cousin, who six years later voted for his death, and seven years later was himself guillotined; and 'the gallant Suffrein,' the Bailli de Suffren, the hero of the recent naval war against England in the West Indies.*

The ceremony of the day was the king's investing the Duke of Berri, son of the Count d'Artois, with the *cordon bleu*. The queen's band was in the chapel where the ceremony was performed, but the musical effect was thin and weak. During the service the king was seated between his two brothers, and seemed by his carriage and inattention to wish himself a hunting. He would certainly have been as well employed as in hearing afterwards from his throne a feudal oath of chivalry, I suppose, or some such nonsense, administered to a boy of ten years old. . . .

After this ceremony was finished, the king and the knights walked in a sort of procession to a small apartment in which he dined, saluting the queen as they passed. There appeared to be more ease and familiarity than form in this part of the ceremony; her majesty, who, by the way, is the most beautiful woman I saw to-day, received them with a variety of expression. On some she smiled; to others she talked; a few seemed to have the honour of being more in her intimacy. Her return to some was formal, and to others distant. To the gallant Suffrein it was respectful and benign. The ceremony of the king's dining in public is more odd than splendid. The queen sat by him with a cover before her, but ate nothing; conversing with the Duke of Orleans and the Duke of Liancourt, who stood behind her chair. To me it would have been a most uncomfortable meal, and were I sovereign I would sweep away three-fourths of these stupid forms; if kings do not dine like other people, they lose much of the pleasure of life; their station is very well calculated to deprive them of much, and they submit to nonsensical customs, the sole tendency of which is to lessen the remainder. . . .

The whole palace, except the chapel, seems to be open to all the world; we pushed through an amazing crowd of all sorts of people to see the procession, many of them not very well dressed, whence it appears that no questions are asked. But the officers at the door of the apartment in which the king dined made a distinction, and would not permit all to enter promiscuously.

Travellers speak much, even very late ones, of the remarkable interest the French take in all that personally concerns their king, showing by the eagerness of their attention not curiosity only, but love. Where, how, and in whom those gentlemen discovered this I know not. It is either misrepresentation, or the people are changed in a few years more than is credible.

Arthur Young [May 27, 1787].

8. COUNTRY HOUSE LIFE

Young has accompanied the Comte de la Rochefoucauld on a visit to the Duc de Liancourt's country seat near Clermont, north of Paris. It would not be safe to assume that all country house life was like this; for the Duke was an admirer of English ideas.

THE ideas I had formed before I came to France of a country residence in that kingdom I found at Liancourt to be far from correct. I expected to find it a mere transfer of Paris to the country, and that all the burthensome forms of a city were preserved without its pleasures; but I was deceived; the mode of living and the pursuits approach much nearer to the habits of a great nobleman's house in England than would commonly be conceived. A breakfast of tea for those that chose to repair to it; riding, sporting, planting, gardening, till dinner, and that not till half after two o'clock, instead of their old-fashioned hour of twelve; music, chess, and the other common amusements of a rendezvous-room, with an excellent library of seven or eight thousand volumes, were well calculated to make the time pass agreeably; and to prove that there is a great approximation in the modes of living at present in the different countries of Europe. . . . The present fashion in France of passing some time in the country is new; at this time of the year and for many weeks past, Paris is, comparatively speaking, empty. Everybody that have country seats are at them, and those who have none visit others who have. This remarkable revolution in the French manners is certainly one of the best customs they have taken from England, and its introduction was effected the easier being assisted by the magic of Rousseau's writings. . . . Women of the first fashion in France are now ashamed of not nursing their own children, and stays are universally proscribed from the bodies of the poor infants, which were for so many ages tortured in them, as they are still in Spain. The country residence may not have effects equally obvious, but they will be no less sure in the end, and in all respects beneficial to every class in the state.

Arthur Young [Sept. 16, 1787].

9. LIFE IN PARIS

The dangers of the Paris streets are a common-place in the literature of the eighteenth century. There were about a thousand fiacres *for hire, at 1 livre 10 sous an hour by day, and 2 livres by night.*

THIS great city appears to be in many respects the most ineligible and inconvenient for the residence of a person of small fortune of any that I have seen; and vastly inferior to London. The streets are very narrow, and many of them crowded, nine-tenths dirty, and all without foot-pavements. Walking, which in London is so pleasant and so clean that ladies do it every day, is here a toil and a fatigue to a man, and an impossibility to a well-dressed woman. The coaches are numerous, and, what are much worse, there are an infinity of one-horse cabriolets which are driven by young men of fashion and their imitators, alike fools, with such rapidity as to be real nuisances, and render the streets exceedingly dangerous without an incessant caution. I saw a poor child run over and probably killed, and have been myself many times blackened with the mud of the kennels. This beggarly practice of driving a one-horse booby hutch about the streets of a great capital flows either from poverty or wretched and despicable economy; nor is it possible to speak of it with too much severity. If young noblemen at London were to drive their chaises in streets without foot-ways, as their brethren do at Paris, they would speedily and justly get very well thrashed or rolled in the

kennel. This circumstance renders Paris an ineligible residence for persons, particularly families, that cannot afford
to keep a coach; a convenience which is as dear as at London.
The *fiacres*, hackney-coaches, are much worse than at that
city; and chairs there are none, for they would be driven
down in the streets. To this circumstance also it is owing
that all persons of small or moderate fortune are forced to
dress in black, with black stockings; the dusky hue of this
in company is not so disagreeable a circumstance as being
too great a distinction; too clear a line drawn in company
between a man that has a good fortune and another that has
not. With the pride, arrogance, and ill-temper of English
wealth this could not be borne; but the prevailing good
humour of the French eases all such untoward circumstances.
Lodgings are not half so good as at London, yet considerably dearer. If you do not hire a whole suite of rooms at a
hotel, you must probably mount three, four, or five pair of
stairs, and in general have nothing but a bed-chamber.
After the horrid fatigue of the streets, such an elevation is a
delectable circumstance. You must search with trouble
before you will be lodged in a private family as gentlemen
usually are at London, and pay a higher price. Servants'
wages are about the same as at that city. It is to be regretted
that Paris should have these disadvantages, for in other
respects I take it to be a most eligible residence for such as
prefer a great city.

Arthur Young [October 25, 1787].

10. COMING TROUBLES

*By the treaty of Versailles (1783) Holland, the ally of France against
England, lost its colony of Negapatam; and when attacked by Prussia in 1787
it did not get the support it expected. These failures, and disappointment at the
results of the American War, brought to a head the criticism of the French
system of government which had been growing for more than half a century.
Hailes foresees that the summoning of the States General, promised by
Lomenie de Brienne, Archbishop of Toulouse, for 1791, and subsequently
moved forward to 1789, will lead to a Revolution; and that France may well
become a more formidable power under the new regime—a limited monarchy on
the English model—than it has been under the old.*

AFTER so much that has been said and published upon the subject of French Finance in general, and after it has been found that even those who have been the nearest to the sources of information have differed widely in their opinion as to the extent and origin of that most important point, the deficiency, I conceive that it would be both superfluous and impertinent in me to offer any thing to your Lordship in addition to so tedious and doubtful an enquiry.

A question of a much more important nature occupies, at present, the minds of the thinking part of the nation: To find out the means, not merely of remedying past abuses in the application of the public Treasure by transitory expedients; not merely to restrain the frequency of arbitrary imprisonments by remonstrances and reclamations of Parliaments without authority; but to insure the country, *in future,* against disorders so much and so justly complained of is the object to which their attention is now directed. Many circumstances have concurred to produce this disposition. The example of the very extraordinary and rapid recovery of Great Britain from the Wounds she received in the late War, has not failed to attract the attention of this people; and the blessings of freedom and justice enjoyed in so eminent a degree under his Majesty's paternal Reign have excited an ardent desire to attain to similar advantages.

A sentiment of shame at the impotence betrayed by France in the late contest in Holland, and the disgraceful political Defeat that followed it, is strongly and generally impressed on men's minds, and is accompanied, no doubt, by the conviction that it is in vain to attempt to struggle with so vicious a Government against a power that possesses an innate and constitutional superiority. But in addition to observations and feelings so natural, it ought, above all, to be considered that there has grown up, of late years, a spirit of enquiry into the measures of Government, an opposition (if I may so call it) of Public Opinion of so forcible a nature, that it has been respected by Ministers even of the most arbitrary Principles. Religion, or rather Superstition of the Church of Rome for a long time upheld the Authority of the Sovereign; but that which may be looked upon to have been in a manner, the Key Stone of the vast Pile of Absolute Power, is now dropt out, or rather worn away from the Building. Human Reason which had been fettered and restrained during so many centuries having at last shaken off the yoke of Spiritual Tyranny is now, in the natural progress of freedom, proceeding to enquire into its Temporal Rights, and perhaps, to contend for a limitation of those powers of Government under which it has been so long oppressed.

In such a point of view, there appears without doubt much ground of apprehension for the interests of Great Britain, for it may be reasonably asked, if France, with all the vices of her Government, has been for so many ages in a situation to act often so brilliant and always so formidable a part in the affairs of Europe, what may not be expected from her when those vices shall have been eradicated, and when she shall be in possession of a constitution (as it is pretended she may) similar to that of her neighbour and Rival?

So strong is the sense of present disgrace and difficulties that it seems to have precluded all ideas of the possibility that a change should prove disadvantageous: an entire revolution in the form of the Government is therefore looked forward to with the greatest eagerness.

By giving, however, a very little extension to the enquiry into the grounds of such expectation, I humbly conceive that it will appear most evident that either this country must shortly be plunged into the most dreadful state of Anarchy, or an end be put to all pretensions to a Constitution.

The little success of the Minister who is at the head of the Finances, in all his operations, owing chiefly to the persevering opposition of the Parliaments, makes it believed that the Epoch of the Assembly of the States is near at hand.

As the Archbishop was *forced* into a promise of that Assembly in the year 1791, it is not to be expected that he will readily consent to its approximation.

Necessity only will bring forward the measure. But, supposing the Representatives of the Nation convened, and even the Majority of them to be animated with a desire to do well, and wisely, they must still be, as they have hitherto been, composed of the Ministers forming a party of the Court, the Clergy, the Nobility, and the Third Estate.

Let it be even supposed (a thing scarcely possible) that the nobility and Clergy should make a voluntary surrender of those privileges which make them, at present, so much the objects of envy and complaint; there must still, should a constitution be attempted to be formed, remain a party to defend the Authority of the Sovereign and another to attack and invade it. To draw the line between the prerogatives of the Prince and the Rights of the people, is a work of such magnitude as could with difficulty be perfected by the most enlightened and disinterested Men, all concurring to the same end. To effect it with opposite and jarring interests is a task that appears next to impossible.

Many parts of the English Constitution, it is said, may be adopted with great advantage to this kingdom—I should rather think that it must be taken whole and entire, with all its Body of Jurisprudence civil and criminal naturally growing out of it, or not at all.

If the abolition of the Lettres de Cachet is to take place, it must be followed by a Law of Habeas Corpus. If the Revenues of the Court are to be strictly applied to the good Government of it, an Annual production of the Public Accounts cannot be withheld.

If the conduct of Ministers is allowed to be enquired into, the liberty of the press must of necessity be established. A partial assumption of these great features of Freedom would only tend to disfigure the French Monarchy, without producing any real advantage.

But, admitting that it were found practicable, by common consent, to adopt the whole or at least all the Essential parts of the British Government (an event that the most chimerical and sanguine speculation can scarcely look forward to) it would then become a great political question how far such a form of Government would be applicable to a Kingdom of such an extent, and situated, on the Continent, as this is. The peculiar advantage of Great Britain (politically speaking) is its insular situation, by which it is exempted from the predicament of a great standing military force for its defense: but France placed between two great Powers in Europe with immense Armies, and having an extended Frontier to guard, is under the most absolute necessity of maintaining one also. How far it is possible to reconcile the freedom of a nation with a power vested in the Prince (and it can be placed no where else) to dispose of one Hundred and sixty-three thousand men (the number which I understand He has declared his intention of completing) I know not; but in all the conversations that I have attended to upon the present fashionable topic of a Revolution, I have yet never heard this difficulty, however obvious, adverted to.

It would require much more knowledge of the general dispositions of the people at large, than I am possessed of, to be able to form any judgment of the degree of energy that might be called forth, and shewn in support of any demands that might be made in their favour: nor would it, I presume, be an easy matter for anyone to foresee what might be the consequence of a dissolution of an Assembly of the Nation, without any thing having been resolved upon (as is most likely to be the case) for the security of the freedom and property of the subject: should that energy prove as great as it is thought to be by some, it might go near to the total subversion of the Monarchy; should it be, on the contrary, as little as it is esteemed to be by others, it would necessarily tend to produce a very great exercise of power and authority in the hands of the Crown. All that can at present be foreseen with great certainty is a long contest and, of course, as long as it lasts, great weakness on the part of Government, as well with respect to Foreign as Domestic Affairs.

Daniel Hailes to Lord Carmarthen [April 17, 1788].

11. 'A VERY CRITICAL TIME'

On July 30, 1787, the Paris Parlement refused to register two new taxes proposed by Brienne. On Nov. 19 it declared illegal the forced registration of a loan, and demanded a meeting of the States-General in 1789. Two of its members were thereupon arrested, and Orleans, who protested, was exiled. The Dauphin, born in 1782, died in 1789; his younger brother, the Duc de Normandie, was born in 1785, and died in the Temple in 1794. Edward Nares was at this time a Student of Christ Church, Oxford, where later he became Bampton Lecturer, and Regius Professor of Modern History.

WE arriv'd at Paris at a very critical time—at the very eve of the Revolution. Things were beginning to be in a ferment, and both the Court and the Country seem'd to expect an explosion. . . . Just as we arriv'd at Paris, the Parliament had refused to register two of the King's Edicts for raising Taxes, and had insisted on his convening the States General, which had not been summoned since 1614. It was, however, thought expedient to check the insolence of the Parliament, and orders were issued for the arrest of two of its members, M. d'Espresmesnil and M. Goelard. This was strongly resented and the King was address'd in very unusual terms. No one seem'd to doubt the good intentions of the King himself, but his Court was profligate, and his Ministers embarrass'd. The plans of reform that were laid before him, met with His Majesty's full approbation, but he could not foresee how much more the nation would demand. . . .

[April 27]. It was, I believe, the very last day on which their Majesties, Louis XVI and Marie Antoinette din'd together in public. We saw much of them during the day, but at dinner were plac'd close to them for some time. The Queen was certainly a most Majestic figure with handsome features, and graceful manners. She did not appear quite at her ease, for which, I apprehend, there was too much reason. She had a plaited napkin plac'd before her, and ate nothing . . . . The King's appearance interested me greatly. His profile was handsome, his countenance was mild and benevolent, and had, in my judgment, more marks of sincerity in it than fell to the lot of the French in general at that time. I saw him in a situation which even habit could scarcely render comfortable to a man of sense, and he appear'd himself to regard it as such. He made a hasty meal, spoke but little, and seem'd heartily glad when the ceremony was ended. Numerous dishes were placed successively on the table, most of which he merely tasted. . . . On retiring from the King's presence, we were conducted to the apartments of his younger son, the Duc de Normandie (afterwards Louis XVII), the Dauphin being too ill to receive us. The young Prince, who was but three years old, was standing on a carpet in the middle of the room. His hair was powder'd, and he was decorated with the order of the St. Esprit. He was a pleasant looking child. On our entrance he advanc'd towards us, show'd us the toy he was playing with, and, having said a few words, drew back again.

Edward Nares [April, 1788].

12. 'RIPE FOR A REVOLUTION'

John Charles Villiers was at this time M.P. for Old Sarum. He became third Earl of Clarendon in 1824.

So much perturbation and heat will not easily subside: and it will be found a matter extremely difficult, if practicable, to reduce their minds, as before, to the yoke of subjection. In fact, the whole kingdom seems ripe for a *Revolution*; every rank is dissatisfied; they despise their King; they detest their Queen; the public walks are now filled in every corner with sets of politicians, and every one seems eager to have some share in the business; in private companies the chief topic is now politics, and they are as much interested, and as much agitated, as in the most troublesome times in England. That fear, which once tied their tongues, and that reverence which restrained their thoughts, is now no more; and where they are not afraid of spies, they can condemn their government, and abuse their King, with as much freedom and as little ceremony as Englishmen; though with fifty times the reason. They begin now to see that so large and rich a territory was never made for the service and the pleasure of one man; and they learn from their increased acquaintance with our country, how much the happiness, the prosperity, and the refinement of a people depend upon well-regulated laws.

If the assembly of the States General takes place, according to the promise of the King, in the ensuing spring, there is little doubt but some revolution in the government will be effected. A constitution, probably somewhat similar to that of England, will be adopted, and limitations affixed to the power of the Crown.

J. C. Villiers (Lord Clarendon).
['On board the Pacquet,' September 2, 1788.]

13. REVOLUTION FORESEEN

By a 'bankruptcy' Young means a repudiation of the National Debt, the interest on which amounted to over 50 per cent. of the total expenditure of the country (Brienne's Comte Rendu au Roi, March, 1788).

DINED to-day with a party whose conversation was entirely political. . . . One opinion pervaded the whole company, that they are on the eve of some great revolution in the government: that everything points to it: the confusion in the finances great; with a *deficit* impossible to provide for without the states-general of the kingdom, yet no ideas formed of what would be the consequence of their meeting: no minister existing, or to be looked to in or out of power, with such decisive talents as to promise any other remedy than palliative ones: a prince on the throne, with excellent dispositions, but without the resources of a mind that could govern in such a moment without ministers: a court buried in pleasure and dissipation; and adding to the distress instead of endeavouring to be placed in a more independent situation: a great ferment amongst all ranks of men, who are eager for some change, without knowing what to look to or to hope for: and a strong leaven of liberty, increasing every hour since the American revolution altogether form a combination of circumstances that promise e'er long to ferment into motion if some master hand of very superior talents and inflexible courage is not found at the helm to guide events, instead of being driven by them. It is very remarkable that such conversation never occurs but a bankruptcy is a topic: the curious question on which is, *would a bankruptcy occasion a civil war and a total overthrow of the government?* The answers that I have received to this question appear to be just: such a measure conducted by a man of abilities, vigour, and firmness would certainly not occasion either one or the other. But the same measure, attempted by a man of a different character, might possibly do both. All agree that the states of the kingdom cannot assemble without more liberty being the consequence; but I meet with so few men that have any just ideas of freedom that I question much the species of this new liberty that is to arise. They know not how to value the privileges of THE PEOPLE: as to the nobility and the clergy, if a revolution added anything to their scale I think it would do more mischief than good.

Arthur Young [Paris, Sept. 17, 1788].

14. 'NOTABLES' AND STATES-GENERAL

The 'Notables' of 1788 were the same as those of 1787 (v. No. 6), except for a few substitutions in case of death. They were divided into 6 bureaux, to each of which the same 52 questions were submitted. The crucial question was the 5th, Quel doit être le nombre respectif des Députés de chaque Ordre? *i.e. should the* Tiers État *be given as many deputies as the Clergy and Nobility put together? Only one bureau voted for this concession, by a majority of one, two were unanimously against it, three rejected it by a majority: the total vote was 33 for, 110 against. But Necker's Report of Dec. 27, 1788, decided in favour of it.*

20 November, 1788.

THE Notables continue their proceedings by Committees and hope to have finished their business by the end of next Month at latest:

Their deliberations have hitherto been carried on with great temper, and though the question (a very important one) in regard to the proportion that is to be allowed to the *Tiers Etat* in the formation of the Etats-Généraux, has occasioned a great difference of opinion, the discussion of it has not been attended with any circumstance to interrupt that harmony which is so essential to render the present proceedings beneficial to the Country.

Nevertheless the Committee, at which Monsieur presides, has determined (differently from the other five) that the Tiers-Etat should be represented more in proportion to the Share it pays of the public expences, so as to make it equal in number to the two Orders of Clergy and Nobility taken together; whereas the other Committees have resolved that one of the Clergy, one of the Nobility, and one only of the Tiers-Etat should be elected in each District; this mode of forming the Etats-Généraux will, with some modification, be conformable to the plan adopted in 1614, and will of course be very disadvantageous to the Tiers-Etat, which thus will be entirely at the mercy of the Clergy and the Nobility.

The Clergy appear to have managed well for themselves in this important discussion since, according to this arrangement, they will be able, by means of the immense property and influence they possess, to over-awe the Tiers-Etat during the holding of the Etats-Généraux and to divide the Nobility, who, in case of a junction (so much dreaded) of their order with that of the Tiers-Etats, might prove very formidable and perhaps fatal to the power of the Church.

How the difference of opinion in Monsieur's Committee will terminate I cannot inform your Lordship, the Numbers uponthedivisionhavingbeenequalviz. 12 —to 12—Monsieur is said to have given the casting vote in favor of the Tiers-Etat: it is however thought probable that this Committee will coincide with the rest rather than risk the delay and confusion which a perseverance in its decision might produce:

The Maréchal de Beauvau and the Duc de Châtelet supported Monsieur's opinion.

The object of the Parliaments is to have the Etats-Généraux convened as nearly as possible in the same manner as in 1614; in this the Clergy and the Magistrates are acting upon similar principles it being equally the interest of both to prevent the Tiers-Etat from having that share in the National Assembly, to which by national right they are entitled. A general dissatisfaction prevails among the Tiers Etat in consequence of the resolution respecting them which they foresee is likely to be passed in the Assembly of Notables: Many Provinces, and particularly Normandy, refuse to send Delegates upon those terms, but seem determined to present themselves in a body in order to insist on their right of voting, and it is imagined that some further indulgence will be granted them to prevent a measure, which would be productive of very serious disorders.

11 December, 1788.

The result of the proceedings of the several Committees will shortly appear in print, I therefore do not attempt to give your Lordship any detail of them; I must however observe that the present temper of the Nation is such that the Provinces probably will not consider themselves as bound to follow any particular mode, that may be dictated to them, for the election of Deputies to represent them at the Assembly of the States-General, unless it shall appear by the records to be conformable to the customs of former times on similar occasions; neither, it is thought, will the Tiers-Etat at any rate submit to a representation of their Order that shall be judged by them inadequate to the magnitude of the proportion they hold in the State; for, by the calculation which has lately been made of the three Orders, it appears that the Clergy, not including the *Religieux*, amounted to 90,000 only: and that of Nobility, even with all those who have purchased their titles, amounted to no more than 500,000: the disproportion therefore between the Tiers-Etat and the other two Orders, taken together, is very considerable, the whole population of France being estimated at 24 millions. Orders have been given for issuing the Letters of Convocation for the States-

General immediately, and they are to assemble at Paris (as it is now said) on the 20th of March, but that being thought a too distant period, the King is to be petitioned to call them together, the 1st of February, which however it is probable cannot be complied with.

Lord Dorset to Lord Carmarthen.

15. SHROVE TUESDAY

Le peuple (*writes Mercier*) fête le Saint-Martin, les Rois, et le Mardi-Gras, *and goes on to detail the usual excitements of the* Carnaval. [Tableau de Paris, *Hamburg*, 1781, *ii*, 312]. This was on Shrove Tuesday.

A CIRCUMSTANCE took place a day or two ago which, as it shews in some degree the spirit of the times and the high notion the people are disposed to entertain of their own consequence, may not be thought unworthy of remark: the ancient custom of going about the Streets in mask is still preserved among the lower sort of people during the few last days of the Carnival: on this occasion an idea struck some young men, a certain number of whom dressed themselves to represent the three Orders of the State, and paraded the Streets of this City in a Coach, hired for the purpose: the Coachman was habited as an Abbé, to represent the Order of the Clergy: the Persons behind the Carriage, in quality of footmen, were decorated with the Order of the Holy-Ghost, representing the Order of the Nobility, and two Savoyards were seated in the inside as Representatives of the Tiers-Etat; this innocent raillery afforded a great deal of mirth without being productive of any disorder or unpleasant consequence.

Lord Dorset to Lord Carmarthen.
[February 26, 1789.]

16. GENERAL ELECTION

The elections for the States-General of 1789 led to disturbances in various parts of the country. At Marseilles the mercantile and working classes took the opportunity to work off old grudges against the clerical and lay aristocracy, and the military garrison. The Comte de Mirabeau was elected, just at this time, deputy for the Tiers État of Aix and of Marseilles.

THE fermentation which has manifested itself lately in different parts of this Kingdom has been carried to a very serious and alarming length, particularly at Marseilles, where the most daring and it may be added cruel outrages have been committed. Amongst the various accounts that are given of this affair the following I have reason to think comes nearest to the truth. On the day appointed for the Meeting of the Nobility for the Election of Deputies to the States-General the populace assembled under pretence of the distress they were suffering on account of the dearness of bread, and surrounded the Assembly-House in a very tumultuous manner; their violence increasing and every effort to appease them proving ineffectual, the Meeting was broken up, and the Members retired to their several homes in the most private manner possible: this served but to increase the tumult, for the populace then proceeded to pillage the houses of those of the Nobility who were most obnoxious to them; amongst others that of the Bishop of Toulon was a marked object of their fury: the Bishop found means to escape in disguise out of the Town, and, as soon as his flight was discovered, the mob, after destroying all the furniture, etc. threw his carriage and horses into the sea; a Gentleman of the place (some accounts say the Mayor, and that he drew upon himself the rage of the Populace by firing at and killing one of them upon the spot) fell a Victim and was butchered in a manner too shocking to be related with all the circumstances of savage cruelty that were exercised upon the body. The Comte de Caraman assembled the Troops, but they were soon overpowered by Numbers, for the populace were provided with Arms, and he, seeing no other chance of restraining the fury of the moment, had recourse to the Comte de Mirabeau for his influence with the people, and his interference succeeded so far as to obtain a temporary cessation of the outrages.

Lord Dorset to the Duke of Leeds.

[April 9, 1789.]

17. PARIS DESCRIBED

Sir Francis Burdett, aged 19, travels on the continent before settling down to married and parliamentary life.

DEAR AUNT JONES,

. . . We intend to leave Paris some time next week, a description of which I shall not pretend to give you, as I find it impossible to give one which can at all convey to you an Idea of Paris, that must be reserved for some future opportunity or for some abler pen. Such a mixture of Pomp and Beggary, filth and magnificence, as may truely be said to beggar all description. Suffice to say, that it is the most ill-contrived, ill built, dirty, stinking Town that can possibly be imagined; as for the inhabitants they are ten times more nasty than the inhabitants of Edinburgh. At the same time there are many Publick buildings, and many parts of the Town which are extremely magnificent. You find the same inconsistency pervade everything here, things the most incongruous, the most opposite in nature to one another, are here united. . . .

believe yours most affectionately,

Francis Burdett.

[April 19, 1789.]

18. THE RÉVEILLON AFFAIR

This incident was an ominous prologue to the opening of the States-General a week later. Réveillon, starting life as a common labourer, had worked his way up, till he owned a wall-paper factory, under royal patronage, and employed 350 men. He regarded himself as a model employer, and said that the agitation against him had been engineered by rivals whom he had undersold. [Ferrières, Mémoires, i. 417.]

THIS City has for some days past been alarmed by a very serious tumult, which began about six o'clock on Monday evening when a number of workmen employed by a considerable manufacturer of painted paper assembled in a riotous manner for the purpose of burning in Effigy their Master, whose name is Réveillon, of whom they had demanded an increase of wages on account of the advanced

price of bread, and who, as they had been designedly made
to believe, had declared in a public Assembly that 15 Sols
a-day were wages sufficient for workmen to subsist on:
however the appearance of some French and Swiss Guards
deterred the mob from committing any material outrage
at that time, but on the following morning (Tuesday) the
rioters assembled again in much greater force, a considerable number of them having furnished themselves with
bludgeons, and thus paraded the Faubourg St. Antoine
menacing everybody who should attempt to obstruct their
proceedings; it happened that on that day there were Races
in the Bois de Vincennes which drew together a large
company of persons of rank and fashion, many of whom in
their road thither through the Faubourg St. Antoine were
prevented passing that way by the vast concourse of
people who were collected and who insisted on their
declaring themselves in favour of the Tiers-Etat: the
Military was called out, and about 2 o'clock the Troops
were under the necessity of firing upon the mob, by which
some few of them were killed and several wounded: this
however did not prevent the people from getting possession
of the house of Mons. Henriot, a manufacturer of salt-
petre, the friend and neighbour of M. Réveillon which
they compleatly stripped of every article and having
piled up all the effects in the Street set fire to and burned
them before the door of the house; most of the persons
employed on this business were either killed in the house
by the soldiers or taken; the.few who were fortunate to
escape got away upon the tops of the buildings, which they
unroofed, and severely wounded some of the Soldiers with
the tiles, etc. which they threw down upon them.

Reinforcements of troops were in the mean time continually arriving, both Cavalry and infantry, and there was
occasional firing upon the mob from six o'clock in the
evening 'till 10 o'Clock at night by which time the streets
were entirely cleared and tranquility thereby obtained: some
accounts say that from three to four hundred of the people
were destroyed. Twelve of the rioters were taken into

custody, two of whom were executed yesterday evening without any attempt being made to rescue them.

Several houses have been threatened with destruction and particularly that of M. du Châtelet, Colonel of the French Guards.

The Hotel Dieu is filled with the wounded, and many more it is imagined must have been conveyed away by their own party. The Boulevards, from the Chaussée d'Autin to the Porte St. Antoine was guarded by detachments of Cavalry posted at certain distances and the Arsenal was protected by a considerable body of Grenadiers from both Regiments, an apprehension having arisen that the mob intended to make themselves Masters of that place with a view to get possession of the Arms: four pieces of Cannon were placed opposite to the Opera-House in readiness to be removed to any Quarter of the Town where a disturbance might arise.

Such was the position yesterday and in all probability the same will be observed for some days to come. No other motive than the dearness of bread has been assigned by the unhappy wretches who were engaged in these excesses, most of whom were intoxicated to a very great degree; though some are disposed to suspect that the friends and supporters of the Parliament have secretly fermented the disturbance.

Reinforcements of Troops have arrived from the environs of this City, and orders have been sent for all the Regiments at a certain distance to approach near to the Capital. The scene of tumult has been confined to the Faubourg St. Antoine tho' some detached parties of vagabonds have paraded parts of the Faubourg St. Germains and laid several carriages under contributions, urging in their behalf the extreme dearness of bread, but it does not appear that they belonged to the principal Mob, nor did they commit any further excesses. Bread is getting dearer every day: a great quantity of flour was brought in from the Country yesterday, but that can be only as a temporary supply and unless Government finds some means of effectually preventing the scarcity that is apprehended, the distress of the people must necessarily become insupportable.

Lord Dorset to the Duke of Leeds.
[April 30, 1789.]

19. THE STATES-GENERAL

(1)

On Saturday, May 2, all deputies to the States-General who had arrived at Versailles were received by the King—Clergy, Nobility, and Commons, separately, and in that order. On Monday, May 4, the Court and the States, after singing the Veni Creator *at Notre Dame, went in procession to St. Louis, to hear Mass and a sermon. The Bishop of Nancy (suffragan of Tréves) was de la Fare; the Garde des Sceaux C. L. F. de P. de Barentin. It is possible to read between the lines of this official report the bitter disappointment of the deputies of the Commons at the tone of the speeches.*

On Saturday last the Members of the States-General had the honor of being presented to His Majesty; and on Monday Their Majesties and all the Royal Family, excepting their Majesties' Children, attended by the Members went in procession to the Parish Church of Versailles, where a Sermon, suitable to the solemn occasion, was preached by the Bishop of Nancy: a great concourse of people attended and gave repeated marks of loyalty and affection to Their Majesties, who about 2 o'clock returned to the Palace. The Sermon delivered by the Bishop was generally much approved, and a particular passage in it addressed to the Members was received with clapping of hands which, as may well be imagined from the novelty of the circumstance, interrupted for some time the devotion of the congregation.

On the following day (Tuesday) His Majesty opened the Assembly of the States-General about 12 o'clock at noon, by a speech from the Throne, which was received with repeated marks of applause evidently manifesting the feelings of that august Assembly in such a manner as could not but be highly flattering and satisfactory to His Majesty.

His Majesty delivered His Speech with great dignity though He was interrupted in the course of it by the repeated acclamation of *Vive le Roi* accompanied by clapping of hands. Her Majesty was seated near to the King on His left-hand: Monsieur and the Comte d'Artois at a small distance on the right: Madame, Madame Elizabeth (His Majesty's Sister) together with Mesdames Victoire and Adelaide (His Majesty's Aunts) on the left-hand behind the Queen. The Comtesse d'Artois was prevented by a slight indisposition, nor were any of their Majesties' Children present.

The other Princes of the Blood with some Dukes and peers were also on the right: the Maréchal of France with others of the same rank were on the left: the Garde des Sceaux on the left, and the other great Officers of state on the right of the Throne. The Duc d'Orleans who is the only Prince of the Blood chosen Deputy to the States-General took his seat as such among the Nobility.

The Ministers were seated close under the platform on which the Throne was placed. As soon as His Majesty had finished His Speech, the Garde des Sceaux delivered a set speech which he read in so low a tone of voice that it was impossible to collect a single sentence of it. M. Necker afterwards addressed His Majesty and the Assembly in a written speech, the whole of which lasted three hours, but M. Necker, after reading a part of it, found himself obliged, on account of hoarseness, the effect of a cold, to crave His Majesty's indulgence in permitting one of the Clerks to read the remainder.

I will not attempt to enter into a full detail of the variety of matter contained in this laborious discourse which was received with bursts of applause. I had flattered myself that the speeches would be published in time for me to send them to Your Grace this day, but I hear that it will be yet some days before they will appear.

M. Necker declared the present annual Deficit to be no more than 56 Millions, and pointed out means of supplying it without any extraordinary burthens upon the people: he gave the States-General to understand that His Majesty had been graciously pleased to call them together more from a desire of fulfilling the promise He had made and of meeting the wishes of His people than from any exigencies of the State, and, if I did not misunderstand the expression, implied that, in case the present assembly of the Nation should manifest a disposition to act in opposition to His Majesty's principles, the King might be induced to dissolve the States-General and have recourse to those methods for supplying the Deficit which the Director General of the Finances engages to provide.

The Establishment of an East India Company, and of a National Bank, consolidating the national debt, and in short whatever may contribute towards securing a national credit, were the principal subjects of the Minister's speech, for which he claimed the sanction of the States-General. He also slightly touched upon the Slave-Trade, observing that an enlightened and distinguished Nation had already set the example of bringing the abuses of that commerce to a thorough investigation.

No mention was made of His Majesty's prerogatives, so as to raise an expectation that any of them would be abandoned. His Majesty only pledged himself to assemble the Nation periodically. M. Necker's speech being finished about 4 o'clock, His Majesty rose from His seat and adjourned the meeting to the following day (yesterday); Their Majesties on Their way back from the Assembly-House received separately very flattering marks of the respect of the public.

Lord Dorset to the Duke of Leeds.

[May 7, 1789.]

(2)

Thomas Blaikie, Scotch gardener and botanist, after travelling in Switzerland (1775) in search of rare plants, entered the service of the Baron de Lauraguais, and afterwards that of the Duc d'Orléans. He lived in France till his death in 1838, aged 89. Extracts from his diary were published as Diary of a Scotch gardener at the French Court *(ed. F. Birrell) in 1931.*

WENT to Versailles and dined with Mr. Brown where I was allways well received both him and Mme being good people. As this was the entry of the Etats-Generaux who came in Procession from the Palais to the church of St. Louis the King and the Princess of his family at the head of the procession, the Duke of Orleans seemed to head the tiers etat or what may be called the communs; this seemed to be the first open opposition to the court which was critisised by some and admired by others; as at this time the Assembly was to be held at Versailles and the wish of the King seemed to do good and to render what good he could to his people and wish those deputies to Settle how they could pay and diminish the nationale debt, this procession was very brilliant and marched in great order into the Church: as we was placed upon the wall of the Potager we had the view of the whole. About this time the whole town was full of Differant pamphelets some for and some against the assemble which was to be held in what they call the Jeu de Paume at Versailles and all the heads seemed to be occupied about this great affaire to be performed by this Assembly.

Thomas Blaikie.

[May, 1789.]

20. THE QUEEN SAD

In the course of his travels (described in Travels Through Spain, *1779, and* Travels in the Two Sicilies, *1783 and 1785) Henry Swinburne made many friends at court; as a result of a second visit to Paris in 1786–8, his eldest son Henry became a page to Marie-Antoinette, and his wife stayed on at Versailles, while he himself returned to England. The Dauphin died on May 14, only two days after this interview.*

I HAD an audience of the Queen two days ago; she is very much altered, and has lost all her brilliancy of look. She was more gracious than ever, and said '*Vous arrivez dans un mauvais moment, chere Madame Swinburne. Vous ne me trouverez point gaie: j'ai beaucoup sur le coeur.*' She is very low-spirited and uneasy about her son, who, by all accounts, lies dangerously ill, and is not likely to recover. She inquired kindly after all our family, and assured me she should consider Henry as under her care, and also spoke of our business, which Madame Campan had told her was my reason for now returning to France. '*Je crains,*' said she, '*que dans ce moment je ne pourrai vous être d'aucune utilité; mais si les tems deviennent meilleurs, vous savez que je n'oublie jamais mes amis.*'.. The whole tenor of her conversation was melancholy, but she said little about public affairs; her child's illness seemed uppermost in her mind. The tears, which I with difficulty restrained in her presence, gushed from me as soon as I had quitted the room. She told me she should like to see me again soon. Poor thing! her kindness and sorrowful manner made me more interested and enthusiastic about her than ever.

Mrs. Swinburne to her husband.
[Versailles, May 10, 1789.]

21. DEADLOCK

For more than a month after the opening of the States-General no business was done, the Clergy and Nobility refusing to sit with the Commons, and the Commons refusing to act as a separate Order.

IT is scarcely possible to give your Grace an adequate idea of the confusion that prevails at present at Versailles owing to the discussions, hitherto fruitlessly, carried on by the several Orders with little if any progress, as your Grace will see by the printed accounts (which are authentic) towards an agreement upon a regular form of proceeding.

The Tiers-État seem to conduct themselves with a determined firmness, and not at all disposed to give way to the Nobility on any point, while on the other hand the Nobility cannot brook the idea of being dictated to by those whom they have ever been used to consider so much their inferiors in point of birth and consideration: the Clergy have evidently shewn a desire to conciliate matters, the nature of their Order forming two interests which on this occasion are incompatible, but the extreme inveteracy of the other two Orders against each other has not admitted of any good effect from their efforts.

In the mean time the public is dissatisfied and becoming

very impatient of delay occasioned by the disunion of the orders at a time the Nation had flattered itself that some salutary measures would have been adopted for its relief: under these circumstances too the Government is placed in a very awkward predicament, for, which appears somewhat extraordinary, none of the Ministers has a seat in the great National Assembly, not one of the Cabinet having been deputed to the States-General, so that whenever the present disputes shall be adjusted in such a manner as to establish a quiet and regular mode of proceeding on business, there will not be a Minister to join in discussing the several Propositions as they are brought forward: it may indeed be urged that the presence of the Officers at the head of the different Departments will be necessary rather to satisfy the States-General in regard to what is past than to assist in providing for the future, and that their attendance in the Assembly will be required for that purpose as shall be occasionally found requisite.

There is every reason to believe that M. Necker is extremely embarrassed at this moment, for as his popularity has hitherto been his chief support, the decline of that Minister's credit, which is already wavering, will unavoidably be attended with a National bankruptcy: and perhaps Government, if it foresees the impossibility of going on, would prefer stopping payment at a moment when the calamity may be attributed to the want of unanimity in the States to whom the Nation is referred for a remedy in its distress.

Stocks have continued to fall since the opening of the Assembly, and the Shares of the Caisse d'Escomte are daily losing in no small proportion.

Lord Dorset to the Duke of Leeds.
[May 28, 1789.]

22. PAMPHLETEERING

The avenues and arcades of the Palais Royal (cp. No. 1) soon became the centre of revolutionary excitement in Paris. In addition to pamphlets, new papers were coming out at the rate of one a week.

THE business going forward at present in the pamphlet shops of Paris is incredible. I went to the Palais Royal to see what new things were published, and to procure a catalogue of all. Every hour produces something new. Thirteen came out to-day, sixteen yesterday, and ninety-two last week. We think sometimes that Debrett's or Stockdale's shops at London are crowded, but they are mere deserts compared to Desein's, and some others here, in which one can scarcely squeeze from the door to the counter. The price of printing two years ago was from 27 livres to 30 livres per sheet, but now it is from 60 livres to 80 livres. This spirit of reading political tracts, they say, spreads into the provinces so that all the presses of France are equally employed. Nineteen-twentieths of these productions are in favour of liberty, and commonly violent against the clergy and nobility; I have to-day bespoke many of this description that have reputation; but inquiring for such as had appeared on the other side of the question, to my astonishment I find there are but two or three that have merit enough to be known. Is it not wonderful, that while the press teems with the most levelling and even seditious principles, that if put in execution would over-turn the monarchy, nothing in reply appears, and not the least step is taken by the court to restrain this extreme licentiousness of publication? It is easy to conceive the spirit that must thus be raised among the people. But the coffee-houses in the Palais Royal present yet more singular and astonishing spectacles; they are not only crowded within, but other expectant crowds are at the doors and windows, listening *à gorge deployé* to certain orators, who from chairs or tables harangue each his little audience: the eagerness with which they are heard, and the thunder of applause they receive for every sentiment of more than common hardiness or violence against the present government, cannot easily be imagined. I am all amazement at the ministry permitting such nests and hot-beds of sedition and revolt which disseminate amongst the people every hour principles that by and by must be opposed with vigour, and therefore it seems little short of madness to allow the propagation at present.

Arthur Young.

[June 9, 1789.]

23. PARLIAMENTARY PROCEDURE

The 'hall of the States' is the Palais des Menus Plaisirs du Roi, *previously used for the sessions of the Notables. For Lazowski v. No. 7. 'Monsieur Baillie' is J. S. Bailly, astronomer, first President of the Assembly of representatives of the Third Estate, which, as a result of this debate, constituted itself, two days later, the 'National Assembly.' Rabaut St. Etienne is the well-known Protestant minister, deputy for the Third Estate of Nîmes. John Hatsell, Clerk of the House of Commons, published his* Precedents of Proceedings in the House of Commons *in 1781.*

THIS has been a rich day, and such a one as ten years ago none could believe would ever arrive in France; a very important debate being expected on what, in our house of commons, would be termed the state of the nation. My friend Monsieur Lazowski and myself were at Versailles by eight in the morning. We went immediately to the hall of the states to secure good seats in the gallery; we found some deputies already there, and a pretty numerous audience collected. The room is too large; none but stentorian lungs, or the finest clearest voices can be heard; however the very size of the apartment, which admits 2000 people, gave a dignity to the scene. It was indeed an interesting one. The spectacle of the representatives of 25,000,000 people, just emerging from the evils of 200 years of arbitrary power, and rising to the blessings of a freer constitution, assembled with open doors under the eye of the public, was framed to call into animated feelings every latent spark, every emotion of a liberal bosom; to banish whatever ideas might intrude of their being a people too often hostile to my own country, —and to dwell with pleasure on the glorious idea of happiness to a great nation—of felicity to millions yet unborn.

In regard to their general method of proceeding there are two circumstances in which they are very deficient: the spectators in the galleries are allowed to interfere in the

36

debates by clapping their hands and other noisy expressions of approbation: this is grossly indecent; it is also dangerous; for, if they are permitted to express approbation, they are, by parity of reason, allowed expressions of dissent; and they may hiss as well as clap; which it is said they have some-times done:—this would be to over-rule the debate and influence the deliberations. Another circumstance is the want of order among themselves; more than once to-day there were a hundred members on their legs at a time and Monsieur Baillie absolutely without power to keep order. This arises very much from complex motions being admitted; to move a declaration relative to their title, to their powers, to taxes, to a loan, etc., etc., all in one proposi-tion appears to English ears preposterous, and certainly is so. Specific motions founded on single and simple pro-positions can alone produce order in debate; for it is endless to have five hundred members declaring their reasons of assent to one part of a complex proposition and their dissent to another part. A debating assembly should not proceed to any business whatever till they have settled the rules and orders of their proceedings, which can only be done by taking those of other experienced assemblies, confirming them as they find useful, and altering such as require to be adapted to different circumstances. The rules and orders of debate in the house of commons of England, as I afterwards took the liberty of mentioning to Monsieur Rabaud St. Etienne, might have been taken at once in Mr. Hatsel's book, and would have saved them at least a fourth of their time.   Arthur Young [June 15, 1789].

24. 'NATIONAL ASSEMBLY'

On June 12, after a final appeal to the Clergy and Nobility to join them, the Commons began to verify the powers of their deputies, i.e. to constitute themselves as representatives of the nation. On the 13th, three clerical deputies joined them, and by the 16th, another sixteen. On the 17th, they called them-selves 'l'Assemblée Nationale,' and declared that taxes should continue to be paid just so long as they remained in session. This assumption of national and sovereign rights was a challenge to which the King might reply by force: but few people shared Dorset's trust in the army.

THE Tiers-Etat finding that there remained no longer any hopes of conciliation between their Order and that of the Nobility resolved the latter end of last week upon proceeding in a regular way to verify the returns of its Deputies which was accordingly done and the whole completed on Monday last: in consequence of an invitation to the two first Orders on the part of the Tiers-Etat to assemble in common with them, a few of the lower Clergy appeared amongst them, but have since retired to their own Order. On Tuesday the Tiers-Etat passed a vote constituting themselves the Representatives of the Nation; in the course of the debate upon this occasion very violent language was held against the Clergy and the Nobility, and the Strangers who were present testified their approbation to such a degree, that those members who were known to be desirous of moderating the animosity that prevailed found it expedient to remove from their places to avoid the insults which seemed to threaten them. The Assembly on that day did not break up, till past 12 o'clock at night.

They met again yesterday when the Resolutions (*Arrêté National*) herewith enclosed were passed by a very great majority, by which, as your Grace will perceive, that Body assume the title of *l'Assemblée Nationale*. . . . .

The Resolutions of yesterday, which I have the honor to send Your Grace, make no mention of others which have been passed, but care has been taken to make known, by Expresses sent for the purpose, to all parts of the Kingdom the particulars of the whole that has been doing, which will no doubt very much inflame the minds of the people.

The Assembly resolved that the Representatives of the Nation do take upon themselves the public debt, and accordingly voted a Loan of at least 80 millions to answer the present exigencies of the State, directing at the same time that any attempt to collect Taxes without their authority should be resisted; they declared also that in case the present Assembly should be dissolved, the people would be justified in refusing to pay any Taxes whatever till such time as that Assembly should be again convoked in a regular and constitutional manner. One of the Members expressed an earnest wish that something might be done immediately to relieve the necessities of the poor.

Such I understand, to be the substance of what passed yesterday (the 17th). Matters are every day growing exceedingly critical yet the King's Authority is still paramount, but if His Majesty once gives His decided approbation of the proceedings, such as they have hitherto been, of the Tiers-Etat, it will be little short of laying His Crown at their feet. The two first Orders, it may be expected, would in case of so marked a preference to their detriment secede: if, however His Majesty on the other hand should espouse the cause of the Clergy and Nobility the people, tenacious of the footing to which they find themselves already advanced, and encouraged by the further advantages they have in view, would, if one may judge by the present temper of the times, be ready to support their cause by force, in which case the contest might at the outset be strongly disputed, but the Army whose zeal and activity are derived wholly from the Nobility, must soon throw the balance into the King's hands. The Army last year was certainly lukewarm in the King's interest, but the disposition of both Officers and Men is much changed, and they have upon all the late occasions shewn themselves to be entirely devoted to the Royal authority.

Lord Dorset to the Duke of Leeds.

[June 18, 1789.]

25. THE TENNIS COURT OATH

A Conseil du Roi was held at Marly on June 19, and resumed at Versailles (where it was attended by the King's brothers, and a Conseiller who could be trusted to vote with them) on the 21st, to decide on the King's reply to the Assembly's declarations of the 17th. This was to be announced at a special session on the 22nd (subsequently postponed till the 23rd). Meanwhile the Hall of Session is closed; and the deputies of the Commons, finding themselves shut out, adjourn to the neighbouring Tennis Court, and take a solemn oath 'never to desert the National Assembly, and to meet whenever circumstances require, until the Constitution of the Kingdom is settled and established on firm foundations.'

NEWS!—News!—Every one stares at what every one might have expected. A message from the king to the presidents of the three orders, that he should meet them on Monday; and under pretence of preparing the hall for the *séance royale*, the French guards were placed with bayonets to prevent any of the deputies entering the room. The circumstances of doing this ill-judged act of violence have been as ill advised as the act itself. Monsieur Bailly received no other notice of it than by a letter from the Marquis de Brézé, and the deputies met at the door of the hall without knowing that it was shut. Thus the seeds of disgust were sown wantonly in the manner of doing a thing which in itself was equally unpalatable and unconstitutional. The resolution taken on the spot was a noble and firm one; it was to assemble instantly at the *Jeu de paume*, and there the whole assembly took a solemn oath never to be dissolved but by their own consent, and consider themselves and act as the national assembly, let them be wherever violence or fortune might drive them, and their expectations were so little favourable that expresses were sent off to Nantes, intimating that the national assembly might possibly find it necessary to take refuge in some distant city. This message, and placing guards at the hall of the states, are the result of long and repeated councils, held in the king's presence at Marly, where he has been shut up for some days, seeing nobody; and no person admitted, even to the officers of the court, without jealousy and circumspection. The king's brothers have no seat in the council, but the Count d'Artois incessantly attends the resolutions, conveys them to the queen, and has long conferences with her. When this news arrived at Paris, the Palais Royal was in a flame, the coffee-houses, pamphlet-shops, corridors, and gardens were crowded—alarm and apprehension sat in every eye—the reports that were circulated eagerly, tending to show the violent intentions of the court, as if it was bent on the utter extirpation of the French nation, except the party of the queen, are perfectly incredible for their gross absurdity; but nothing was so glaringly ridiculous but the mob swallowed it with indiscriminating faith.

Arthur Young.
[June 20, 1789.]

26. THE ROYAL SESSION

At the special session of the Assembly on June 23, speeches were made by and on behalf of the King, announcing a limited programme of reform, but annulling the 'National Assembly.' Necker's absence showed his disapproval of this démarche, and it is unlike Young's usual shrewdness to be surprised at the Commons' rejection of it.

THE ferment at Paris is beyond conception; 10,000 people have been all this day in the Palais Royal; a full detail of yesterday's proceedings was brought this morning, and read by many apparent leaders of little parties, with comments, to the people. To my surprise, the king's propositions are received with universal disgust. He said nothing explicit on the periodical meeting of the states; he declared all the old feudal rights to be retained as property. These, and the change in the balance of representation in the provincial assemblies, are the articles that give the greatest offence. But instead of looking to, or hoping for further concessions on these points, in order to make them more consonant to the general wishes, the people seem, with a sort of frenzy, to reject all idea of compromise, and to insist on the necessity of the orders uniting, that full power may consequently reside in the commons, to effect what they call the regeneration of the kingdom, a favourite term, to which they affix no precise idea, but add the indefinite explanation of the general reform of all abuses. They are also full of suspicions at M. Necker's offering to resign, to which circumstance they seem to look more than to much more essential points. It is plain to me, from many conversations and harangues I have been witness to, that the constant meetings at the Palais Royal, which are carried to a degree of licentiousness and fury of liberty that is scarcely credible, united

41

with the innumerable inflammatory publications that have been hourly appearing since the assembly of the states, have so heated the people's expectations, and given them the idea of such total changes, that nothing the king or court could do would now satisfy them; consequently it would be idleness itself to make concessions that are not steadily adhered to, not only to be observed by the king, but to be enforced on the people, and good order at the same time restored. But the stumbling-block to this and every plan that can be devised, as the people know and declare in every corner, is the situation of the finances, which cannot possibly be restored but by liberal grants of the states on one hand, or by a bankruptcy on the other. It is well known that this point has been warmly debated in the council: Monsieur Necker has proved to them that a bankruptcy is inevitable if they break with the states before the finances are restored; and the dread and terror of taking such a step, which no minister would at present dare to venture on, has been the great difficulty that opposed itself to the projects of the queen and the Count d'Artois. The measure they have taken is a middle one, from which they hope to gain a party among the people and render the deputies unpopular enough to get rid of them: an expectation, however, in which they will infallibly be mistaken.

Arthur Young.

[June 24, 1789.]

27. THE KING GIVES WAY

Two days after the session of June 23, a large body of deputies of the Nobility, led by the Duc d'Orléans, joined the Commons. In view of this, and of the threatening temper of the general public, the King on the 27th ordered the deputies of both the privileged Orders to join the Third Estate. It was a complete victory for the Commons. The Comte de Montmorin, Minister for Foreign Affairs, who had supported Necker and protested against the policy of the 23rd, now shared his popularity.

I LOSE no time in communicating to Your Grace the

important occurrences of yesterday at Versailles, and the sudden change effected thereby in the Constitution of this Kingdom.

The greater part of the Clergy having already joined the Tiers-Etat it remained only to be seen whether or not the Nobility would follow the example of that Order, as well as of a certain number of their own Members, headed by the Duc d'Orleans.

The whole day of Friday was passed in deliberating upon this important question, and yesterday, in consequence of the final resolution, the remainder of the Clergy and the whole of the Nobility (excepting three, whose names I have not hitherto been able to learn) went and joined the Tiers-Etat forming by this means a regular National Assembly, which will be confirmed by the King in due form on Tuesday next.

Your Grace may easily imagine what was really the case, that nothing but the pressing urgency of the moment could have induced the Nobility to relinquish at once all further design of persevering in their original determination; but when it was seen that the King's personal safety was actually endangered, that was a motive for giving way which could not be resisted: the fermentation of the people, from the moment when the Tiers-Etat had so far gained their point as to bring over to their Body a part of the other two Orders, for the purpose of verifying their returns in common, became very alarming, added to which some of the Military joined in the popular cry, and the French Guards had even been wrought upon to bind themselves by oath not to support the King under the present circumstances many of these paraded the capital in small bodies, openly boasting of the engagement they had entered into not to obey their Officers: it may well be conceived the effect this had upon the populace who now became quite ungovernable at Versailles, as well as at Paris, insomuch that the King and the Royal Family were no longer secure from outrage even in the Palace: in this situation of things His Majesty, after consulting with the Presidents of the two first Orders on Friday evening, decided upon writing the Letter, which I have the honor of sending Your Grace herewith inclosed, and which was addressed to the Duc de Luxembourg, President of the Nobility, at that time assembled: this Letter occasioned a very warm and interesting debate, and there is reason to think would not after all have produced the desired effect, had it not been followed by one from the Comte d'Artois whereby His Royal Highness earnestly entreats that Assembly to comply with the King's wishes, representing the extreme danger to which His Majesty's person would be exposed, if that Body continued any longer to persist in their refusal to join the Tiers-Etat. No sooner was this Letter read than most of the Members started from their seats and declared themselves ready to give every proof in their power of their zealous affection to His Majesty, and tender regard for the safety of his person; immediately after which they proceeded to join the rest of the Deputies in the Common-Hall.

As soon as this event was known out of doors the greatest demonstrations of joy were manifested by the people, who assembled in great numbers under the windows of Their Majesties, crying: *Vivent le Roi et la Reine.* The King and Queen appeared for some minutes at the balcony, and upon their retiring, the people went in the same manner to the several apartments of the Royal Family.

They afterwards proceeded to M. Necker's House, where they remained a considerable time testifying their approbation of that Minister's conduct.

M. de Montmorin had also a share of the popular applause, but none of the rest of the Ministers were noticed: this circumstance gives room for suspicion that the mob had been properly instructed and perhaps influenced, probably by pecuniary consideration, to take the part they did.

Nothing can equal the despondency of the Nobility upon this occasion, forced as they have been by an extraordinary and unexpected impulse to sacrifice in one moment every hope they had formed and the very principles from which they had resolved and flattered themselves that no consideration whatever should oblige them to depart.

Lord Dorset to the Duke of Leeds.

[June 28, 1789.]

28. APPEAL TO ARMS

The mutiny and prison-breaking of the Gardes Françaises, *and other instances of disaffection on the part of French regiments, induced the King to mobilise his foreign troops at Versailles. The suspicion and alarm caused by this move led to the arming of Paris, and the attack on the Bastille.*

2 July, 1789.

TUESDAY evening exhibited a very extraordinary scene in the Gardens of the Palais Royal; some few days before fifteen of the French Guards had been taken up for various misdemeanours which they had committed and were confined in a prison, called *l'Abbaye*, in the Faubourg St. Germains, from whence it was intended to send them privately to Bicêtre in order to their being punished according to their deserts: they contrived however to get a Letter conveyed to the Caffé de Foix making known their situation, upon which a mob to an amazing amount, proceeded immediately to the prison and rescued the Soldiers, whom they carried in triumph to the Palais Royal where they paraded them amidst the acclamations of a prodigious Number of people: the following morning a man with a basket in his hand made a collection, to which everyone who passed, contributed for the benefit of the Soldiers who had been thus taken under the protection of the populace.

Yesterday a numerous body of citizens signed a petition in favor of these delinquents and presented it to the *Assemblée Nationale* with a view of obtaining their pardon; in the mean time they are at liberty. The mutinous spirit which has shewn itself pervades the whole Regiment of French Guards, and at Versailles the men who have been ordered upon duty at the entrance of the avenues leading to the House of Assembly have gone so far as to lay aside their fire-locks while at their posts. The Swiss Guards as well as two other Swiss Regiments have been extremely attentive to their duty, as have likewise been the Dragoons and other Cavalry which have lately been quartered in this City and the environs . . . .

His Majesty has appointed the Maréchal de Broglie Commander-in-Chief of the Troops both at Versailles and Paris. Several Regiments are on their march from different parts which are to be encamped in the neighbourhood of the Capital during the summer. Orders have been given to erect Batteries on the heights above Sève and St. Cloud, and many hundred men are now employed on the declivity of Montmartre preparing a spot for the same purpose.

9th July. M. Necker has more than once expressed his uneasiness at the appearance of so large an Army, which sufficiently proves that that Minister was not consulted upon the measure, and consequently is not in the full confidence of His Sovereign.

The Maréchal de Broglie, to whom the command of the Army is given, is a man of a very determined character, and is what the French call *un bon serviteur du Roi*: such a Person in the King's Council must be a great check upon the encroaching advances of the representations of the Tiers-Etat, if anything can check them; for it is well understood that the Maréchal will not, so far as shall depend upon his exertions, suffer His Royal Master's authority to be impaired in the smallest point.

His Master's lenity towards the French Guards who were released from prison by the populace, in granting their pardon at the interposition of the States-General in their behalf, has had the good effect of stopping the fermentation which for some days agitated this Capital, to which also the continual arrival of Troops has probably contributed very much, for the spirit of popular party is not a little overawed by the unexpected reinforcements of German and Swiss Auxiliaries, whose military discipline is perhaps of itself sufficient dependence for Government to rely on, and with whom, a further security against corruption, it will be difficult to tamper on account of their ignorance of the French language.

A camp is already formed, of about 2500 men, in the

Champ de Mars, adjoining to the *Ecole Militaire:* strict orders have been given not to admit any visitors, and every possible precaution taken to prevent the soldiers from having any intercourse with the common people.

A small camp is also to be formed immediately at St. Denis, but no large encampment can take place 'till after the harvest: the whole number of men in the environs will amount to 30,000.

Lord Dorset to the Duke of Leeds.

29. CRISIS AT VERSAILLES

Edward Rigby, a well-known Norwich physician, visited Paris just at this time, and his Letters from France give a lively picture of the early days of the Revolution. It was on July 11, whilst the Assembly debated whether to preface the Constitution with a Declaration of Rights, that the King dismissed Necker, the other Ministers resigned, and nothing was left but an appeal to arms. G. J. B. Target was a deputy for the Commons of Paris, and one of the best known lawyers in the Assembly.

EARLY on Saturday morning (July 11) we went to Versailles, and entered the Assembly—a glorious sight! Everyone was admitted without difficulty. We were in time to hear La Fayette make the motion for a declaration of rights, which will probably be considered one of the most prominent events in this revolution. His speech was short, but animated and expressive. Lally de Tollendal supported the motion. Neither of them delivered long speeches, but they were received with enthusiastic approbation by the greater part of the Assembly, and by the crowd of auditors who surrounded them. A curé, habited in the shabby dress of an humble ecclesiastic, but with an expressive and ingenuous countenance, stood near us, and seemed to catch every patriotic sentiment; reiterating his approbation with actions and gestures the most enthusiastic. One of our party having letters to Mirabeau, Target, and some others of the popular characters in the Assembly, we called upon them in the afternoon. Target was the only one at home. He conversed very freely on the state of France. He said that the crisis was fast approaching; that the court was driven to an extremity. But he knew they had resolved to get rid of the control of the Assembly, to strike a decisive blow against the growing resistance of the people, and to exonerate themselves from the public debt. 'We,' said he, 'Mirabeau, La Fayette, myself, and others, are all proscribed; but we are sure of the people, and not without a reasonable hope that the army will declare for us. We know the imbecility which prevails in the Court, and the want of vigour in the administration. We therefore,' said this member of the Assembly, 'have great confidence that the struggle will terminate favourably to the people. . . .'

In the afternoon we walked in the parks, gardens and woods belonging to the Palace—a fine country, but the grounds badly laid out. In these walks we saw many members of the Assembly, particularly of the Tiers-Etats in black gowns, conversing apparently with much earnestness. It reminded us of the Athenian groves filled with philosophers. Nor could we see the splendour of the Palace, nor witness the King and Queen going to mass, gazed upon by such a mixed multitude, without adverting in thought to the peculiar situation of the country; nor could we behold the face of Marie Antoinette, and not see symptoms of no common anxiety marked on it. The dignity of countenance which, according to various descriptions, formed at an earlier period of her life a most interesting addition to those claims of natural beauty so profusely bestowed on her, might be said, indeed, to remain, but it had assumed more of the character of severity. The forehead was corrugated, the eyebrows thrown forward, and the eyes but little open, and, turning with seeming caution from side to side, discovered, instead of gaiety or even serenity, an expression of suspicion and care which necessarily much abated of that beauty for which she had once with truth been celebrated.

Edward Rigby.
[1789.]

30. THE FALL OF THE BASTILLE

(1)

The 'Barriers' were the gates in the mur d'octroi *erected round Paris by Calonne to facilitate the collection of customs on goods entering the city. Lord Dorset's account of the attack on the Bastille is not entirely accurate. The fortress was protected by an outer and an inner drawbridge. The crowd which broke down the first was fired at by the garrison to prevent its attacking the second; there was no 'breach of honour,' or 'massacre.' The firing on the 'flag of truce' was a later, not an earlier incident, and probably due to a misunderstanding. J. F. X. Whyte, born at Dublin in 1730, became an officer in a Franco-Irish regiment, married in Paris, was incarcerated at Vincennes by his family in 1781 on account of mental derangement, and transferred to the Bastille in 1784. He had thus been in prison not 30 but only 8 years.*

I WROTE to Your Grace on the 12th Inst. by a messenger extraordinary to inform you of the removal of M. Necker from His Majesty's Councils: I have now to lay before Your Grace an account of the general revolt, with the extraordinary circumstances attending it, that has been the immediate consequence of that step. On Sunday evening a slight skirmish happened in the Place de Louis XV, in which two Dragoons were killed, and two wounded of the Duc de Choiseuil's Regiment: after which all the troops left the Capital, and the populace remained unmolested masters of everything: much to their credit however, uncontrouled as they now were, no material mischief was done; their whole attention being confined to the burning of some of the Barriers. Very early on Monday morning the Convent of St. Lazare was forced, in which, besides a considerable quantity of corn, were found arms and ammunition, supposed to have been conveyed thither as a place of security, at different periods from the Arsenal: and now a general consternation was seen throughout the Town: all shops were shut; all public and private works at a stand still and scarcely a person to be seen in the Streets excepting the armed *Bourgeoisie*, a temporary police for the protection of private property, to replace the established one which no longer had any influence.

In the morning of Tuesday the Hospital of Invalids was

summonsed to surrender and was taken possession of after a very slight resistance: all the cannon, small arms and amunition were immediately seized upon, and every one who chose to arm himself was supplied with what was necessary: two of my servants, whom I had sent out on messages and directed, for private reasons, to put off their liveries, were compelled to go to the Hospital where they received two very good muskets which they brought away with them: the cannon was disposed of in different parts of the Town: in the evening a large detachment with two pieces of cannon went to the Bastille to demand the ammunition that was there, the *Gardes Bourgeoises* not being then sufficiently provided: a flag of truce was sent on before and was answered from within, notwithstanding which the Governor (the Marquis de Launay) contrary to all precedent fired upon the people and killed several: this proceeding so enraged the populace that they rushed to the very gates with a determination to force their way through if possible: upon this the Governor agreed to let in a certain number of them on condition that they should not commit any violence: these terms being acceded to, a detachment of about 40 in number advanced and were admitted, but the drawbridge was immediately drawn up again and the whole party instantly massacred: this breach of honor aggravated by so glaring an act of inhumanity excited a spirit of revenge and tumult such as might naturally be expected: the two pieces of cannon were immediately placed against the Gate and very soon made a breach which, with the disaffection that as is supposed prevailed within, produced a sudden surrender of that Fortress: M. de Launay, the principal gunner, the tailer, and two old invalids who had been noticed as being more active than the rest were seized and carried to the Hôtel de Ville where, after a very summary trial before the tribunal there, the inferior objects were put to death and M. de Launay had also his head cut off at the Place de Grève, but with circumstances of barbarity too shocking to relate: besides the abovementioned the *Prévôt des Marchands*, M. de Flesselles, who the day before was

unanimously called to preside at the Assembly at the Hôtel
de Ville for forming regulations relative to the tranquility
of Paris and to means of furnishing the Town with provisions was, upon a suspicion that was raised against him,
seized in his own house, when a letter (said to be from the
Baron de Breteuil) was found upon him, in which he was
desired to amuze the citizens as well as he could for the
reasons *he knew*; this was sufficient to draw upon him the
fury of the people; he was immediately shot with a pistol,
and his head was cut off, which, with M. de Launay's and
the tailer's hand, all placed upon pikes, was exhibited at the
Palais Royal and afterwards in several of the neighbouring
Streets. In the course of the same evening the whole of
the *Gardes Françoises* joined the Bourgeoisie with all their
cannon, arms and ammunition: the Regiments that were
encamped in the *Champ de Mars*, by an Order from Government left the ground at 2 o'Clock yesterday morning and
fell back to Sêve, leaving all their camp equipage behind
them; the magazines of powder and corn at the *Ecole
Militaire* were immediately taken possession of and a *Garde
Bourgeoise* appointed to protect them. Nothing could
exceed the regularity and good order with which all this
extraordinary business has been conducted: of this I have
myself been a witness upon several occasions during the
last three days as I have passed through the streets, nor had
I at any moment reason to be alarmed for my personal
safety.

Since Tuesday morning the police has been most strictly
observed: the principal inhabitants of every parish were
summonsed to meet at their respective Churches in order
that each parish should undertake to furnish a guard for its
own protection. No one however has been allowed to go
out of Paris and all those who have come in, especially on
the Versailles side, have been strictly searched and any
letters found upon them have been taken to the *Hôtel de
Ville* to be examined: M. de Crosne, *Lieutenant Général de
Police*, owing to a discovery that was made by this means
has found it necessary to secrete himself, as has also the

Baron d'Ogny, *Maître des Postes* on a similar account. M. de Crosne's house has already been forcibly entered and all the books and papers relative to the police destroyed.

Nothing material happened in the course of yesterday (Wednesday) morning, but about 3 o'clock in the afternoon a Deputation arrived from Versailles at the Palais Royal, to announce that the King had been present at the States-General where He made the speech, which I have the honor to send Your Grace enclosed, and which was communicated to the Hôtel de Ville: the Deputation returned the same evening to Versailles: the coolness with which this news was received seems to have thrown everybody again into the utmost consternation, and, to judge by circumstances, the diffidence of the people is greater than ever for all the barriers are doubly guarded.

The general wish now is that the King would come to Paris and it was hoped yesterday that His Majesty would be induced to shew Himself here on this day, but it is said that He is prevented coming by indisposition: it is thought difficult to foresee what measures the people will have recourse to: the general idea however is that an armed Body of Citizens to the number of at least 50,000 will go to Versailles and forcibly bring their Sovereign to the Capital. The disposition of the people at this moment is so unfavorable to the Court that I should not be surprized if the States-General, by appearing to give too much credit to the King's professions, should lose the consideration in which they have hitherto been held by the Nation.

The Populace will not easily forgive the removal of M. Necker; for they seem determined to push their resentment to the utmost lengths: but God forbid that should be the case, since they have already got the upperhand, for who can trust to the moderation of an offended multitude?

The regularity and determined conduct of the populace upon the present occasion exceeds all belief and the execration of the Nobility is universal amongst the lower order of people . . . .

Upon searching the Bastille not more than 4 or 5

prisoners were found, of whom none had been there any length of time, except an Englishman who calls himself Major White, and who had been confined in a dungeon upwards of 30 years: he was questioned by some English Gentleman who happened to be near while he was conducted away, but the unhappy man seemed to have nearly lost the use of his intellects and could express himself but very ill; his beard was at least a yard long; what is very extraordinary he did not know that the Bastille was the place of his confinement, but thought he had been shut up at St. Lazare, nor did he appear to be sensible of his good fortune in being released; he expressed however a strong desire of being taken to a *Lawyer*.

Everybody since Monday has appeared with a cockade in his hat: at first green ribbons were worn but that being the colour of the Comte d'Artois' livery, red and white in honor of the Duc d'Orléans, have been substituted.

Thus, My Lord, the greatest Revolution that we know anything of has been effected with, comparatively speaking, if the magnitude of the event is considered, the loss of very few lives: from this moment we may consider France as a free Country; the King a very limited Monarch, and the Nobility as reduced to a level with the rest of the Nation.

Lord Dorset to the Duke of Leeds.

[July 16, 1789.]

(2)

The Caisse d'escompte *was the almost National Bank founded by Turgot in* 1776. *Of the six prisoners liberated from the Bastille with Whyte* (*v. above*) *four were forgers, a fifth was confined for indecency, and the sixth, like Whyte insane, had declared himself an accomplice in the attempted murder of Louis XV* (*Alger,* Englishmen in the French Revolution, *p.* 333). *If this last was the Count d'Auche, he had been in prison* 32 *years. The Archbishop of Paris was Leclerc de Juigné; his carriage had been stoned by a crowd on June* 24.

AT about eleven o'clock on Monday (July 13) we went to the Post-office and found all in confusion; one of the clerks in an agony of distress, crying and biting his hands. We also called at Sir John Lambert's, our banker, but could get no cash, the *Caisse d'escompte* refusing to do any business. The populace still continued parading the streets in large bodies. We met one containing at least four thousand going into the Palais Royal, who insisted on our taking off our hats. All the prisons except the Bastille were opened on this day, and we saw one prisoner, Lord Massareene, an Irish nobleman, pass through the streets. He is said to have been a captive twenty-three years; he was dressed in a white frock, like a cook, and had a bar of iron on his shoulders. Paris had not before perhaps been in such real danger as on this day, with such numbers of exasperated rabble within its walls, such a formidable army without, and at Versailles an enraged and disappointed Court ready to strike the moment an opportunity should offer of renewing the attack. Symptoms of general apprehension exhibited themselves, with all the circumstances likely to be produced in a populous and so variously peopled city. Crowds of strangers and even of the inhabitants hastily left Paris. . . . Business of all kinds was immediately at a standstill and the shops shut. . . . The magistrates assembled at the Hôtel de Ville, and the inhabitants of the several districts were called together in the churches, to deliberate upon the measures proper to be taken under circumstances of such peculiar danger and urgency. It was resolved that a certain number of the more respectable inhabitants should be enrolled and immediately take arms; that the magistrates should sit permanently at the Hôtel de Ville, and that committees, also permanent, should be formed in every district of Paris, to convey intelligence to the magistrates, and receive instructions from them. This important and most necessary resolution was executed with wonderful promptitude and unexampled good management. It was necessary not only to arm a description of persons who could be relied upon, but to disarm those from whom little protection was to be expected, and who might become disorderly and mischievous; and the effecting this required considerable address. Early in the afternoon (July 13) we began to perceive among the motley groups of mob who paraded the streets with such symptoms of irritation as must soon have produced excess, here and there a man of decent exterior, carrying a musket, and assuming a respectable military appearance. The number of these gradually increased, and it was evidently their intention at once to conciliate and disarm the irregular band; and this appeared to be principally effected before the evening, at which time the regularly armed citizens almost exclusively occupied the streets, and were divided into different parties, some forming posts of guards at different stations, others patrolling, and all arranged under leaders. About this time some of them began to be distinguished by a cockade, but its colour was green. I should also observe that large bodies of citizens, previous to their arming, exhibited themselves in the Palais Royal soon after they had recorded their names at the Hôtel de Ville; and these in several instances consisted of persons of similar occupations, forming something like Companies. Not the least numerous, least respectable, and least manly was the company of the *Maitres Perruquiers*, said to be a thousand of them, each having four or five *Garçons*. Many of them were remarkably fine fellows.

This disarming the populace and establishing a well-armed military body of citizens, may be considered one of the most important steps which could have been taken by the Parisians at this period of the revolution, and the extraordinary address and temper they discovered in doing it will probably ever be mentioned with admiration.

July 14. A Canadian Frenchman, whom we found in the crowd and who spoke good English, was the first who intimated to us that it had been resolved to attack the Bastille. We smiled at the gentleman, and suggested the improbability of undisciplined citizens taking a citadel which had held out against the most experienced troops in Europe; little thinking it would be actually in the hands of the people before night. From the commencement of the struggle on Sunday evening there had been scarcely any time in which the firing of guns had not been heard in all quarters of the city, and, as this was principally produced by exercising the citizens in the use of the musket, in trying cannon, etc., it excited, except at first, but little alarm. Another sound equally incessant was produced by the ringing of bells to call together the inhabitants in different parts of the city. These joint sounds being constantly iterated, the additional noise produced by the attack on the Bastille was so little distinguished that I doubt not it had begun a considerable time, and even been completed, before it was known to many thousands of the inhabitants as well as to ourselves.

We ran to the end of the Rue St. Honoré. We here soon perceived an immense crowd proceeding towards the Palais Royal with acceleration of an extraordinary kind, but which sufficiently indicated a joyful event, and, as it approached we saw a flag, some large keys, and a paper elevated on a pole above the crowd, in which was inscribed '*La Bastille est prise et les portes sont ouvertes.*' The intelligence of this extraordinary event thus communicated, produced an impression upon the crowd really indescribable. A sudden burst of the most frantic joy instantaneously took place; every possible mode in which the most rapturous feelings of joy could be expressed, were everywhere exhibited. Shouts and shrieks, leaping and embracing, laughter and tears, every sound and every gesture, including even what approached to nervous and hysterical affection, manifested, among the promiscuous crowd, such an instantaneous and unanimous emotion of extreme gladness as I should suppose was never before experienced by human beings. . . .

The crowd passed on to the Palais Royal, and in a few minutes another succeeded. Its approach was also announced by loud and triumphant acclamations, but, as it came nearer, we soon perceived a different character, as though bearing additional testimony to the fact reported by the first crowd, the impression by it on the people was of a very different kind. A deep and hollow murmur at once pervaded them, their countenances expressing amazement mingled with alarm. We could not at first explain these circumstances;

but as we pressed more to the centre of the crowd we suddenly partook of the general sensation, for we then, and not till then, perceived two bloody heads raised on pikes, which were said to be the heads of the Marquis de Launay, Governor of the Bastille, and of Monsieur Flesselles, *Prévôt des Marchands*. It was a chilling and a horrid sight! An idea of savageness and ferocity was impressed on the spectators, and instantly checked those emotions of joy which had before prevailed. Many others, as well as ourselves, shocked and disgusted at this scene, retired immediately from the streets. . . .

The night approached; the crowd without continued agitated. Reports of a meditated attack upon the city that night by a formidable army under the command of the Count d'Artois and the Maréchal Broglie were in circulation, and gained such credit as to induce the inhabitants to take measures for opposing them. Trees were cut down and thrown across the principal approaches to the city; the streets were impaved, and the stones carried to the tops of houses which fronted the streets through which the troops might pass (for the fate of Pyrrhus was not unknown to the French) and the windows in most parts of the city were illuminated. The night passed with various indications of alarm; guns were firing continually; the tocsin sounded unceasingly; groups of agitated citizens passed hastily along, and parties of the *Milice Bourgeoise* (for such was the name already assumed by those who had taken arms the day before) paraded the streets. . . .

I went (July 15) and was led by the sound of an approaching crowd towards the end of the Rue St. Honoré, and there I witnessed a most affecting spectacle. The Bastille had been scarcely entered and the opposition subdued, when an eager search began to find out and liberate every unhappy captive immured within its walls. Two wretched victims of the detestable tyranny of the old Government had just been discovered and taken from some of the most obscure dungeons of this horrid castle, and were at this time conducted by the crowd to the Palais Royal. One of these was a little feeble old man, I could not learn his history; he exhibited an appearance of childishness and fatuity; he tottered as he walked, and his countenance exhibited little more than the smile of an idiot. . . . The other was a tall and rather robust old man; his countenance and whole figure interesting in the highest degree; he walked upright, with a firm and steady gait; his hands were folded and turned upwards, he looked but little at the crowd; the character of his face seemed a mixture of surprise and alarm, for he knew not whither they were leading him, he knew not what fate awaited him; his face was directed towards the sky, but his eyes were but little open. . . . He had a remarkably high forehead, which, with the crown of his head, was completely bald; but he had a very long beard, and on the back of his head the hair was unusually abundant. . . . His dress was an old greasy reddish tunic; the colour and the form of the garb were probably some indication of what his rank had been; for we afterwards learned that he was a Count d'Auche, that he had been a major of cavalry, and a young man of some talent, and that the offence for which he had sustained this long imprisonment had been his having written a pamphlet against the Jesuits. Every one who witnessed this scene probably felt as I did, an emotion which partook of horror and detestation of the Government which could so obdurately as well as unjustly expose human beings to such sufferings; and of pity for the miserable individuals before us. . . .

It had been reported that the King was to come to Paris on the Thursday (July 16), and great crowds filled the streets through which it was expected he would pass: but his coming did not take place till the Friday (July 17). We were very desirous of witnessing the spectacle of the monarch thus, I might almost say, led captive. The spectacle was very interesting, though not from the artificial circumstances which have usually given distinction to royal processions. The impression made on the spectator was not the effect of any adventitious splendour of costly robes or glittering ornaments—the appearance of the King was simple, if not humble; the man was no longer concealed in the dazzling radiance of the sovereign. . . . The streets were lined with the armed bourgeois, three deep—forming a line, as we were assured, of several miles extent. The procession began to pass the place where we were at a quarter past three. The first who appeared were the city officers and the police guards; some women followed them, carrying green branches of trees which were fancifully decorated; then more officers; then the Prévôt des Marchands and different members of the city magistracy. Many of the armed bourgeois followed on horseback: then some of the King's officers, some on horseback and some on foot; then followed the whole body of the Etats Généraux on foot, the noblesse, clergy, and Tiers-Etats, each in their peculiar dresses. That of the noblesse was very beautiful; they wore a peculiar kind of hat with large white feathers, and many of them were tall, elegant young men. The clergy, especially the bishops and some of the higher orders, were most superbly dressed; many of them in lawn dresses, with pink scarfs and massive crosses of gold hanging before them. The dress of the Tiers-Etats was very ordinary, even worse than that of the inferior order of gownsmen at the English universities. More of the King's officers followed; then the King in a large plain coach with eight horses. After this more bourgeois; then another coach and eight horses with other officers of state; then an immense number of the bourgeois, there having been, it was said, two hundred thousand of them in arms. The countenance of the King was little marked with sensibility, and his general appearance by no means indicated alarm. He was accustomed to throw his head very much back on his shoulders, which, by obliging him to look upwards, gave a kind of stupid character to his countenance by increasing the apparent breadth of his face, by preventing that variation of expression which is produced by looking about. He received neither marks of applause nor insult from the populace, unless their silence could be construed into a negative sort of disrespect. Nor were any insults shown to the noblesse or clergy, except in the instance of the Archbishop of Paris, a very tall thin man. He was very much hissed, the popular clamour having been excited against him by a story circulated of his having encouraged the King to use strong measures against the people, and of his attempting to make an impression on the people by a superstitious exposure of a crucifix. He looked a good deal agitated, and whether he had a leaden eye or not I know not, but it certainly loved the ground. The warm and enthusiastic applause of the people was reserved for the Tiers-Etat. . . . *Vivent les Tiers-Etats! Vive la Liberté!* were loudly iterated as they passed.

.   .   .   .

On the Saturday (July 18) we visited more of the public places, but the most interesting object, and which attracted the greatest number of spectators, was the Bastille. We found two hundred workmen busily employed in the destruction of this castle of despotism. We saw the battlements tumble down amidst the applauding shouts of the people. I observed a number of artists taking drawings of what from this time was to have no existence but on paper.

.   .   .   .

And this reminds me of our having a second time seen the other prisoner, the feeble old man. He was placed conspicuously at a window opposite the house where we saw the King pass, and at that time he was brought forward and made to wave his hat, having a three coloured cockade on it.

Edward Rigby.

31. A BLOODLESS REVOLUTION

This 'extract of a letter from Paris' is printed in Despatches from Paris, 1784–1790. *Emigration, led by the Comte d'Artois, began on July 16, the day after the King's decision to disband his troops, and to visit Paris. A first* Comité de Constitution, *of 30 members, had been set up on July 6: a second, of 8 members, was nominated on the 14th, including J. J. Mounier, deputy for Dauphiné, the abbé E. J. Sieyès, deputy for Paris, and the Comte de Clermont-Tonnerre, deputy for the Nobles of Paris. J. L. De Lolme, of Geneva, published* The Constitution of England *in 1775.*

THE Revolution in the French Constitution and Government may now, I think, be looked upon as compleated, beyond all fears of any further attempts being made by the Court Party to defeat it. The entrance of the King into Paris was certainly one of the most humiliating steps that he could possibly take. He was actually led in triumph like a tame bear by the Deputies and the City Militia. The whole party, inimical to the rights of the people, are dispersed. The Count d'Artois and his whole family (except the Countess, who is much beloved) the Condés, Contis, Polignacs, Breteuils, Vaudreuils, etc., are all fled and people are talking of confiscating their estates. The news we have from the Provinces are much more favorable than could have been expected. Everywhere the people and the soldiers seem to have been animated with the same spirit. In Brittany, where the greatest apprehensions were entertained, not a drop of blood has been spilt. The soldiers refused to obey their officers, and many of them joined the people. Fifty thousand Bretons were in arms, ready to march to the assistance of the Parisians, and there is no doubt, that if the King had not come round, they would not have left a Nobleman's house standing thro' the whole Province.

There certainly never was an instance of so astonishing a Revolution operated almost without bloodshed, and without the people being led on by any leader, or by any party, but merely by the general diffusion of reason and philosophy. We shall soon be able to form a guess what is the nature of the constitution that is intended to be adopted in France. A Committee of 8 members is chosen to form a plan, which will afterwards be laid before the whole Assembly for its approbation. The three people who will probably have the greatest share in this important work are M. Mounier, the Abbé Sieyès and the Count of Clermont Tonnerre, all three men of first rate abilities. From what is known of their ideas and principles it is thought the Executive Power will be left solely to the King, who will be deprived of all share in the Legislative Authority, which will be lodged in the National Assembly, formed into one

Body, without distinction of Orders. The best French Politicians (contrary to the opinion of de Lolme) look upon the division of the Legislative Authority in England as a great defect in our constitution, and the principal source of that system of corruption which takes place with us. Another circumstance in which it is thought the French Constitution will differ essentially from ours, will be to have a power in the State superior to that of the National Assembly, by leaving to the people in great and important Constitutional points the right of controuling the proceedings of their Representatives, in the manner which takes place in the United States of America. Several years must pass over, before we can judge of the advantages, and disadvantages of such a form of Government.

Anon.
[July 22, 1789.]

32. LAFAYETTE AND THE NATIONAL GUARD

J. G. Millingen's Recollections of Republican France (1848) *reproduce memories of such extreme youth—he was only 8–10, when his father held a position at the Paris mint between 1790 and 1792—that something must be allowed for later reflexion. The Marquis de Lafayette, deputy for the Nobles of Paris, was nominated first Commandant of the* milice parisienne *on July 15. Only 'active' citizens, i.e. those paying taxes to the value of three days' labour, were at this time recruited for the National Guard, which was accordingly regarded as undemocratic.*

LAFAYETTE did not belie his distinguished birth. He looked essentially aristocratic, even when mixing familiarly amongst the very lowest orders. He seemed to be the idol of the multitude. I recollect him well; his affable smile, his ingratiating manner, his dignified calmness, amidst surrounding conflicts, that threatened the destruction of all social order, gave him a power of fascination that could lay the gathering storm.

In this he might have succeeded, had he not committed a great fault, by producing a feeling of hostility between the National Guard and the people, trusting to the armed force for the repression of excesses. The people, therefore, soon looked upon the burgher guard as an aristocratic and privileged body, which had something to lose, and therefore something to protect. It was from this circumstance that, in many of the numerous outbreaks of the reckless and heedless rabble, the National Guard neither did nor could repress their turbulence. They were citizens, divided in interests and opinions, and only uniting for security; whereas their opponents formed numerous masses, inspired by one sentiment—havoc and revenge—and at the orders of any faction that paid them, or excited their evil passions. Had Lafayette amalgamated the National Guard with the people, it would have been a much wiser plan, and might possibly have guarded the country against many future fearful contingencies, as the fusion might have neutralized many of the mistaken notions of the lower orders.

J. G. Millingen.

33. PROVINCIAL IGNORANCE

The Gazette de France, *a kind of Court Circular, and the* Mercure de France, *a literary magazine, were the only French papers dating from the 17th century. The* Journal de Paris, *dating from 1777, was almost the only other pre-revolutionary paper. By the* Courrier de l'Europe, *Young probably means the* Journal général de l'Europe, *which began to appear in 1788, and dealt with politics, agriculture, and commerce.* Affiches *and* placards *were posters, sometimes containing as much matter as papers, stuck up on walls or street corners.*

THE backwardness of France is beyond credibility in everything that pertains to intelligence. That universal circulation of intelligence, which in England transmits the least vibration of feeling or alarm, with electric sensibility, from one end of the kingdom to another, and which unites in bands of connection men of similar interests and situations, has no existence in France. Thus it may be said, perhaps with truth, that the fall of the king, court, lords, nobles, army, church, and parliaments is owing to a want of intelligence being quickly circulated, consequently is owing to the very effects of that thraldom in which they held the people: it is therefore a retribution rather than a punishment. From Strasbourg hither, I have not been able to see a newspaper. Here I asked for the *Cabinet Literaire*. None. The gazettes? At the coffee-house. Very easily replied, but not so easily found. Nothing but the *Gazette de France*, for which, at this period, a man of common sense would not give one *sol*. To four other coffee-houses; at some no paper at all, not even the *Mercure*; at the *Caffé Militaire*, the *Courier de l'Europe* a fortnight old; and well-dressed people are now talking of the news of two or three weeks past, and plainly by their discourse know nothing of what is passing. The whole town of Besançon has not been able to afford me a sight of the *Journal de Paris*, nor of any paper that gives a detail of the transactions of the states; yet it is the capital of a province, large as half a dozen English counties, and containing 25,000 souls—with, strange to say! the post coming in but three times a week. At this eventful moment, with no licence, nor even the least restraint on the press, not one paper established at Paris for circulation in the provinces with the necessary steps taken by *affiche*, or *placard*, to inform the people in all the towns of its establishment. For what the country knows to the contrary, their deputies are in the Bastile, instead of the Bastile being rased; so the mob plunder, burn, and destroy in complete ignorance: and yet, with all these shades of darkness, these clouds of tenebrity, this universal mass of ignorance, there are men every day in the states who are puffing themselves off for the FIRST NATION IN EUROPE! the GREATEST PEOPLE IN THE UNIVERSE!

Arthur Young.
[July 17, 1789.]

34. BEGGARS

The poor harvest of 1788 *sent up the price of corn to the highest figure it had reached for over fifty years ; and the bad winter that followed, coinciding with a climax in the price of living, caused intense distress among the poor, particularly in the towns. Samuel Ireland, author and engraver, published a* Picturesque Tour through France, *etc., in* 1790.

SOME recent disturbances have taken place in this city, for

want of bread, a plea, I fear, that has much truth in it, as I never remember to have seen so great a number of beggars in any city I have passed through: they flock through the streets in immense crowds, and are sometimes exceedingly vicious, on being refused their request, or rather demand. . . . On our return to Amiens we prepared for our route to England, when in getting into our chaise, to exemplify what I have before remarked of the poverty of this place, we counted no less than sixty-four beggars, who surrounded our carriage, and with one voice, in full cry, implored our charity.

Samuel Ireland.
[Amiens, Sept. 1789.]

35. CHAOS

The debate on the King's veto, Aug. 29—Sept. 11, was the first in which the Assembly definitely split into a Right and a Left Party, and in which Paris opinion, inspired by leaders of the Commune (Hotel de Ville, Town Hall), and expressed by speakers at the Palais Royal, made itself feared. The Marquis de Lally-Tollendal was a deputy for the Paris Nobility, and a member of the Comité de Constitution. *Early in August Necker had made a report on the financial situation, and proposed a loan of 30 million* livres. *William Eden, first Baron Auckland, had negotiated the commercial treaty with France in 1786 and was British Ambassador at the Hague during the Revolution.*

THE Plan of a Constitution recommended by the Committee of the Assemblée Nationale and opened by Monsieur de Lally Tolendal would probably have procured a period of tranquillity, and would have allowed the entering upon the great work of providing for the Debt and the Deficit, both of which in the present state of things are increasing every hour: but the Assemblée Nationale is ill circumstanced in all respects. The Members of the Noblesse and of the Clergé cannot bring themselves to wish cordially for any result which, however necessary to the Kingdom for the sake of its internal tranquillity, may sanctify the violences done to their respective classes; and the representations of the Tiers Etat, considered collectively, are factious, ignorant and absurd. There are in all the Orders some individuals of great integrity, right meaning, and good talents; but in general they are under intimidation from the lower people of Paris and of the chief Provincial Towns; and there is not yet any man who stands forward with talents and weight to guide the others: In effect the Kingdom of France is at this hour governed by some nameless individuals who assemble every morning and evening at the Hotel de Ville de Paris. The Court of Versailles is not only in appearance but in fact in a state of imprisonment. The nominal Ministers of the Country avow without reserve that they are merely nominal. The Church is not only without influence but without respect, and is soon likely to be without bread. The Army is without discipline, and almost without soldiers. The treasury is without money, and nearly without credit; tho' M. Necker's last Rapport (which is an excellent composition) will probably effectuate the new loan of forty millions: and lastly the Magistracy is without power or functions. It is certainly possible that from this chaos some creation may result; but I am satisfied that it must be long before France returns to any state of Existence which can make her a subject of uneasiness to other nations. . . .

Mr. Eden to the Duke of Leeds.

[Sept. 3, 1789.]

36. THE OCTOBER DAYS

(1)

On Sept. 23, the Flemish Regiment, ordered up from Douai ten days before, arrived at Versailles. At regimental dinners on Oct. 1 and 3, royalist toasts were drunk, and (it was said) the tricolour cockade was insulted. On Oct. 5, some Paris fish-women (Poissardes) protesting against the food-shortage, marched to Versailles to ask the King for bread, and to punish the troops who had insulted the national colours. The National Guard forced Lafayette to lead them there too, for the same purpose. He arrived in time to keep the peace at Versailles that night; but early next morning (Oct. 6) the crowd broke into the Palace, killed some of the King's guard, and put the Queen's life in danger. Thereupon the King promised to come and live in Paris, and the Royal Family

was escorted back by the crowd the same evening, and lodged in the Tuileries.
Mr. B. Garlike, previously private secretary to Lord Auckland, was at this
time attached to the Embassy. Later he became Minister in Denmark.

My Lord,—I take the advantage of a few minutes to inform your Lordship that, in consequence of the alarm occasioned by what passed at Versailles on Friday, and the un-accountable continuance of the scarcity of bread, the Poissardes assembled yesterday morning from every part of Paris, and, forcing men and women into their party, went off in furious disorder to Versailles. Mr. Bailly's consternation and fears were such that he intended resigning and escaping; and the Marquis Lafayette, without orders from the Hôtel de Ville, could come to no resolution he was sure would be safe. The troops assembled in every district and the Gardes Françaises (who also began to fear for themselves in case of any turn against them) and some others of the troops surrounded M. de Lafayette's house, and insisted on his leading them instantly to Versailles, and, mentioning the *Lanterne* as an alternative, told him he must either go on or go up. About 40,000 troops, armed men, and some women, left Paris about five o'clock, headed by the marquis. On their arrival at Versailles, they found the King's household had surrendered to the mob of women in Versailles militia that had attacked the Gardes de Corps in the morning. Five or six of this Corps were taken, and either cut to pieces or beheaded, and sixteen or seventeen were saved by the arrival of the city troops. The heads of two of these young gentlemen were paraded through the streets this morning, without a sigh for their fate from any of the spectators, and amidst more insults and cruelty from men, women, and children, than I could have conceived in any people, and in any people with such a spectacle before them, in any state of humanity whatever.

The King and Queen, and royal family arrived at Paris about seven o'clock this evening, and are to remain at the Tuileries. Many of the Gardes de Corps have escaped: those now in Paris have taken the common oath, and are incorporated with the National Militia.

In the mobbing on Monday I saw many genteel women forced from their coaches to go to Versailles; means, however, were found to prevent the greater part from being taken there. Several went, and some, fainting in the streets, were left to the mercy of the bystanders.

Mr. Garlike to Lord Auckland.
[Tues., Oct. 6, midnight.]

(2)

Lord Robert Fitzgerald succeeded Hailes as Chargé d'Affaires *for Lord Dorset in October, 1789, and remained in that post under Lord Gower till June, 1790. His account exaggerates the slaughter at Versailles on Oct. 6.*

7 Oct., 1789.

I DISPATCH a messenger extraordinary to give Your Grace some account of the unprecedented events of the day and for that purpose must carry Your Grace as far back as Thursday last which gave birth to the scenes of horror and confusion I have since been witness to.

It being customary, My Lord, as I am informed, for the *Gardes du Corps* at Versailles to give an entertainment to any new Regiment that arrives in that Town, the Regiment *de Flandres* was that Day sumptuously entertained with a Dinner by that Corps in the Palace.

After Dinner Their Majesties judged proper to honor the Company with their presence, and to shew much seeming satisfaction in the general joy that prevailed among the guests.

On their appearance the music instantly beat up to the tune of *O Richard O mon Roi*, and the company joyning in a chorus seemed to unite all ideas in the one unanimous sentiment of loyalty, and a love for the King, and nothing was heard but repeated shouts of *Vive Le Roi*, within and without the Palace. Happy would it have been had their Festivity ended in noise and singing, but unfortunately they forgot themselves, and in the height of imprudence and mistaken zeal they all tore the National Cockade from their Hats and trampled them underfoot, with many oaths against all those who wore them and whom they considered as traitors to the King. The Garde du Corps supplied themselves with black Cockades in the room of those they had thrown away in such disdain, and this circumstance, My Lord, however trifling it sounds, was of lamentable consequences and proved the ruin of that fine corps of men. The news of this day soon reached Paris and general ill-humour spread visibly throughout.

On Saturday the Palais Royal was much disturbed, and it became unsafe to walk the streets with black Cockades, as several strangers experienced, from whose hats they were torn with much violence and abusive language. On Sunday the confusion encreased and in consequence of some motions made in the Palais Royal a vast concourse of people tumultuously proceeded to the Town House, which it is said they pillaged of some money, altho' many affirm it was only to demand bread and to enquire into the real causes of the extreme scarcity of it at this season of the Year.

On Monday morning, My Lord, we were much surprised and at first much entertained with the ludicrous sight of a female army proceeding very clamourously, but in order and determined step towards Versailles.

I do not exaggerate when I assure Your Grace that there could not have been less than five thousand women who, armed with every weapon they could possibly pick up, proceeded on this expedition, which bore a more serious aspect when we perceived they were followed by the numerous inhabitants of the Fauxbourgs St. Antoine and St. Marceau, besides many detachments of the Milice Bourgeoise. In the evening our alarms for Versailles encreased with our astonishment when we found that 20,000 of the Milice Bourgeoise with M. de La Fayette at their head were under march to the support of the numerous bands of disorderly people who had preceded them in the course of the day. We waited the events with much anxiety all night and on Tuesday morning received the unpleasant account of there having been blood spilt. The Gardes du Corps were the first who fired on the Parisians and five or six people, chiefly women, were killed: the regt. *de Flandres* was also drawn out to oppose this torrent, but the word to fire was no sooner given than they, to a man, clubbed their arms and with a shout of *Vive La Nation* went over to the Parisians. Some troops of Dragoons that are quartered at Versailles also laid down their Arms, and the Swiss detachments remained motionless having received no orders from their officers to fire. The Garde du Corps being thus abandoned and overpowered by numbers fled precipitately into the gardens and woods, where they were pursued and vast numbers were killed and taken prisoners.

I wish, My Lord, the vengeance of the Parisians had ended there, but seeming desirous their fellow citizens should share and witness their triumph, they carried some of the heads of their unhappy victims to Paris, and paraded them through the Streets on spikes. These dreadful scenes occupied the curiosity of all on Tuesday morning, when the sudden and unexpected report came that the King, Queen, and Royal Family were on their way to Paris. I confess I entertained doubts of the possibility of the Royal Family's moving from Versailles to Paris at so short a notice and was only convinced of the truth of what I heard when I saw the people flocking from all parts of the town and above 50,000 Militia proceeding to line the Streets and the Road to Versailles. Their Majesties and the Royal Family arrived between 7 and 8 o'clock in the evening after having been 6 hours on the Road. The carriages all proceeded to the Town House, but for what purpose I have not yet been able to learn; the concourse of People that attended is not to be described and the shouts of *Vive La Nation* filled the air. From the Town House they were conducted to the Palace of the *Thuilleries*, totally unprepared for their reception, but where it is said they are to remain and fix their future residence. Such, My Lord, is the hasty but impartial account of what has passed here; any comments of my part must necessarily fall short of the occasion, as I believe the event is unparalleled, but I shall hope by Thursday to give Your Grace particulars of it all, which the shortness of my time prevents me from supplying you with at present.

The conduct of the Regt. de Flanders in which the utmost reliance and confidence was laid, much astonished and confounded everybody.

Mons. de La Fayette's life, I must also remark, was menaced in case He refused to conduct the *Milice Nationale* to Versailles.

8 Oct., 1789.

To resume the subject that occasioned my Dispatch express yesterday morning, I shall inform your Grace that, H.M.C. Majesty and Royal Family having taken up their residence Tuesday night at the *Thuilleries*, those Gardens were on the morning following crowded with People from all quarters of the Town, who called loudly and impatiently out of them, and especially the Queen, to shew themselves. The whole day passed in that fatiguing but necessary Ceremony, and it is to be believed and hoped that Her Majesty gained many hearts by her condescension and affability as those very People who the day before vowed her death and loaded her with the most opprobrious language now shouted *Vive La Reine* and said aloud that She had been much wronged by those who wished her ill, but that they would prove her defence and support at the expence of their lives.

This day their Majesties received the foreign Ministers and I shall freely confess to your Grace that their situation excited much compassion and was extremely moving.

The Palace seemed in the utmost disorder, was crowded with all sorts of people without distinction and the dignity of Majesty was confounded in the chaos.

The King was much dejected and said little. Her Majesty's voice faltered and the tears ran fast down her cheeks as she spoke, and all their Attendants seemed impressed with the deepest melancholy and concern: during this time, My Lord, altho' the second day since their arrival, the gardens were still thronged with people and nothing was heard but repeated screams and shouting, and, from the marked pain and distress on the countenance of all the Court, I do not doubt that they all, from what they had so lately experienced at Versailles, considered themselves in a most precarious situation and by no means secure from popular violence, which, indeed, it is impossible for anybody to say they are. The people pressed so thickly this day on all sides the Palace that Mons. de la Fayette judged proper to post strong Guards of *Milice Nationale* and Cannon at the chief entries and gateways. The Persons of the Royal Family were also guarded by the *Milice Bourgeoise*, and the *Gardes du Corps*, who alone did their duty at Versailles on Monday, and who saved the Queen's life on that occasion when the Poissardes broke into her bed chamber at 2 o'clock in the morning, as I have since learnt are to be disbanded. Those unfortunate men can only shew themselves here in company with the *Gardes Nationales* with whom they are seen walking about the Town arm in arm for protection.

From the Thuilleries we went to pay our court to Monsieur and Madame at the Luxembourg.

In a few days, My Lord, we may be better able to judge how matters will turn out, which at present it is impossible to see, as the blind and headlong will of the Populace directs all, and all submit with fear and trembling to their Government as the dangerous maxims that all men are equal, and that numbers can overcome a few, are in the mouths of every vagabond at present: Nothing is now left to the superior class of people but submission and the well proportioned exercise of that Policy, reason and education which may in time give them again the superiority over the Multitude.

Fitzgerald to the Duke of Leeds.

(3)

Mrs. Swinburne (v. No. 20) was living at Versailles, to be near her son, and would have the story from him.

We have had dreadful doings. On the 6th, at night, a set of wretches forced themselves into the chateau, screaming '*La tête de la reine! à bas la reine! Louis ne sera plus roi—il nous faut le Duc d'Orleans—il nous donnera du pain celui-là!*' Monsieur Durepaire, one of the Gardes du Corps, defended the Queen's door, and was killed. Others took his place, and were thrown down. ' *Sauvez la reine !* ' was the cry of the Gardes du Corps. Madame Thibaud awoke the Queen, who threw a coverlid of the bed over her, and ran into the King's room, and, soon after he was gone, her door was burst open. The King ran and fetched his son, and all together they waited the event. They owed their rescue to M. de la Fayette and the Gardes Françaises. He insisted upon the King taking up his abode at Paris, without which he would not promise him safety. At one, next day, therefore, they all went, partly escorted by the poissardes and their bullies. They were six hours going from Versailles to Paris.

Mrs. Swinburne.

[Versailles, Oct. 9, 1789.]

(4)

The heads of the slaughtered Gardes du Corps *were not carried in the main procession, but by a small body which preceded it, and arrived at Paris six hours earlier.* Mitron *is a 'baker's apprentice.'*

[Oct. 5] About this time every one was afraid of another and round the place groups of people some proposing one thing some another but few realy knew what they wanted. . . . As the fermentation continued and the Assembly pretended they were not free at Versailles and the people imagining the falt of the Government so they formed the resolution to go to Versailles and force the King and family with the Assembly to come to Paris. As this was the project of the Jacobin club who Stuck at nothing all those revolutionary went of for Versailles to bring in the King and endeed such a rable was hardly ever seen; as they approached Versailles the gardes desired to defend the King but he ordered them to make no resistance although several of them was massacred and M. L'Heretier who was with the Paris Gardes got into the appatements and saved the Queen who was in the greatest danger as the people hated the

Queen as some people ensinuated that it was her that was the cause of the Scarcity of Bread &c. which was all done by other intrigues. However she was conducted into the King's appartement and the whole brought to Paris but the Scene was most chocking to See the poissards mounted up on the Cannon some with one of the gards coats or hatts and the poor gardes obliged to be conducted along with them in this manner and the heads of their comerades that was killed at Versailles brought along with them. The King and Queen and Dauphin was likewise conducted in this humiliating condition; the Maire of Paris was at the Barriere des Bonnes hommes below Passy to receive them and as a form to present the Keys of the town to the King which might be looked upon rather as a Mockery than otherwise. The people was all roaring out 'Voila le Boulanger et la Boulangère et le Petit Mitron' saying that now they should have Bread as they now had got the Baker and his wife and Boy. The Queen sat at the bottom of the Coach with the Dauphin on her Knees in this condition while some of the Blackguards in the rable was firing there guns over her head. As I stood by the coach one Man fired and loaded his gun four times and fired it over the Queen's head. I told him to desiste but he said he would continue but when I told him I should try by force to stop him and not have people hurt by his imprudence some cryed it was right and so he Sluged of very quietelly and after the corte went on and they lodged the King and his family in the thuilleries. So that everything now began to change and the Jacobin club to triumph and the royale familly keept as prisoners.

Thomas Blaikie.

37. THE MOVE TO PARIS

Following rumours that he was implicated in the events of Oct. 5–6, and an interview with Lafayette, the Duc d'Orléans applied for a passport (Oct. 14), and left for England. An inquiry was also set on foot by the Châtelet (the chief criminal court in Paris).

A MOST mysterious and impenetrable veil covers all at

this moment, and from the dark face of things since the residence of the Royal Family in this Town, most fatal conclusions drawn: there are few people who do not believe that a third Revolution in affairs will shortly take place, and none who do not suppose it will be more bloody than the two former. Party, long kept low and humble by popular violence, which exhibited a false scene in which all played the same part, now gains strength and courage and it daily becomes more evident that there are ill-intentioned men in the State, who will strike any blow to obtain their purposes. Those very men who once stood most forward and high in the esteem of the people have not only fallen extremely low in their opinion, but are now suspected by them to have acted like other men in other Revolutions who, by making use of plausible pretexts and the arm of the multitude, obtain their own ends and neglect the interests of the people.

The Duke of Orleans, to the astonishment of everybody, quitted Paris yesterday morning early for England, and as by a late Decree of the National Assembly, no members can absent themselves without making known their reasons to the Assembly, those He desired might be given for his departure were, that H.M.C. Majesty had charged him with a private commission to England. His departure is considered as the summit of imprudence at a moment when numberless accusations appear against him as the chief promoter of all the troubles and misfortunes of this Country, in which ungracious service it is said he has expended the greatest part of his fortune. Endless conjectures, as your Grace may well imagine, are found on this hasty measure of His Highness, which is no small triumph to his enemies who do not spare the deep die with which they at present stain the Prince's character.

There is, I am assured at this moment, much bustle in the Palais Royal on account of his departure but not of a flattering kind to him, as he is reproached for it in the vilest terms by all. On Tuesday he had a short conversation with the King, who it is said received him most coldly.

It is impossible to say, My Lord, if any conspiracy was

really forming here, but certain it is that many people have been lately taken up and imprisoned on suspicion, among others are a Mons. de Livret, Mad^lle de Bissy and Mons. L'abbé de St. Génies, all people of some distinction and upon whom it is pretended that papers of a treasonable nature have been found. These circumstances, attended with the marking of houses with chalk, which was observed for some nights together, spread much terror and alarm, which it seems from the accounts given by those people who were seized in the fact was the only motive. These matters however were considered in a serious light by Mons. de la Fayette and the Guards at the Palace were doubled for some time till the minds of people became more easy and the general alarm was in some measure abated.

During this time, My Lord, your Grace may conceive how unpleasant the situation of the Royal Family must be, deprived of their Body Guards and usual attendants, they are now surrounded by the *Milice Nationale* and guarded more like prisoners than Princes. It is now the tenth day since they have been at Paris and His Majesty, altho' accustomed to much exercise and hunting has not been once out into the air, indeed a walk in the garden is deprived them, as it is constantly crowded with people, and suffered to remain a thoroughfare.

The Riding House at the Thuilleries has been fixed on by the Assembly to hold their future sittings in, and is preparing for the reception; 'till it is ready, they are to meet at the Archbishop's Palace here. They are to come to Paris to-morrow but business will be suspended until Monday next, that they may have time to settle. It is not to be told, my Lord, how many of the members of that Assembly have lately retired home, but I believe I may without exaggeration say that two hundred at least are gone and among them some of their best speakers, viz., Mons. de Lally Tolendal, M. Mounier and one or two more whose names I do not recollect at this moment. This emigration, if I may use the term, arose to that height as to give alarm, and caused that Decree of the Assembly which I mentioned in the former part of my Dispatch in speaking of the Duke of Orleans.

Fitzgerald to the Duke of Leeds.

[Oct. 15, 1789.]

38. THE ROYAL FAMILY AT THE TUILERIES

The garden between the Tuileries and the Manège was no longer private.

AFTER breakfast walk in the gardens of the Tuileries, where there is the most extraordinary sight that either French or English eyes could ever behold at Paris. The king walking with six grenadiers of the *milice bourgeoise*, with an officer or two of his household and a page. The doors of the gardens are kept shut in respect to him, in order to exclude everybody but deputies or those who have admission-tickets. When he entered the palace the doors of the gardens were thrown open for all without distinction, though the queen was still walking with a lady of her court. She also was attended so closely by the *gardes bourgeoises*, that she could not speak, but in a low voice, without being heard by them. A mob followed her talking very loud, and paying no other apparent respect than that of taking off their hats wherever she passed, which was indeed more than I expected. Her Majesty does not appear to be in health; she seems to be much affected and shows it in her face; but the king is as plump as ease can render him. By his orders, there is a little garden railed off for the Dauphin to amuse himself in, and a small room is built in it to retire to in case of rain; here he was at work with his little hoe and rake, but not without a guard of two grenadiers. He is a very pretty good-natured-looking boy of five or six years old, with an agreeable countenance; wherever he goes, all hats are taken off to him, which I was glad to observe. All the family being kept thus close prisoners (for such they are in effect) afford, at first view, a shocking spectacle; and is really so if the act were not absolutely necessary to effect the revolution; this I conceive to be impossible; but if it were necessary no one can blame the people for taking every measure possible to secure that liberty they had seized in the violence of a revolution.

Arthur Young.

[Jan. 4, 1790.]

39. THE JACOBIN CLUB

The Société des Amis de la Constitution *was called the Jacobin Club because, just at this time, it had taken up new quarters at the Dominican (nicknamed Jacobin) Convent in the Rue St. Honoré.*

AT night, Monsieur Decretot and Monsieur Blin carried me to the revolution club at the *Jacobins*. . . . There were above one hundred deputies present, with a president in the chair; I was handed to him, and announced as the author of the *Arithmetique Politique*; the president standing up repeated my name to the company and demanded if there were any objections—None; and this is all the ceremony, not merely of an introduction but an election: for I was told that now I was free to be present when I pleased, being a foreigner. Ten or a dozen other elections were made. In this club the business that is to be brought into the National Assembly is regularly debated; the motions are read that are intended to be made there, and rejected or corrected and approved. When these have been fully agreed to, the whole party are engaged to support them. Plans of conduct are there determined; proper persons nominated for being of committees, and presidents of the Assembly named. And I may add that such is the majority of numbers, that whatever passes in this club is almost sure to pass in the Assembly.

Arthur Young.

[Jan. 17, 1790.]

40. 'A CITADEL BESIEGED'

The acquaintance of William Taylor, the literary critic and historian, with Goethe had made him such an admirer of the Revolution that when he landed at Calais on May 9, he wrote 'At length I have kissed the land of liberty.' For his disillusionment, v. No. 42.

THE French seem to love what we call standing in hot water, and seem able to bear it longer than any other people. All Paris is still in a ferment. The last sound which dies away upon the sleeping ear is the rattle of the patriot drums, and the first murmur which disturbs our rest is the martial music of the national militia. Every morning they are marched, exercised, and reviewed, each division in its turn: every evening they parade the streets with ostentatious bustle. They guard every palace, and are stationed in every playhouse. It is like living in a citadel besieged. In every street you are surrounded by hawkers of pamphlets with terrific titles, and every hour is startled with some new tale of terror. I have already thrown away many a sol for these whole sheets and half sheets, these hand-bills and pamphlets; but I find them in general trifling in matter, though declaratory and lofty in language. All tend to accuse the aristocrats of little or great treasons, to blacken their schemes and their persons, and to protract as much as possible a change, which is certainly begun in the minds of the people, from hate of an oppressive nobility, to pity for a vanquished foe. The clergy seem to fall unpitied even by their allies; of all the approbrious titles by which the enemies on the new government are known, that of the priest-ridden party, or "parti des Capucins," seems to teaze them most.

William Taylor.

[May 14, 1790.]

41. 'THURST FOR WAR'

On May 14, 1790, in view of the Nootka Sound affair, which seemed likely to involve France, as an ally of Spain, in hostilities against England, Montmorin, Minister for Foreign Affairs, informed the Assembly that the King intended to mobilise a French fleet. The result was a long and heated debate which ended on May 22 in a declaration that 'the right of declaring peace or war belongs to the nation.'

THE same thurst for war still prevails here among the fallen Nobility and Clergy as well as His Most Christian Majesty's Ministers, notwithstanding the assurances of

these last to the contrary and, if I may judge from appear-
ances, I should conceive that Her Most Christian Majesty
joined in the same wish. Her Majesty's marked attention of
late to the Spanish Ambassador and her very affable manner
in conversation with him at her Majesty's last public Card
Party attracted the notice of many people present and was
even blamed as being very indiscrete at a moment when so
many watchful and suspicious eyes were upon her, but
supposing this to be the case it by no means follows that
war is nearer at hand for as I have before repeated, the
majority of the Assembly and the Nation is much against it,
altho' I will confess that I am much come off from the idea
which I had entertained of justice being done to England,
with respect to her present differences with Spain, by the
popular side of the National Assembly and I was not a little
surprised some days ago to hear Mons. de la Fayette tell me
he believed that we had sought the cause of quarrel in the
intention to interrupt the French Revolution by involving
France in the contest and to dismember, at the same time,
the Spanish Empire by rousing and assisting Spanish
America to throw off the yoke. In the first instance he said
we should never succeed as the Spirit of Liberty was grafted
in the heart of every French peasant in the Kingdom, and in
the second he thought that our attempts were premature,
but that, if we would wait for a more favourable opportunity, France would assist us in our laudable endeavours
for that it was the sincere wish of this Country to see a
similar Revolution to the present one take place all over the
World and the National Cockade universally worn. However extravagant this may be I conceived it not to be amiss
to give your Grace an idea of the principles entertained by a
principal character in the present Revolution, and to shew
how much further he carries his republican doctrines he did
not scruple to assure me that he saw with regret the necessity that existed in this Country's being a Monarchy but
that he hoped it might be a most limited one that he did
not despair of seeing a still more perfect equality take place
among men and that the only means to bring that about was

an impartial division of landed property which must, he added, some day or other take place and that until it happened, all would not be complete.

Fitzgerald to the Duke of Leeds.

[June 4, 1790.]

42. GROWING PAINS

The marc d'argent was the qualification for candidates, not electors. The 'fictitious decree' was mentioned in a report by Target to the Assembly on June 2.

I HAVE spent nine days in the National Assembly, and heard almost all the eminent speakers. . . . Of the wisdom, talent, and taste displayed in every decree emanating from the National Assembly, I remain the most unqualified admirer. That their conduct is governed by the lofty motives they profess, is, I must think, extremely problematical. If however they be from interest generous, and from prudence forgiving, it is much the same to their enemies and to posterity. The deed still contributes to the happiness and instruction of society. Neither is information by any means so diffusive in France as I imagined. Of the active citizen (persons paying a yearly tribute of a mark of silver) nearly half, particularly in the country, can neither write nor read. Four provinces are now in a state of most dangerous anarchy, in consequence of a fictitious decree of the N.A., promulgated by the disinterested party, fixing the price of bread at a halfpenny a pound, and of meat at twopence. It will be some years before rank recovers its stability, and prosperity its security, in this country. But indeed this state of things began to be wanted. The complete depravity of the higher orders of society was such, and their indifference to the unsettled state of the lower so great, that it was proper they should suffer, in order that they might learn to feel.

William Taylor [June 5, 1790.]

81

43. THE CHAMP DE MARS

Parisians of all classes took part in preparing the Champ de Mars (later Champ de Réunion, where the Eiffel Tower now stands) for the Fédération *on July 14, 1790—a festival of national unity, attended by representatives of the National Guard from every part of the country.*

As the federation which happened the 14 Jully to Commemorate the taking and destruction of the Bastille and what they said the beginning of their Liberty, this preparation had employed the Parissiens for some time and all the classes of People went work at the Champ de Mars where they hollowed out the Midle of this great inclossure and raised all arround a bank a Amphetheatre for the People; here was Ladys wheeling the barrow and loading allong with Shoe blacks and all promiscus; all the whole seemed a sorte of rage and many absurditys invented at that time to Amuse the people. At this everything seemed to be changed as the first principles was changed; the first motives of the King was to do good and he wished to Make the people happy but soon this Systeme was turned to anomisity every one trying to destroy there Neighbour and everything seemed at a Stand, Pamphlets vomiting all sorts of absurditys against the King, and the Nobles deserting the country and turning off their Servants. Such conduct as this created them Still more enimys and the General cry was against the Nobles and Clergy and the people everywhere began to destroy the game.

Thomas Blaikie.
[July, 1790.]

44. FÉDÉRÉS AT THE TUILERIES

From 'a letter to Madame Walpole from her sister at Paris.'

ON the 13th arrived at Paris fifteen hundred Bretons on foot, the commander alone mounted. They marched to the *pont tournant* of the Tuileries. The Garde Nationale would have stopped them, and have obliged the Commander to dismount—*point du tout*. They advanced into the garden under the windows of the King, who appeared in the balcony, and gracieused them. They demanded admission to him, and were admitted, when the Commandant, bending one knee, laid his sword at the King's feet, and said, 'Sire, je suis chargé par la nation bretonne de venir jurer amour et fidélité à votre Majesté, et je verserai la dernière goutte de mon sang pour vous, pour la Reine, et pour Monseigneur le Dauphin.' The King embraced him. The whole troop then went to a little garden parted off for the Dauphin on the terrace of the Tuileries, where he was gathering flowers. The pretty boy gave a flower as long as they lasted to every Breton, and then gathered lilac leaves, and for fear they should not last, tore them in two, and gave half a leaf apiece to the rest.

[July 23, 1790.]

45. THE FEDERATION

(1) AT RHEIMS

C. B. Wollaston, a naval lieutenant, travelling with his step-brother James Frampton, writes to Mrs. Frampton, who printed the letters in her Journal.

On Wednesday, 14th July, was held the ceremony of the Fédération. All the Bourgeois were dressed in the national uniform, with arms, etc., up to the number of between 2000 and 3000, and were drawn up on the promenade, a fine spacious walk near the town. At half-past eleven all the bells in the city began to ring, and some guns were fired, when the mayor pronounced the oath, to which they assented by holding up their hand, after which the *Te Deum* was sung. It rained so exceedingly hard during the ceremony, and there was such a mob of People, that we could hardly see anything that was going on, and indeed there was little to be seen. This ceremony was performed at precisely the same hour in every town in the Kingdom, and there is something very well conceived and magnificent in the idea of the bells all over the Kingdom ringing at the same instant of time, and the whole nation assembling to take the oath.

C. B. Wollaston.

[July 18, 1790.]

(2) IN PARIS

Helen Maria Williams, from whose Letters on the French Revolution *this and the following extract are taken, was an authoress of revolutionary sympathies, who visited Paris on the eve of the event she here describes, lived there during most of the Revolution, and wrote a number of enthusiastic and uncritical accounts of her experiences.*

THE weather proved very unfavourable during the morning of the federation; but the minds of people were too much elevated by ideas of moral good, to attend to the physical evils of the day. Several heavy showers were far from interrupting the general gaiety. The people, when drenched by the rain, called out with exultation, rather than regret, 'Nous sommes mouillez à la nation.' Some exclaimed, 'La revolution Françoise est cimentee avec de l'eau, au lieu de sang.' The national guard, during the hours which preceded the arrival of the procession, amused the spectators with dancing in a circle, and with a thousand whimsical and playful evolutions, highly expressive of that gaiety which distinguished the French character. . . . The people had only one subject of regret; they murmured that the King had taken the national oath in the pavilion, instead of at the foot of the altar; and some of them, crowding round Mons. de la Fayette, conjured him to persuade the King to go to the altar and take the oath a second time. 'Mes enfans,' said Mons. de la Fayette, 'le serment n'est pas une ariette, on ne peut pas le jouer deux fois.'

.   .   .   .

On the following Sunday the national guards were reviewed by Mons. de la Fayette in the Champ de Mars, which was again filled with spectators, and the people appeared more enthusiastic than ever in their applauses of their General. The Champ de Mars resounded with repeated cries of 'Vive Mons. de la Fayette.' On this day carriages were again forbidden, and the evening displayed a scene of general rejoicing. The whole city was illuminated, and crowds of company filled the gardens of the Thuilleries, from which we saw the beautiful facade of the Louvre lighted in the most splendid manner. In the Champs Elysées, where a fête was given to the Deputies, innumerable lamps were hung from one row of trees to another, and shed the most agreeable brilliance on those enchanting walks; where the exhilarated crowds danced and sung, and filled the air with the sound of rejoicing. Several parties of the national guard came from the Champs Elysées, dancing along the walks of the Thuilleries with a woman between every two men: and all the priests, when they met in their way, they obliged to join in the dance, treating them as women, by placing them between two soldiers, and sometimes sportively dressing them in grenadier's caps. Fireworks of great variety and beauty were exhibited on the Pont Neuf, and the statue of Henry the fourth was decorated with the ornament of all others the most dear in the eyes of the people, a scarf of national ribbon. Transparencies of Mons. de la Fayette and Mons. Bailly were placed, as the highest mark of public favour, on each side of this revered statue.

Helen Maria Williams.
[July 1790.]

(3) IN THE COUNTRY

Montauban, capital of the Department of Tarn-et-Garonne, was one of the most Protestant centres in France.

I have just read a private letter from a little town two leagues from Montauban, called Negre-Pelisse, where the inhabitants, on the day of the Federation, displayed a liberality of sentiment, which reflects honour, not only on themselves, but on the age in which we live. The national guard of this little town and its environs, were assembled to take the national oath. Half of the inhabitants being

Protestants and the other half Catholics, the Curé and the Protestant Minister ascended together one altar, which had been erected by the citizens, and administered the oath to their respective parishioners at the same moment, after which, Catholics and Protestants joined in singing Te Deum. . . . This amiable community, when their devotions were finished, walked in procession to a spot where fireworks had been prepared; and, it being considered as a mark of honor to light the fireworks, the office was reserved for Mons. le Curé, who however insisted on the participation of the Protestant Minister in this distinction; upon which the Minister received a wax taper from the Curé and with him led the procession. The fireworks represented two trees. One, twisted and distorted, was emblematical of aristocracy, and was soon entirely consumed: when a tall straight plant, figurative of patriotism, appeared to rise from the ashes of the former, and continued to burn with undiminished splendour.

Helen Maria Williams.

[July, 1790.]

46. FRENCH JOURNEY

William Wordsworth, an undergraduate at Cambridge, excited by the news of the Revolution, took the opportunity of the Long Vacation of 1790 to go on a walking tour in France, with his friend Robert Jones of Ruthin. They landed at Calais on July 13, and tramped via Arras, Soissons, Troyes, and Bar-le-Duc to Châlons, and thence went down the Saône to Lyon (July 30). From Lyon they took boat again down the Rhone to St. Vallier, and walked to the Grande Chartreuse (Aug. 3).

(1) BY ROAD

We chanced

To land at Calais on the very eve
Of that great federal day; and there we saw,
In a mean city, and among a few,
How bright a face is worn when joy of one
Is joy for tens of millions. Southward thence
We held our way, direct through hamlets, towns,

Gaudy with reliques of that festival,
Flowers left to wither on triumphal arcs
And window-garlands. . . .
Unhoused beneath the evening star we saw
Dances of liberty, and, in late hours
Of darkness, dances in the open air
Deftly prolonged, though grey-haired lookers on
Might waste their breath in chiding. . . .

(2) BY RIVER

           A lonely pair
Of strangers, till day closed, we sailed along,
Clustered together with a merry crowd
Of those emancipated, a blithe host
Of travellers, chiefly delegates returning
From the great spousals newly solemnised
At their chief city, in the sight of Heaven.
Little bees they swarmed, gaudy and gay as bees;
Some vapoured in the unruliness of joy,
And with their swords flourished as if to fight
The saucy air. In this proud company
We landed—took with them our evening meal,
Guests welcome almost as the angels were
To Abraham of old. The supper done,
With flowing cups elate and happy thoughts
We rose at signal given, and formed a ring
And, hand in hand, danced round and round the board.
All hearts were open, every tongue was loud
With amity and glee; we bore a name
Honoured in France, the name of Englishmen,
And hospitably did they give us hail,
As their forerunners in a glorious course;
And round and round the board we danced again.
                       William Wordsworth.
                       ['The Prelude'.]

47. NEWS FROM PARIS

For the Duc d'Orléans and the October days, in which rumour also implicated Mirabeau, v. No. 37. The demolition of the Bastille was ordered immediately after its capture: but there were difficulties with Palloy! the contractor, and the work was held up in June, 1790.

I HAVE been twice to the National Assembly, on Thursday through the whole of the sitting, and this morning for two or three hours. You shall hear more when we meet, at present I can only say that the President's 'bell' does not keep such good order there as the speaker's mace in the House of Commons in England.

The Duke of Orleans was there on Thursday. He does not make his appearance much in public. He has some friends, but the generality of people look very shy upon him. You may have seen in the papers that he has been accused of having been concerned in the affair at Versailles in October last, and of a design to murder the King; this, however, is not true. One of the members of the National Assembly made use of some strong expressions relating to that affair, for which he was reprimanded, and has since been imprisoned for eight days for publishing a pamphlet to the same effect. It was supposed that he alluded to the Duke of Orleans and Mirabeau.

Paris is certainly a very pleasant residence. Everybody dresses in the English fashion, and even to the extreme, as boots are not uncommon in the first boxes at the opera. This is fortunate for us. It is much less expensive living at Paris than in London; we dine every day at one of the first coffee-houses in the Palais Royal, where there is always very good company, and get our dinner very good and cheaper than in the coffee-houses in the neighbourhood of Lincoln's Inn.

Yesterday we visited the remains of the Bastille, and picked off a bit of stone as a present for Miss Fauquier.

C. B. Wollaston [August, 1790.]

48. PARIS CHANGED

William Augustus Miles, the political writer, had lived in France since 1783, and died in Paris, in 1807, when collecting materials for a history of the Revolution. His Correspondence on the French Revolution *was published in 1890.*

PARIS, at all times interesting, both to the libertine and the philosopher, is more so now than ever, and the man who is fond of scrutinising the human character, and of developing the most secret recesses of the heart and mind, will find ample employment for his talents at research, and will discover every moment new matter to excite his admiration or provoke his abhorrence. I am wonderfully amused at times, and, having seen this place under the stern vigour of absolute monarchy, everything appears in its present disorganized state as in masquerade. I fancy myself in the midst of a grand Carnival, and would enter *de bon coeur* into all the mirth and ridicule of the diversified characters that jostle me and each other perpetually in the street, were it not that I am frequently called from the folly of the actors to a commiseration of their sufferings, and to a horror of their crimes. They do not, however, suffer or feel disgusted at atrocities that would freeze our blood: they will mount the scaffold on which they are to perish with a hop, step and a jump, take a pinch of snuff, crack a joke with the executioner, and die with a *bon-mot* or a pleasantry in their mouths.

. . . .

The inhabitants of Paris are so changed that you would scarcely acknowledge them to be the people whom you formerly knew. That attention to dress which once characterised the natives of this country, and forbade a Frenchman to appear at dinner except in full dress, or with a sword, prevails no more. I find a revolution in their manners as well as in their government; and, although their prejudices will not be totally removed for some time, there is little doubt but the succeeding generation will be relieved from all that frivolity which marked their ancestors. The share which every individual now has in the Legislature

gives him a turn for thinking more consonant to manhood.
It is inconceivable the change that has taken place in the
minds of men. The Palais Royal, the Tuileries, the bridges,
and all the public places, are inundated with newsvendors and
politicians; all ranks of men begin to reason on the principles
of Government; and the Minister who would dare to
divert the current into another channel would risk something more than his place or character. We mistake these
people very much in England by imagining that their
manners will remain the same as they were under the
despotism of their ancient Government.

W. A. Miles.

[Aug. 13, 1790.]

49. THE QUEEN AT SAINT-CLOUD

*This was the last visit of the royal family to the Queen's 'summer palace' of St.
Cloud. At Easter, 1791, they were prevented from going there by a crowd,
which suspected an attempt to escape. After the flight to Varennes in June
1791, they never left the Tuileries.*

We heard at Versailles that the King and Queen were at
Paris that day, and were to return to St. Cloud the next,
and that by going to St. Cloud we might see them pass by.
Accordingly, on Sunday night, we slept at St. Cloud. We
were told there that we might go into the palace and see
them get out of their carriage; we therefore waited two
or three hours in the apartments, to which everybody had
free access: they were full of strangers and the National
Militia. About two o'clock the King, Queen, Dauphin,
Madame Royale, and Madame Elizabeth, the King's sister,
arrived in one carriage. We saw them get out, pass close
by us going upstairs, and afterwards we stood in the ante-
chamber, where they passed by two or three times, and stood
talking for ten minutes before they went to dinner. I shall
never forget the Queen's stepping out of the carriage, and
then waiting and taking the Dauphin by the hand, leading
him upstairs, and afterwards appearing at a balcony

between her two children. I assure you, Mrs. Siddons
was never finer in any of her parts.

C. B. Wollaston.

[Aug. 17, 1790.]

50. THE NANCY MUTINY

*Trouble between counter-revolutionary officers and revolutionary rank and
file in the army came to a head in the Châteauvieux regiment, and the Nancy
affair became a trial of strength between two parties in the Assembly and
the country. Lord Gower (Duke of Sutherland, 1833), another Old Westminster, succeeded Lord Dorset as ambassador in June, 1790. His Despatches
were edited by Oscar Browning (1885).*

AUGUST 20, 1790. A most alarming insurrection of the garrison of Nancy has obliged the National Assembly to give
to the King the full power of the sword in case persuasion
may not have the desired effect. The three regiments, Du
Roy, Mestre de Camp cavalry and de Chateauvieux a
Swiss regiment, in short the whole garrison of Nancy,
have risen against their officers, broke open the military
chest and divided the money contained in it. The Assembly
have unanimously decreed that the instigators of this
rebellion as well as the soldiers are guilty of the crime of
lèse-nation; that those who have taken any part whatever
in it and who shall not have declared, by writing, if it is
thought necessary, within the space of twenty-four hours
after the publication of the present decree, that they
acknowledge and repent of their error, shall be punished
accordingly and, in order to enforce it, they have requested
his Majesty to appoint some general officer with power to
collect together the troops and national guards of the
Département de la Meurthe and all the neighbouring
departments. The King has in consequence, named Mr.
Malseigne, a Maréchal de Camp and Brigadier des Carabiniers, to that post.

The Regiment du Roy is remarkably well furnished with
cartridges but the cannons have fortunately no carriages.

.   .   .   .

91

September 3, 1790. By the activity and good conduct of Mr. de Bouillé the insurrection of the troops in garrison at Nancy is supprest, but not without considerable slaughter. On the first day of this month he appeared before the town with all the troops and Gardes Nationales he could collect in the neighbourhood: the latter requested to be placed in the first ranks, which was granted, in hopes that their appearance might prevent the seditious soldiers from firing; but unfortunately this had not the desired effect: some of the regiment having fired it soon become general. The Regiment du Roy, the first which capitulated, is sent to Verdun, of the Regiment de Chateauvieux those who are not killed are taken prisoners and the Regiment de Mestre de Camp is ordered to Toul. The following event had obliged Mr. de Bouillé to send to the Assembly requesting them to appoint commissioners to assist him in enforcing their decree.

Mr. Denoue, who commands the Regiment du Roy in the absence of their colonel Mr. de Châtelet, was forced into a dungeon and Mr. Malseigne, to avoid the same fate, had escaped by force out of the town and was pursued but not overtaken before he had joined the Carabiniers at Lunéville who after a slight engagement were obliged to bring him back; but what principally operated with Mr. de Bouillé was a report industriously spread about, not only at Nancy but throughout the country, that he was sent by the ministry and the aristocratical party in order to effect a counter-revolution. He is now reproached by the club of the Jacobins and some few members of the Assembly for having approached the town before the arrival of the commissioners, but his conduct is applauded by all impartial men.

Lord Gower.

51. 'PARIS GOVERNING'

William Wellesley-Pole, third Earl of Mornington, who afterwards held various Government posts, and was a member of Lord Liverpool's Cabinet (1814–23) was at this time (aet. 27), M.P. for East Looe. The air O Richard O mon roi, *from Grétry's opera* Richard Cœur de Lion, *was associated with the regimental dinners of October (v. No. 36), and its performance could not but be provocative.* Les Enragés *was a nickname applied to more than one party of extremists during the Revolution: here it seems to mean members of the Cordeliers Club, founded in the summer of* 1790. *The '89 Club' was founded in June,* 1790, *by a secession of the more conservative members from the Jacobin Club, with which Lord Mornington wrongly identifies it.*

You are well able to judge how strange the contrast must be between Paris governed, and Paris governing; but it is so strange in so many ways, that I own I find great difficulty in attempting to answer your question of what strikes me most, for I am quite perplexed by the number and variety of ridiculous and absurd things, which I hear and see everywhere, and every day. The common people appear to me to be exactly as gay as I remember them, though it is undoubtedly true that the greater part of them is starving for want of employment, especially the tradesmen; and notwithstanding they all talk the highest language in favour of the Revolution, they laugh at the National Assembly without scruple, and say they had rather have Aristocratical Louis, than Democratical Assignats. The streets are crowded with newsmen and hawkers, crying about libels of all sorts from morning till night, exactly in the manner you must have observed in Dublin; nothing is too indecent or abusive. There being an end of the police, it is not possible to imagine any kind of bawdy print that is not publicly stuck up in the Palais Royal, and on the Boulevards: the Attorney General's blood would boil at the sight of such audacious bawdery. The object seems to be everywhere to mark a contempt for all former regulations. At the *spectacle*, they have introduced monks and nuns and crucifixes on the stage; and the actors are violently applauded, merely for wearing these forbidden garments. The *parterre* is more riotous than twenty English upper galleries put together; a few nights ago Richard Coeur de Lion was acted, and a woman of fashion was absolutely forced to leave the house, because she clapped with too much violence while the famous song of *O Richard, O mon roi!* was singing; a hundred fellows started up together roaring *à bas la femme en éventail blanc*, and would not suffer the actors to proceed till this *Aristocrate* left the house. . . . Nothing can be more tiresome than all their new plays and operas; they are a heap of hackneyed public sentiments on general topics of the rights of men and duties of Kings, just like Sheridan's grand paragraphs in the *Morning Post*: these are applauded to the skies. I do not know whether you have heard that many of the Petits Maitres, in order to show their attachment to the Democracy, have sacrificed their curls, *toupées*, and *queues*; some of them go about with cropped locks like English farmers without any powder, and others wear little black scratch wigs, both these fashions are called *Têtes à la Romaine*, which is a comical name for such folly. I must not forget that I have seen several wear gold earrings with their black scratches. . . . I understand from everybody whom I have seen that nothing can be more changed than the whole of their manners. The *Democrates* out of the Assembly are very few indeed among the people of any distinction, and the *Aristocrates* are melancholy and miserable to the last degree; this makes the society at Paris very gloomy; the number of deserted houses is immense, and if it were not for the Deputies, the Ambassadors, and some refugees from Brussels, there would be scarcely a gentleman's coach to be seen in the streets. You have certainly been informed of the principles of the two clubs, the *Enragées*, whose name is easily understood, and the *Quatre Vingt Neuf*, the latter is something like our armed neutrality . . .; for this club acting together, can give a majority either to the *côté gauche* or *droite* in the Assembly. . . . I have never been at this club of 1789, although they admit English members of Parliament, because I understand nothing is done publicly excepting the recital of speeches and motions intended for the Assembly; and with these I have been sufficiently tired at the Assembly itself. I have been there several times, and it is not possible to imagine so strange a scene; the confusion at times surpasses all that ever has been known since government appeared in the world. . . . They have no regular forms of debate on ordinary business; some speak from their seats, some from the floor, some from the table, and some from the tribunes or desks; . . . they speak without preparation, and I thought many of them acquitted themselves well enough in that way, where only a few sentences were to be delivered; but on these occasions the riot is so great that it is very difficult to collect what is said. I am certain that I have seen above a hundred in the act of addressing the Assembly together, all persisting to speak, and as many more replying in different parts of the House, sentence by sentence; then the President claps his hands on both ears and roars order, as if he was calling a coach; sometimes he is quite driven to despair; he beats his table, his breast; . . . wringing his hands is quite a common action, and I really believe he swears. . . . At last he seizes a favourable moment of quiet, either to put the question or to name who ought to speak; then five hundred reclamations all at once renew the confusion, which seldom ends till the performers are completely hoarse, and obliged to give way to a fresh set. On great occasions the speakers deliver their speeches from the tribune, and these are always written speeches, or so generally, that I believe Mirabeau and Maury and Barnave are the only exceptions; and even these often read their speeches. Nothing can be more fatiguing than these readings, which entirely destroy all the spirit and interest of debate. . . . I heard Mirabeau and Maury both speak a few sentences in the midst of one of the riots I have mentioned, and I preferred Maury, whose manner is bold and unaffected, and his voice very fine; Mirabeau appeared to me to be full of affectation, and he has a bad voice, but he is the most admired speaker. There are four galleries which contain above twice the number admitted into the gallery in England, and here a most extraordinary scene is exhibited; for the galleries approve and disapprove by groaning and clapping, exactly as if the whole was a *spectacle*. . . . While the orators are reading their speeches, the Assembly frequently shows a most singular degree of patience such as I am certain the English House of Commons is not capable of. . . . Dulness and monotony are borne in perfect silence; and during such speeches, the President generally amuses himself with reading some pamphlets or newspapers. . . . I forgot to mention one circumstance that had a most comical effect. The *Huissiers* of the Assembly walk up and down the room during times of great tumult, bellowing silence as loud as they can hollow, and endeavouring to persuade the disorderly orators to sit down.

I went to Court this morning at the Tuilleries, and a most gloomy Court it was; many of the young people of the first fashion and rank wear mourning always for economy. . . The King seemed well, but I thought his manner evidently humbled since I was introduced to him before; he now bows to everybody, which was not a Bourbon fashion before the Revolution. The Queen looked very ill; the Dauphin was with her, and she appeared anxious to shew him. They say here that he is her shield; she never stirs out without him.

Lord Mornington.

[Sept. 27, 1790.]

52. PARIS AND THE ASSEMBLY

The site of the Manège *(originally built as a riding-school for Louis XV)*
is marked by a tablet on the north wall of the Tuileries Gardens, facing the
Rue de Rivoli. Mary Berry the authoress, a friend of Horace Walpole, had
travelled to France and other parts of Europe in 1783–5.

FRIDAY, 15th. The first city in the world is at present much in déshabille; for what with the number of emigrants caused by the violence and prejudices of the people, the number of others who, without being actually in danger, choose to stand aloof, and see how matters will go, together with another description of people, perhaps not less numerous, who from motives of economy and quiet have retired to their own country-houses, or to those of their relations, or to the provincial towns—the streets of Paris, the Palais Royal, the Tuileries—in short, all places of public resort, exhibit a very different appearance, and seem filled with very different people, from what I remember them five years ago. The streets are full of fiacres and carts, hardly a gentleman's carriage or a voiture de remise to be seen, at least not one for twenty, and the Palais Royal and Tuileries filled with people of the lowest class, with a very small proportion of those one can suppose above it.

Saturday, 16th. At half-past two found M. de Levis waiting for us in the Terrace des Feuillans in the Tuileries. The Salle of the National Assembly joins it, and is what was formerly a Manège. We entered it under the auspices of our friend M. de Levis, who is Député de la Noblesse de Dijon.

The members have all in their turn, alphabetically, so many tickets to give away. It was not his turn, but as the debate was a dry one—upon the equal taxation of different sorts of *biens fonciers*—many people had left the gallery, and we got very good places. The room is long, very commodiously fitted up for the purpose, with six or seven rows of benches, one above another, all round, and covered with green cloth, and a door, such as is in our Westminster Hall fitted up for a court of justice. In the middle of one side sits the President at a small table, elevated as high as the last row of benches; and under him is another larger table, at which sit the clerks and short-hand writers. Opposite the President is a sort of pulpit, in which those who wish to make a speech place themselves; those who have only an amendment to move, an objection to make, or only wish to say a few words, speak in their place. While we were present, there were seldom fewer than three or four speaking at once—often many more—with such a noise that it was impossible anything could be heard; the President in vain ringing a great bell, which stands by him on the table, by way of enforcing silence or drowning other noises, and the criers in vain demanding it; and when at last some one with strong lungs and much perseverance overcame the

97

rest, he never got a hearing for more than three or four sentences, in the course of which something was sure to occur which met with the approbation, or blame, of the major part of the Assembly, and was expressed in an equally vociferous manner by every individual according to his own particular sentiments. Their appearance is not more gentlemanlike than their manner of debating—such a set of shabby, ill-dressed, strange-looking people I hardly ever saw together.

Mary Berry.

[Oct. 1790.]

53. MIRABEAU AND LAFAYETTE

The sacking of de Castries' house by a mob (Nov. 13), and the manifesto of the Paris sections against the Ministers, had at this time alarmed the Court, and thrown them on the protection of Lafayette; whilst Mirabeau's anti-clerical attitude in the debate on the Civil Constitution (Church Establishment) had offended the Queen, and weakened his influence at Court.

MIRABEAU, more distinguished by his crimes than by his abilities, and whose character in any other country would exclude him from all public and private confidence, aspires to govern this distracted kingdom; but the principle on which he wishes to carry his point is ill adapted to the character of the nation, and is to the full as barbarous as it is happily impracticable. There are more than the Queen in his way. . . Mirabeau is the declared enemy of your friend the Marquis de Lafayette, whom I firmly believe to be a good citizen, and to possess as much moral rectitude and to be as sincere as it is possible for mankind to be . . . I am convinced that Lafayette wishes to see France free for the sake of his fellow-citizens more than for his own, whilst Mirabeau wishes to see his country emancipated from the shackles of monarchy merely to enslave it more effectually and more disgracefully by those of a turbulent and remorseless democracy. . . . Believe me, the French are not so enlightened as is generally thought; there is a great deal of intellectual capacity in the nation, but there is very little

98

knowledge, and still less principle. I know no people so corrupt as the higher orders of Frenchmen: and it is the extreme profligacy of the clergy and nobility that retards the completion of the work in hand.

W. A. Miles.

[Nov. 27, 1790.]

54. THE KING AND QUEEN

The King and Queen were known to sympathise with the resistance of the clergy to the Civil Constitution, which was just at this time rousing bitter anticlericalism among the Paris public.

THE imbecility of the royal mind renders the King incapable of any wise or vigorous effort to recover what he has lost; and to the same cause may be attributed his insensibility to the affronts that are daily offered to him with impunity. Those who are disposed to emancipate him from the abject state into which he is fallen are forbidden even to think on a scheme of the kind; to those who are the most attached to him he says the least, and when he speaks, it is to desire that they will be quiet. The Queen, whatever her guilt may have been, has more than atoned for all the offences she could possibly have committed. Her degradation alone is a punishment beyond the measure of her vices, if she had any, and gives her a claim to the admiration, compassion, and affection of every man awake to a sense of justice or humanity. But the vulgar, insolent, and unjust triumph in her disgrace and insult her in misfortune. The people in this country have become brutal, nor were the cruelties exercised in the worst times in England so atrocious as those committed by the rabble at Paris since the Revolution.

W. A. Miles.

[Jan. 5, 1791]

55. PARIS DIARY

Samuel Rogers, the poet, was at this time 28, *and taking a holiday from his father's bank. The Abbé Maury, deputy for the clergy of Péronne, was an uncompromising opponent of the Civil Constitution. The Club Monarchique was founded by Clermont-Tonnerre towards the end of* 1790. *The 'affair of La Chapelle' was a fight on Jan.* 25, 1791, *between smugglers and customs officers at the barrière on the road to St. Denis.*

Jan. 23. As we changed horses at St. Denis, one of them was restive and broke the traces. 'Ha, ha! Monsieur l'abbé Maury,' said a boy as he passed by, 'ne voulez-vous pas rester tranquille?' Over the arch of every nobleman's gateway the coat of arms was erased, and printed advertisements of the sale of the Church lands were fixed on every wall. As we approached Paris we saw an infinite number of avenues leading from it in all directions, like the radii of a circle. Passed at the foot of Montmartre, a hill of granite covered with windmills. The clumsy coaches of all shapes that rumble along without springs; the ladies hurrying out of their way with rouged cheeks and without hats; the gentlemen parading with their national cockades, immense muffs, and copper buckles; and the very beggars accosting us with a powdered head, a muff, and a cockade—everything was new to an Englishman; but who could attend a moment to such *minutiae* when so many thousands were beating as it were with one pulse in the cause of liberty and their country, and crowding every coffee-house and public walk to congratulate each other on an event so favourable in its consequences to the best interests of mankind?

In the evening walked under the piazzas of the Palais Royal, a very elegant square, full of shops and coffee-houses, glittering with lights, and crowded with belles and beaux who were taking their evening promenade.

Jan. 30. Went at ten to the Salle Nationale—the tribune crowded, the subject uninteresting—respecting the alienation of the incomes of the hospitals. Barnave, Rochefoucauld, and Mirabeau spoke a few words; the last is the best speaker in the National Assembly. On the table was a bust of Monsieur Désiles who fell a victim to the soldiery at Nancy. The bell rung frequently by the President Mirabeau to obtain silence. . . .

Drove to the Théatre François and saw 'La Liberté conquise'—a simple representation of the taking of the Bastille, interspersed with noble sentiments but laid in a distant province. Between the acts 'Ça ira' was played by the orchestra, and the audience beat time by clapping. When soldiers clubbed their arms and embraced their fellow-citizens the house resounded with shouts for some minutes. An English nobleman is introduced, who utters fine sentiments of liberty, and concludes the piece with this address, 'François, vous avez conquis la liberté, tâchez de la conservir.'

Feb. 2. Went to the Club of '89. A debate on three different motions to the same purpose, the exclusion of the members of the Club Monarchique. That of M. de Condorcet carried. Was afterwards told that the Club Monarchique were friends to despotism under the mask of moderation; that the Club of '89 and that of the Jacobins are much the same in principle, and act in concert in the Assembly, but that the first are less precipitate in their measures, and that the leaders of each have a degree of jealousy of each other; that a motion had been made more than once to exclude those of '89 from the Jacobins, but without success; that [those] of '89 are about four hundred. The Jacobins much the largest.

Feb. 3. The Jacobins about twelve hundred in Paris, with six hundred corresponding societies in the country; the Monarchique about four hundred, professing a desire to establish a constitution like that of England, but in fact something worse; that and the Club of '89 have no other branches in the country. . . .

Feb. 4. Saw the Place Vendôme; the Hospital des Invalides, with a most beautiful dome, the military school, and the Champ de Mars, the scaffold of which is still standing, with the elegant heights of the village Chaillot. In the centre of the area, on an eminence, is the *maison* in which the oath was administered—on one side is written this inscription: C'est dans ce champ où ils venoient de jurer d'être fidèles à la Nation, à la Loi, et au Roi.

Feb. 5. Saw the family go to Mass through the apartments of the Louvre. The King came first with a good-humoured unmeaning face, afterwards the Queen bowing courteously to all about her, with the dauphin, a little pale-faced boy with a kind of night-cap on his head. She has a beautiful profile, but her eyes are heavy. Then Monsieur, very like the King, his eldest brother, and his sister.

Feb. 8. Dined with Mr. Keay. Went afterwards to the Société des Amis de la Constitution. Passed through a long arched passage, and ascended by a stone staircase into a long narrow room, with a low vaulted roof, formerly the library of the Jacobins. Over the recesses for the books were written 'Historiae profanae,' 'Interpretes Scripturae,' 'S.S. Patres,' etc., with several portraits of nuns and abbots. An inquiry into the affair of La Chapelle was before them, the room full, 300 or 400 present. A fulmination against the Société Monarchique. The conquerors of the Bastille presented themselves, three plain modest men, thanked them for having been chosen members of their Society, presented them with a book, and desired leave to put themselves under the protection of the Society, as they had reason to expect every moment to be assassinated.

Feb. 10. A beautiful day. Walked with Mr. Keay in the Tuileries—full of company. Saw the Dauphin's garden and duckery at the end of it, in which his name was sown in mustard seed—Louis Dauphin.

Feb. 13. At the Church of Notre Dame, from a gallery, saw three *curés* elected by the Electoral Assembly in the great aisle; each from the pulpit delivered a short discourse expressive of his attachment to the present constitution. He said that his office as preacher was to enlighten the people and give energy to the laws; that heaven approved of the Confederation, and that to inculcate these sentiments would be the last employment of his life.

Samuel Rogers [1791.]

56. PARIS FINANCE

On Feb. 8, a deputation from the Paris Commune asked the Assembly to reduce the Paris octroi to the level of that of other towns. The Assembly replied by abolishing all octrois—a great boon to poor townspeople.

THE reduction of the number of municipalities, a consummation most devoutly to be wished for by all who are enemies to anarchy and confusion, would have been agitated before this time in the Assembly had it not been for the interruption, which a remonstrance from the city of Paris, and the business brought forward in consequence of that remonstrance has occasioned.

The municipality has stated to the Assembly that Paris is no longer able to bear the weight of those taxes which the former abuses of Government enabled it to pay: that in proportion to their decrease of wealth they suffer an increase of expence. That they are obliged to maintain twenty-seven thousand adventurers and needy persons (the fact is that, under the name of workmen and labourers those people receive fifteen sous a day although they scarcely work at all). That they have still to pay four millions for the expence of the revolution, and one million two hundred thousand livres for the works in the Champ de Mars for the Federation. That it is unjust that they who were the most active in bringing about the revolution should be the greatest sufferers by that event. In this state of distress they request the Assembly to decree that six millions should be paid to them by the public treasury; they being able to prove that fifteen millions are owing them by the public.

The payment of the six millions has accordingly been decreed, and Mr. Dupont, by order of the Comité d'Impositions, has laid before the Assembly a plan for levying taxes to be paid at the entrance of towns in proportion to their population; according to which plan it is calculated that every inhabitant of Paris will pay annually eighteen livres per head instead of forty livres ten sous. The towns of France formerly paid in droits d'entrée seventy millions per annum, of which forty-six went to the service of Government, the other twenty-four were employed by the towns themselves.

Paris alone contributed thirty-six millions, twenty-eight of which were paid to the public. It is now proposed to reduce the forty-six millions, which were formerly paid to Government, to twenty-four and that of Paris from twenty-eight to ten.

Lord Gower.
[Feb. 11, 1791.]

57. 'TWO CONSIDERABLE MOBS'

(1) AT THE LUXEMBOURG

The departure of the King's aunts—Mme. Adelaide and Mme. Victoire— for Italy on Feb. 20 made the people suspect that the Comte de Provence and the King himself were planning to escape from Paris.

THE departure of the King's aunts has been the cause of two considerable mobs, but which, owing to the vigilance of Mr. la Fayette, have been attended with no bad consequences. The first gave me an opportunity of being witness to great firmness and presence of mind in the King's brother; I happened to dine, on Tuesday, at the Luxembourg with a company which was honored by his presence: while we were at coffee, one of his attendants, with signs of the greatest alarm, rushed into the room and informed us that the mob threatened to force their way into the Petit Luxembourg where Monsieur resides, declaring that they were certain that he intended to quit Paris that night: he immediately without the least signs of emotion gave orders for a *deputation* to be admitted into the court, where he went and informed them that they were perfectly mistaken, and at the same time gave them his word of honor that he would not leave the kingdom at present. This deputation consisted entirely of women. Having done this, he proceeded to the Thuileries, where he goes regularly every Tuesday, in order to attend the *Jeu de la Reine*, accompanied on this occasion by a troop of *Poissardes* and populace. When Monsieur entered the gates the guard endeavoured, but in vain, to prevent their following him into the court; upon this Mr. la Fayette ordered the cavalry to force them out of it, Mr. Bailly and some municipal officers arrived at that instant and insisted upon their sheathing their swords, but informed the mob that, if they did not retire, it would be impossible for them any longer to prevent the guards from firing upon them: this had the desired effect! they retired, and Monsieur was suffered to return quietly to the Luxembourg. I understand that Mr. de la Fayette complains much of Mr. Bailly's want of resolution, last night when the latter was giving a circumstantial account of the different disturbances to his Majesty the King was heard to say: It is impossible to continue to act any longer in this manner, something must be done! or words to that effect.

Lord Gower.

[Feb. 25, 1791.]

(2) AT THE TUILERIES

Miles is wrong about Théroigne de Méricourt, who had left Paris before this date (v. No. 97).

I was at the château in the Tuileries in February 1791, when one part of the rabble, on a report that Monsieur was going to leave Paris, proceeded to the Hotel de Luxembourg, while another, conducted by Mademoiselle Théroigne, assailed the Tuileries. It was the most violent commotion that had occurred since the month of October 1789, and the people had nearly forced their way into the royal apartments. It was some time before M. Bailly arrived. He came in pale and trembling. The King, with a firmness and tone of voice he had never used before, inquired the cause of his being exposed to these perpetual insults, and the city to these false alarms, and insisted on these tumults being suppressed. It was the firm manner in which Lafayette acted that imposed on the multitude, and protected the lives of the King and Queen, who, you may be assured, will certainly perish in some of these tumults. I was present at this distressing scene, and was astonished to find the King more collected and less alarmed than the Mayor.

W. A. Miles.

[Feb. 28, 1791.]

58. ROBESPIERRE

*Robespierre's persistence as a speaker, and his intransigeant liberalism, had
already got him a name in the Assembly, and it was only a few weeks later that
Mirabeau's death cleared the way for his rise to power. Miles' prophecy is
none the less remarkable.*

THE man held of the least account in the National Assembly
by Mirabeau, by Lafayette, and even by the Lameths and
all the Orleans faction, will soon be of the first consideration. He is cool, measured, and resolved. He is *in his heart*
Republican, honestly so, not to pay court to the multitude,
but from an opinion that it is the very best, if not the only,
form of government which men ought to admit. Upon this
principle he acts, and the public voice is decidedly in favour
of this system. He is a stern man, rigid in his principles,
plain, unaffected in his manners, no foppery in his dress,
certainly above corruption, despising wealth, and with
nothing of the volatility of a Frenchman in his character.
I do not enter into the question of the forms of Government, but I say that Robespierre is *bonâ fide* a Republican,
and that nothing which the King could bestow on him,
were his Majesty in a position to bestow anything, could
warp this man from his purpose. In this sense of the word,
that is, *in his heart meaning well*, as to the destruction of the
monarchy, he is an honest man. I watch him very closely
every night. I read his countenance with eyes steadily fixed
on him. He is really a character to be contemplated; he is
growing every hour into consequence, and, strange to
relate, the whole National Assembly hold him cheap,
consider him as insignificant, and, when I mentioned to
one of them my suspicions, and said he would be the man
of sway in a short time, and govern the million, I was
laughed at.

W. A. Miles.
[March 1, 1791.]

59. 'DAGGER DAY'

(1)

On Feb. 28, a mob attack on the state prison at Vincennes (another Bastille) was repulsed by the National Guard under Lafayette. Meanwhile, fearing an attack on the Tuileries, a number of the King's supporters had gathered there, carrying weapons, and were disarmed by the National Guard. This incident, which gave rise to rumours of a royal flight, was called the Journée des poignards.

A Mr. DE COURT, a gentleman from the West Indies, having by accident let fall from under his coat a short couteau de chasse in the Queen's appartment at the Thuilleries last Monday morning was the cause of the extraordinary scene which passed there on that evening. On the Tuesday and Thursday, preceding when, on account of the mobs that surrounded the palace, it was supposed that the persons of the Royal Family might be in danger, many gentlemen, from motives of duty or principle, went to the royal apartments, and being in haste were of course in undress, but, as it is usual at present, had pistols in their pockets, and many had short couteaux de chasse or daggers, in so doing they shewed greater marks of zeal than prudence, it being contrary to law to enter the palace thus armed. On account of what had happened in the morning, the National Guard thought themselves entitled to search the persons of those who had arrived that evening; the search was very productive; many baskets being soon filled with pistols and daggers: this however was not done without violent opposition from the wearers of them, some of whom declared they would sooner die than give up their arms: the King, seeing the danger of this resolution, laid his commands upon them to deliver them up, saying that he would be defended only by the National Guard. Some of those who were most obstinate have been sent to prison, many have suffered much from the ill-treatment of the soldiers. The measure was right, the means were undoubtedly wrong.

In the midst of this scene of danger to all present, for had any one pistol gone off by accident a massacre must have ensued, Mr. de la Fayette arrived from Vincennes. He thanked the Guard for their conduct and congratulated them that for the future there would not be a body of men between their Sovereign and them. The next day he signified in writing, the language of which is curious on account of the novelty of some of the expressions, that he had given his Majesty's orders to the *chefs de la domesticité*, a new term for the chief officers of the household, to prevent the introduction of arms into the palace; it being the will of the King of the Constitution to be guarded only by the soldiers of liberty.

Lord Gower.

[March 4, 1791.]

(2)

Henry Redhead Yorke (the 'Yorke' was a later addition to his name) visited Paris as a young man (aet. 19) and consorted with Paine and his friends. But he could not agree with their views, and was denounced by John Oswald for opposing the invasion of England. Returning to England, he was denounced as a spy there, and put into prison (1795–8). In his later Paris *in* 1802 *he included some reminiscences of the earlier visit.*

I was present on the occasion, and was a calm spectator of the scene. An immense concourse of people collected about the Chateau, and I heard a great noise about concealed daggers and brandished weapons, but I saw none. Every man repeated whatever he heard from his neighbour, with many additions of his own; but I declare I saw no blade but that of La Fayette, who, mounted on his white charger, was galloping to and fro, as if the fate of the world depended that night upon him. At one instant, he was forming the National Guards in line: at the next, he was ordering them to file off: then he dismounted, and bolted into the Palace; in a trice he was again on horseback: the little man was so busy, that he created more alarm among the people than if an Austrian army had reached their barriers. At length, after a deal of marching and counter-marching, bustling and puffing, the Marquis assured the mob that all was safe, and from the measures *he* had taken, he would be responsible for the safety of the monarch. Here followed great applause, and the populace quietly dispersed.

H. R. Yorke.

60. THE KING'S HEALTH

The 'new bishop' is J. B. J. Gobel, who, being elected for episcopacy by three departments, chose (March 15) the see of Paris, and was consecrated by Talleyrand, bishop of Autun—the first such ceremony under the Civil Constitution. In Oct. 1793, he renounced his Orders, and in March, 1794, was guillotined with the Hébertists.

March 11, 1791.

The King of France, naturally of a full habit of body, has never been sufficiently abstemious in his diet; but, while he resided at Versailles, a constant course of hard exercise prevented the bad effects which an excess of food would otherwise have produced: at Paris he has been debarred the advantage of exercise; to this cause and perhaps, in some degree, to agitation of mind in consequence of what happened lately at the Thuilleries, is to be attributed a fever under which he has suffered for some days past. On Sunday we were informed that, on account of a slight indigestion, his Majesty could not see us, but on Tuesday the disorder had risen to an alarming height, and on Wednesday his throat was so swelled that he articulated with the greatest difficulty. The fever is since considerably abated and there is every reason to suppose that he is now out of danger.

March 18, 1791.

The King is so far recovered from his late indisposition that no bulletins have been given out since Wesnesday. There was a general illumination last night, by desire of the municipality; on Sunday there will be another and Te Deum will be sung in the cathedral, at which the new bishop will officiate: although the King's recovery is the ostensible reason the election of the bishop has a great share in these proceedings.

Lord Gower.

61. THE POLITICAL SITUATION

George Hammond had been secretary to David Hartley the younger in Paris in 1783, and was now, after being Chargé d'Affaires at Vienna (1788–90), temporarily attached to the Embassy there. He became the first British Minister at Washington the same year. He is writing to James Bland Burges, under-secretary for Foreign Affairs (1789–95). The Assignats—a paper currency based on nationalised Church property—were to depreciate almost continuously, till by the end of 1794 they ceased to have any value.

THERE is one point upon which all parties seem to be agreed—that the restoration of the ancient form of government is become totally impracticable, from any quarter or by any means whatsoever. The three descriptions of persons *in the Kingdom*, the most interested in the event, are the Sovereign, the Nobility, and the Clergy; but it is evident that their exertions alone, unaided by foreign Powers, are absolutely inadequate to the accomplishment of it. That loyalty and attachment to their Sovereign, which were formerly the characteristics of this nation, exist no longer. The mental imbecility of the present King, and the profligacy of some branches of the royal family, have implanted contempt and aversion so deeply in the bulk of the people, that his present melancholy state of captivity and humiliation, so far from creating a spirit of indignation against those who have usurped his authority, has afforded a subject of ridicule and triumph to a great majority of the nation. In regard to the nobility, their dispersion, their want of concert, of pecuniary resources and of a leader, but chiefly the circumstances of their estates being at the mercy of their enemies, all concur to prevent them from forming or carrying into execution any enterprize of much magnitude and moment. The respect that used to be paid to the character and functions of the clergy has long been dwindling away, and the influence which that body derived from their great territorial possessions, now act as an instrument against them. Not only inasmuch as their estates have been wrested from them, but also as the individuals who have purchased those estates under the national faith are now materially interested in protecting them, *by every means*, against any invasion of their newly acquired rights, and the possibility of their ever reverting to their original possessors. With respect to the prospect of any *external* interference, you, Sir, are better able to judge of that than I can be. I am, however, firmly persuaded that no serious apprehensions on that head are entertained here. The ruling party, indeed, do not rely on the three millions of men (now trained to arms) alone—they assert they have a more effectual pledge for the non-intervention of foreign Powers, in possessing the persons of the King, and of such of the Aristocratical party as have not chosen to expatriate themselves, both of whom they would not scruple to deliver up to the fury of an exasperated populace on the first appearance of a foreign invasion. . . .

There is no assertion of Mr. Burke's more true than this —that the French have shown themselves much more skilful in destroying than in erecting. As I am convinced that no man in this country, *even at this moment*, has any clear notion of the new order of things that is to arise in the place of the old, it is therefore needless to enter into any discussion of the numerous speculative theories that now swarm in the nation, which have no other foundation than the heated imaginations of their fabricators.

No party in the National Assembly seems to be actuated by an adherence to a regular well-defined system, which is, I think, pretty clearly proved by the contradictory decrees that are every day issuing out to answer the emergency of the moment. And even if there was a system, there does not appear to be any man of abilities so transcendent, or of patriotism so unsuspected, as to be capable of giving direction and energy to the movements of any compact *concentrated* body of individuals. This is a circumstance which separates the French Revolution from every preceding one in any other country, and renders it impossible to discern a clue to the present and future operations of that body, in whom all authority is at present centered. . . .

In the meantime they avoid rendering themselves obnoxious and unpopular, by throwing the execution of everything that is either odious or absurd in their own numerous decrees on the King and his ministers. They have stripped royalty of everything that could make it either respectable or amiable, and by perpetually separating the *function* from the *person* of the monarch, they insensibly confound him in the general mass of citizens. Indeed their affectation is carried to so ridiculous a pitch, that I am rather surprised that we do not hear of the *pouvoir executif's* looking out of the window, or going to bed to *its* wife.

In the midst of all this wretched scene of political confusion, it is strongly suspected that several members of the National Assembly have enriched themselves by stock-jobbing and other arts, and Mirabeau in particular. That arch-patriot is now living in great magnificence, and indulges his ruling passion for buying up valuable books with unexampled profusion.

As you may have been perhaps surprised that the late discussion of the question of Regency should have appeared to be a matter of such urgency, I think it necessary to remark that the King's health, not from extreme sensibility, but from want of exercise, and from indulging too freely in the pleasures of the table, has suffered so much that it is not expected his Majesty can survive many years.

I must not omit to mention two circumstances that have struck me greatly in my present residence in this capital— the tranquillity which now appears to subsist in it, and the little interruption that the newly-created paper money has had to encounter in its circulation. Excepting a greater number of men in military uniforms parading the streets, all the common occupations of life proceed as smoothly and regularly as if no event of consequence had occurred, and the public amusements are followed with as much avidity as in the most quiet and flourishing periods of the monarchy. In regard to the *Assignats*, although they are now at a discount of 7 per cent. and are expected to fall lower, no person seems to murmur at taking them in payment, or to express any doubts of their validity.

George Hammond to Mr. Burges.

[March 25, 1791.]

62. THE DEATH OF MIRABEAU

Mirabeau died on April 2, 1791, and was buried in the newly-built church of St. Geneviève, set apart thenceforth as a Panthéon, 'to receive the ashes of great men belonging to the era of liberty.' For Voltaire's reburial there v. No. 74. Mirabeau's body was thrown out again in 1793.

(1)

MY father was a great admirer of Mirabeau, and, during the illness that terminated his singular and erratic career, he used to send me and a servant every day to his hôtel, to bring a report of the *bulletin*, published to satisfy the thousands who surrounded his house. . . .

His obsequies I can well remember. The *cortège* extended from the Chaussée d'Antin to the Boulevard du Temple, and the dense mass of citizens of every class of society, must have numbered three or four hundred thousand. The body was borne on a funeral car, drawn by eight black horses, and covered with a pall of black velvet, studded with silver stars, surmounted by a figure of Fame. The mass of mourners gradually increased during the procession to the church of St. Geneviève—then transformed into a National Pantheon.

J. G. Millingen.

(2)

If Mirabeau had been an honest man, or if he had possessed either virtuous pride or noble sentiments, he might, by his talents and acquired knowledge, have rendered his country most essential service; but he was mercenary: though extravagant, and vain, vulgar, and mean —ready to sell himself to any party who thought him worth buying. I knew him personally. You may form some idea of him when I inform you that he was an object of dread and contempt to all parties. The confidence which his countrymen had in his capacity and superior attainments obtained him a degree of influence in the National Assembly; this influence be preserved to the last, and it would be an injustice to his memory to deny that the Revolution owed much to his collected firmness. You will not suspect me of partiality towards him when I inform you that he decided that important event by his courage and presence of mind in a moment of alarm and consternation, and when his colleagues, intimidated by an order from the Court to separate, and by the appearance of a military force, were on the point of abandoning their mission. It was then that Mirabeau stood forth the champion of their honour and the vindicator of the nation's freedom. It was a moment worth ages. It has immortalised his name: and if his subsequent conduct had been as glorious and consistent, it would have atoned for all the vices and irregularities of his former life.

W. A. Miles.

[April, 1791.]

63. THE SAINT-CLOUD AFFAIR

On Palm Sunday (April 17), mass was said for the King and royal family by Cardinal de Montmorency, a prêtre réfractaire or non sermenté, i.e. one who had refused to take the oath prescribed by the Civil Constitution. The next day, when the royal family were starting for St. Cloud, to spend Holy Week there, a crowd, indignant at the King's attitude, and suspecting a plan to escape from Paris, made it impossible for them to go.

THE extraordinary events of this week have given manifest proofs of the absolute anarchy under which this country labours. An endeavour to compel the King to attend mass celebrated by priests who have taken the oath has caused the constitutional laws and liberty of the country to be violated by those who were especially armed for the defence of them: for it was the National Guard, not the mob, which prevented the King from going to St. Cloud.

On Sunday, it was with the greatest difficulty that Mr. la Fayette could persuade them to do duty at the King's Chapel: during which time, those who attempted to enter the Church of the Theatins, where the late curate of St. Sulpice was to officiate, were threatened with the fashionable punishment of flagellation. The next day, when His

Majesty, the Queen and the Royal Family entered their carriages in order to go to St. Cloud, where they had, some days before determined to pass the Holy Week; they were surrounded by a multitude of people, who insisted that they should not depart. Having remained an hour and three quarters in his carriage, having seen the few nobility that remained about his person ill treated, and having heard, during all that time, the Queen abused with the most harsh and indecent language the King was obliged to return to his palace or rather to his prison. The presence of Mr. Bailly had, as usual, no effect upon the people, and Mr. de la Fayette discovered that Commandant General was become an empty title. The National Guard confessed that they were acting against the law but insisted that the *premier fonctionaire public* should obey the supreme will of the people.

The next morning the Directory of the Department issued a proclamation for assembling the sections in order that they should decide whether the King should be desired to fulfill his intentions of going to St. Cloud, or whether he should be thanked by them for having preferred to remain at Paris least he should disturb the public tranquillity.

The majority of the sections wisely agreed that *il n'y avoit lieu à deliberer*.

The Directory at the same time presented an address to the King requesting him, in strong language to dismiss the *refractaires* who surrounded his person, and advising him to announce to foreign nations the glorious revolution which has taken place in France and that he is King of a free people.

The King went to the Assembly and read a speech, a copy of which together with the President's answer I inclose.

The only measure which the Assembly took upon the subject was to order them to be printed by way of a proclamation for the reestablishment of public tranquillity.

The next day the chief officers of the household the King's and Queen's almoners and most of the inferior officers of the court sent their resignations, and yesterday the King received us accompanied by a few remaining attendants on his way to a mass celebrated by a solitary priest.

Lord Gower.

[April 22, 1791.]

64. THE POPE

For a long time Pope Pius VI hesitated to condemn the Civil Constitution: but in Briefs of March 10 and April 13, 1791, he did so openly; and refused to receive de Ségur, who had been nominated to replace the counter-revolutionary Cardinal de Bernis as French ambassador at Rome. On May 4, when the Brief of April 13 became known, the Pope was burnt in effigy at the Palais Royal.

THE Pope's conduct in the present crisis is not to be accounted for by the rules of cool policy. Why he should refuse to receive an Ambassador because he has taken the Civic Oath, distinct from, but which he seems to have confounded with, that which the clergy are obliged to take, it is difficult to account for; the more so as he suffers the present Chargé d'Affaires to transact business at Rome although equally stigmatized in that respect. His Holiness, they say, begins to doat; his *bref*, a copy of which, in print, and of a second, which is lately arrived, I send to your Lordship, rather favours that opinion. The Nuncio did not appear at Court yesterday; he pleaded illness, which is in part founded, for the irksomeness of his situation has had a visible effect on his health; his decent behaviour in these ticklish times has gained him a general esteem. The effigy of his master drest in robes ridiculously costly was publickly burnt the other day in the Palais-royal, not by the mob but by a set of wild enthusiasts of what is called the better sort.

Lord Gower.

[May 6, 1791.]

65. A BEGGAR

Miss Miles, a daughter of W. A. Miles (v. No. 48) was living in Paris at this time, and wrote regularly to her father.

REFUSE a beggar charity, and you will be called a '——

116

aristocrate.' This happened to me the other day. We were sitting on the bench at the bottom of the garden, when a beggar woman came and attacked us. There are such numbers in the Champs-Elysées that if you give to one the rest will also expect, and you will be persecuted out of your life. I said civilly to her, 'Je n'ai rien, ma bonne—une autre fois.' She immediately answered, 'Comment osez-vous dire que vous n'avez rien? Je vois par là que vous êtes une aristocrate, et c'est vous —— aristocrates qui êtes causes de nos misères. Sors un peu de ton jardin, si tu en as le courage, et je te tordrais le nez comme je te tordrais le cou, si je pouvais en faire à ma guise.' A woman standing next to her with a child in her arms, asked if she did not blush to hold such language, and whether the ladies were not at full liberty to dispose of their money to those they thought deserving. She added that she was as poor as she could be, but when she got anything she was thankful. This reasonable beggar obtained some partisans, and the other was obliged to quit the walk.

Miss Miles.

[May 6, 1791.]

66. THE QUEEN AND THE GARDENER

Madame Elisabeth was the King's sister, ten years younger than himself; she was guillotined in 1794. For Blaikie, v. No. 19 (2).

ONE day Mme. Elizabeth came and walked in the garden and amongst some Conversation about the revolution I told her what I thought and that they had to do with a bad set of People who wished to Sacrifice them and many other things which surprized her; after coming and resting herself in my house which she admired for its cleanlyness she returned to Paris and told the King and Queen what I had said, so that some days afterwards the Queen came and enquired of the Porter where I was, who said I was Somewhere in the Park. So I soon joined her who told her Suitte that She did not want them as she was with me and would see the

Garden; she told me 'You had a Visite from my Sister Elizabeth who told me what you said. I know your way of thinking and I shall never forget you. I have known you long. I will go and see your house which I hear is neat and clean.' After all this conversation when she went off She repetted she would not forgett me.

Thomas Blaikie [1791].

67. THE REVOLUTION IN ALSACE

John Owen, secretary and historian of the British and Foreign Bible Society, was at this time (aet. 25) a Fellow of Corpus Christi College, Cambridge. His Travels into different parts of Europe, etc., *were published in 1796.*

I WAS amused with the very sudden change which I discovered in the appearance, the dress, and the air of the inhabitants, in passing from the headquarters of Aristocracy. The people all wear, without exception, the national cockade; and each town has its *Garde Nationale*. I never saw people more at their ease. They appear not yet to have recovered from those paroxysms of transport, into which the Revolution first threw them; and they are frolicking without apprehension, at a time when the exiled noblesse are plotting schemes for their destruction, at a distance of half a dozen leagues from their frontier. . . .

The town of Lauterbourg was enlivened by the notes of military music; and the popular air of 'Ca ira' resounded in every street. . . .

All is political at Strasbourg. The corner of every street is covered with *Programmes*, and the walls of every church decorated with Proclamations and Decrees. The greater part of the latter, advertise the sale of the national effects. . . . One scarcely walks twenty yards now, without meeting in places of public observation a declaration of civil rights; and all the shops of music and prints are hung with national ballads and political caricatures. . . .

I must assure you, that I found the state of the people in this part of France very different from what it had been represented. At Manheim and Worms, reports prevailed of the most serious tumults now reigning in France; and we were more than once cautioned against trusting ourselves amongst a *canaille*, who would hang us up at the lamp-post for a word or a look. This statement has so little connection with truth, that everything passes with the utmost order; and, so far as I can judge from observation and report, freedom of remark encounters less danger here than at the court of Manheim. . . .

The day after our arrival, was rendered festive by a new enrolment of National guards. This was formed out of the citizens over the age of eighteen years, and was effected without the least symptom of disorder. Beside the guard thus regularly embodied, the citizens are seen every evening in different parts of the town, learning, against an emergency, the use of arms. It certainly is animating to read, in a thousand conspicuous places, proclamations setting forth the right of private judgment; allowing to every man the free exercise of his opinion in matters of religion; and establishing to each individual the liberty of adopting that mode of worship he best approves.

John Owen.

[At Strasbourg and Basle, June 7–10, 1791.]

68. THE FLIGHT TO VARENNES
(1) IN PARIS

It was thought at first that the King and his family had taken the road to Brussels, as the Comte de Provence did. The Logographe *(later* Logotachy-graphe) *reported the debates in the Assembly: there were several papers called* Postillon; *probably that* de l'Assemblée Nationale *is intended. J. N. Mangin of Varennes had sat as* suppléant *deputy for the Commons of Sedan since Dec.* 1789. *His son's arrival is reported in the minutes of the Paris Commune under the name of Mougins on the 22nd.*

JUNE 22, 1791. I take the first opportunity of informing your Lordship of the surprizing event which happened yesterday, no person whatever having till this moment been permitted to leave Paris.

Between seven and eight in the morning it was discovered

that the King and all the Royal Family had left the Thuilleries unknown to the Guard. It is supposed that they quitted the Palace between one and two o'clock, and it is imagined that they have taken the rout through the forests of Compiègne and the Ardennes to the Low Countries but nothing certain is as yet known. Monsieur and Madame have also left the Luxembourg.

Owing to the activity of the National Guard the exertions of the municipality and the prudent deliberations of the National Assembly, for the heat of party, has, for the present entirely subsided, the tranquillity of this town has been perfectly preserved.

As soon as the Assembly was met, the President informed them that he had received from the mayor intelligence of the departure of the King and of the Royal Family: couriers were immediately ordered to be sent to every department with orders to prevent any body from quitting the kingdom and the Ministers were summoned to attend the Assembly.

The *Ministre de la Justice* was authorized to continue to make use of the Seal of the State, which measure was thought necessary, as a letter had been delivered to him that morning signed by the King forbidding him to do so till further orders. That Minister delivered a memorial which Mr la Porte (*Intendant de la Liste Civile*) had put into his hands, having had the King's orders to communicate them to all the Ministers.

The National Assembly sits night and day, and the Ministers transact business in an adjoining appartment.

I send inclosed the Logographe which gives the most accurate account of every thing that passes in the Assembly, and some other printed papers by way of supplement. In the Postillon of this morning there is mention made of the fears of some of the Ambassadors for their personal safety: if any of them have exprest such fears they have had very little reason for so doing: for myself I never had any.

I walt with impatience for instructions from your Lordship at this critical period.

P.S. The inclosed notes from Mr Montmorin will prove

to your Lordship the difficulty I had to obtain a passport for my messenger.

June 23, 1791.

I received the inclosed paper from Mr. de Montmorin last night.

The most recent account of the King's situation was brought this afternoon by a Mr Mangin, son to a member of the Assembly, who resides at Varennes, a small town between Stenay and Clermont in Argonne. He says that early on Wednesday morning the King and Royal Family passed through Sainte Menehould in a Berline with six horses but with only two attendants on horseback: the post-master of that place suspected that they were not common travellers and questioned them particularly about their rout; they said that they were going to Verdun the first town on the great road, he followed them but seeing them take the bye road which leads to Varennes, he rode in haste to that town and gave the alarm: when the King arrived at the inn the inhabitants insisted that he should not proceed on his journey untill they knew for certain who he was and the motives of it. His Majesty was therefore obliged to enter the inn where he was seen by Mr Mangin who, being acquainted with his person, informed the astonished multitude that they possest their King.

A courier arrived at the Assembly last night about nine o'clock with an account of his Majesty's being stopt at this place, he at the same time delivered a letter from the municipal officers of Sainte Menehould informing the Assembly that Mr Bouillé, who commands at Metz, had sent detachments of troops to that town and other places in the neighbourhood, having given out that a large quantity of money for the pay of the garrisons on the frontiers was expected to pass that way and that they were to convoy it. It appears that when the King was first stopt some hussars were seen riding through the town who finding the alarm too general passed quietly on. The Assembly has given orders to secure Mr Bouillé and it has also appointed three of its members Mr Barnave Mr Pethion and Mr la Tour-Maubourg commissioners with power to give orders to the troops the National Guard and the administrative bodies: their principal business however is to protect the persons of the Royal Family on their return to Paris. According to Mr Mangin's account, the King slept last night at Chalons and intends to sleep this night at Epernay; it is therefore possible that he may arrive in the capital to-morrow, but more probably on Saturday. Monsieur and Madame are safely arrived at Mons.

The way in which the Royal Family contrived to leave the Thuilleries is not yet known; the thing is wonderful and the more so because the Mayor and Mr la Fayette had been apprized of their intention for some days before and had accordingly taken all possible precautions to prevent it: they both staid with his Majesty till one o'clock, when they retired perfectly secure that no attempt of the sort could be made that night; having left a double guard and an extra-ordinary number of officers upon duty against whom there is no suspicion of corruption.

The Assembly continues to sit night and day adjourning sometimes for an hour or two and in the intervals of urgent they proceed with the ordinary business.

Lord Gower.

(2) IN THE PROVINCES

Stephen Weston, antiquary and man of letters, had travelled as a tutor on the Continent in 1771, and visited Paris in 1791–2. His Letters from Paris during the summer of 1791 show more signs of first-hand knowledge than his Letters from Paris during the summer of 1792.

There never was a greater change worked in the course of five minutes in the looks and gestures of any people, than in the inhabitants of this place on the arrival of the messenger from the National Assembly. The whole town I may say, that is, an immense crowd, was collected together in the great square before the town-house, all apparently sullen, and discontented, and full of suspicion, endeavouring from time to time to force their way into the court of the

Hotel de Ville, which the guards at the gates had some difficulty to prevent. The great fear of the people was, that the castle would be surprized, and the assignats fell 50 per cent. before the next day. But as they had no distinct idea of what was to befal them, their trepidation was the greater, *major est ignotarum rerum timor*. I was contemplating this representation to the life of a troubled city, when on turning my head round I saw a courier advancing through the crowd towards the town-house, as fast as the waves of the people could retire on both sides to make a lane for him. The messenger rode immediately into the court of the Hotel de Ville, and very soon after the municipality came out to declare that the King was stopped at Varennes, and on his road back to Paris. But the courier had told the tale long before, and the transition from the deepest dejection to the highest elevation had already taken place. The whole square formed itself into a ring, and danced round like an Indian tribe, with a hoop and a halloo. All at once you saw five hundred hats in the air, and the place re-echoed with screams of joy. These frantic exultations continued till eleven at night, and the town was in a blaze, illuminated through all its streets.

Stephen Weston.
[Lisle, June 24, 1791.]

(3) THE RETURN

Louveteau is 'a wolf's cub'—a reflexion on the Queen rather than the Dauphin. There are many accounts of the scene on June 25: all agree that the King was received in complete silence, and with no sign either of insult or respect.

The King, Queen, and royal family arrived in town yesterday, escorted by 150,000 men. The crowd assembled to see them enter was astonishing. The interment of Mirabeau did not produce such a number. The King, Queen, Dauphin —whom they call her *louveteau*—Madame Royale, and Madame Elisabeth, are in separate apartments, with separate guards. The Dauphin is to have a governor named by the nation; the King is no longer regarded as such. The

National Assembly is to finish the Constitution; and when it is settled a deputation is to be sent to Louis XVI to know whether the mode of government that is adopted suits him: if it does he is to be their sovereign, if it does not a Regent is to be chosen until the Dauphin is of an age to be crowned. The King and Queen are to be conducted to the National Assembly to answer the questions that will be asked them. A report goes about the town that the enemy has entered France, and it is advised, if that is the case, to chop off the King's head, and to tie the Queen to the tail of a horse and drag her through Paris till she dies.

... I forbear all comments on what has passed, judging it imprudent to trust my sentiments in a letter. The dread we had of yesterday is not to be described, but, thank God, everything passed off astonishingly quiet. The King and Queen were suffered to enter Paris without receiving the least insult; this I did not expect, because I think the former acted a cowardly part in sneaking off, after appearing to be so well satisfied with the present Constitution. He has certainly perjured himself, and given his enemies an opportunity of triumphing over him.

Miss Miles.
[June 26, 1791.]

(4) PUBLIC FEELING

J. B. Drouet, maître de poste at St. Ménéhould, recognised Louis when his coach stopped there on June 21, and rode by a short cut to Varennes, just in time to stop the fugitives there. He arrived in Paris on the 24th.

Child as I was, I partook of the general opinion, despite the admonitions of my mother, who was constantly asserting the sacred inviolability of the sovereign. When the King was brought back, after his flight to Varennes, I was walking with her on the Boulevard of the Bains Chinois, when Drouet, the post-master of Sainte Ménéhould, who had stopped the fugitive royal family, crowned with a wreath of laurels, was conducted about the streets amidst popular bursts of enthusiasm. Every woman the mob met was obliged to kiss the supposed saviour of the country, and my poor mother, despite her remonstrance in broken French, was compelled to submit to the rude embrace, which was reiterated amidst shouts of laughter: when the poor, dear soul wiped her mouth and face, shedding bitter tears, amidst roars of *c'est une Anglaise! c'est une Anglaise!*

The populace were roving about the streets in frantic turbulence—effigies of the King and Queen were carried about and burnt, whilst the mob danced round the *auto-da-fe* singing '*Ah ça ira,*' and '*La Carmagnole.*' Wooden heads, fantastically dressed up, with straw stuffed in their mouths, representing the Monarch and Marie Antoinette, were carried about stuck upon pikes, and wherever the word *Royal* was inscribed over theatres, lottery offices, tobacconists, etc., etc. it was effaced with mud or paint, and every symbol of royalty was dashed to pieces, or torn down by the infuriated multitude.

J. G. Millingen.

(5) SECRET HISTORY

Quintin Craufurd was a rich Englishman, once British Resident at Manila, who had since 1780 been living in Paris with Mrs. Eleonora Sullivan, formerly mistress of the Duke of Wurtemberg and the Emperor Joseph II. A friend of the Queen, he was in close touch with her Swedish admirer, Count Axel Fersen, who was concealed in Craufurd's house during his last dangerous visit to the Tuileries in February, 1792. He was therefore in the best possible position to hear the truth about the part Fersen played in the flight to Varennes. The extract is from 'a paper delivered to Mr. Pitt and Lord Grenville,' printed in his Notices sur Marie Stuart et sur Marie-Antoinette *(Paris, 1819).*

It was hinted to me some months ago, that the Count de Fersen frequently saw the King and Queen of France in private, both at the Tuileries and St. Cloud; but the difficulty and danger seemed so great, that I scarcely gave credit to it. I have since understood from him, that, from towards the end of October, 1789, about three weeks after their Majesties were brought from Versailles to Paris, he generally saw them once or twice a week, and sometimes oftener, according as he had business with the King. The place where he constantly saw their Majesties was the King's Closet. He went to the Palace after it was dark, dressed in a frock, with a round hat, and was admitted into the apartments by means of one of those passes which were given to persons of the Household. . . .

The confidential correspondence of their Majesties, both within and without the Kingdom, was carried on by means of M. de Fersen. The infidelity of some, and the indiscretion of almost all, made them now extremely cautious whom they trusted: but they were under the necessity of employing someone on whom they could depend; and he seems to have enjoyed and to have merited their entire confidence. I know him intimately, and think him a man of unquestionable honour and veracity. He is calm, resolute, and uncommonly discreet, without being reserved. The only person abroad who was fully authorised to treat for the King with foreign powers, was the Baron de Breteuil. Though the King loves the Count d'Artois, he seems to be mistrustful of his prudence; and the King and Queen have shown the most decided disapprobation of his employing M. de Calonne.[1]

I left Paris on the 3rd of May last to come to England; and I left London on the 17th of June to return to Paris. On my arrival at Boulogne on the 18th, a letter was delivered to me, by which I was advised not to come to Paris, but to go immediately to Brussels. I did so, and on the 22nd advice was received there of the King's escape. M. de Fersen, who had conducted it, left the royal family about seven miles from Paris. He pressed the King to permit him to accompany him, but he positively refused, saying, 'If we should be stopped, and you taken, it would probably be impossible for me to save you: besides, you have a letter for the Emperor,[2] which in case of my being arrested may be of importance: I therefore order you to go to the Low

[1] Had the King arrived safely at Montmédy, the Baron de Breteuil and the Archbishop of Bordeaux (the late Garde des Sceaux) were immediately to have joined him. Monsieur was to have remained with the King, but the Count d'Artois was to have been sent back to Turin, to act in the Southern Provinces as circumstances might require. Q.C.

[2] This letter served to transmit a copy of the manifest that the King left behind him. He observed to the Emperor that should he be prevented from going away, it would serve to announce his real sentiments; and requested him in that case not to abandon him, or words to that effect. Q.C.

Countries as fast as you can; and, added he, 'Que Dieu vous conserve, acceptez l'offre que je vous fais de mon amitié, et, arrive ce qui veut, Je n' oublierai iamais votre zèle et vos services.' M. de Fersen told me that he felt himself much affected at the manner in which the King spoke to him; and, looking after the carriage as it went away, was strongly tempted to disobey an order that was merely the effect of goodness, and to follow it. He arrived at Mons on the 22nd early in the morning; and having delivered a message to Monsieur, who came there about the same time, he set out to join the King at Montmédy; but at Arlons he met Monsieur de Bouillé, and being informed by him of what had happened at Varennes, he came to Brussels.

Quintin Craufurd.

[Aug. 3, 1791.]

69.   'PRIVATE TRUTHS'

In his declaration of June 26, the King said he had intended to go to Mont-médy, because it was a safe town, near the frontier, where he would be in a position to oppose any foreign invasion, and whence he could 'move to any other part of the country that seemed convenient.'

I AM going to write private truths which might be un-pleasant to a royal eye. If this country ceases to be a mon-archy it will be entirely the fault of Louis 16th. Blunder upon blunder, inconsequence upon inconsequence, a total want of energy of mind accompanied with personal cowardice, have been the destruction of his reign. In this last affair, when he had undertaken to escape from Paris, or if you will, to go to Montmédi, he ought to have effected his plans or perished in the attempt. It will be difficult to persuade me that he intended to stay at Montmédi, especially after the hopes that Monsieur unwarily gave the emigrants in the Low Countries of his brother's speedy arrival among them. . . . It has always been the fate of this unfortunate monarch that whenever the enemies of his Government have begun to suffer the public opinion, he has adopted some measure which has reinstated them. How he can extricate himself out of the present difficulty I know not. Foreign forces would, in my mind, serve only to unite the country still stronger against him, and would compel the French to form a good government: who, if left to themselves, would have frittered it away into a nondescript metaphysical permanent anarchy, or rather ochlocracy.

Lord Gower to Lord Greville.

[July 1, 1791.]

70. TOM PAINE AND HIS FRIENDS

Thomas Paine visited Paris for the second time during the Revolution in 1791. Given French citizenship by the Constituent Assembly, and elected a deputy to the Convention, he came again to Paris in 1792, was involved in the fall of the Girondins, and spent 11 months (Jan.–Nov. 1794) in prison. Horne Tooke was not in France during the Revolution. 'Macintosh' is Sir James Mackintosh, whose Vindiciae Gallicae, *published in this year, was an answer to Burke's* Reflections on the French Revolution. *Thomas Withers served with Nelson, and fought at the battle of Cape St. Vincent. Jean-Baptiste Cloots, a rich and eccentric 'Prussian baron' from Cleves, settled in Paris, 'dechristianised' his name to Anacharsis, and became a propagandist of international revolution. He was guillotined with the Hébertists in March, 1794.*

SEVERAL Englishmen at this period frequented our house; among them was Thomas Paine, who drew up an address to the French people, under a fictitious name. In this insidious production, he insisted that the King had, *de facto*, abdicated, and that the short absence of the monarch had produced an *interregnum* far more desirable for the future welfare of the country than his perfidious misrule. I recollect this address was read at my father's, who then received Horn Tooke, Macintosh, Withers, and other English gentlemen, with Anacharsis Clootz, a most extraordinary foreigner, with long bushy hair, and who appeared to me, by the violence of his frantic gestures, to be out of his mind. He was the first person I saw who wore a red Phrygian cap—the emblem of liberty—which was afterwards generally adopted.

J. G. Millingen.

71. REPUBLICAN MANIFESTO

On the King's flight to Varennes, Paine drew up this manifesto, which his friend Achille Duchâtelet translated into French, and posted on the door of the Manège. *He also engaged in a press controversy on republicanism with the abbé Sieyès.*

BRETHREN AND FELLOW CITIZENS:

The serene tranquillity, the mutual confidence which prevailed amongst us, during the time of the King's escape, the indifference with which we beheld him return, are unequivocal proofs that the absence of a King is more desirable than his presence, and that he is not only a political superfluity, but a grievous burden, pressing hard on the whole nation.

Let us not be imposed upon by sophisms; all that concerns this is reduced to four points.

He has abdicated the throne in having fled from his post. Abdication and desertion are not characterized by the length of absence; but by the single act of flight. In the present instance, the act is everything, and the time nothing.

The nation can never give back its confidence to a man who, false to his trust, perjured to his oath, conspires a clandestine flight, obtains a fraudulent passport, conceals a King of France under the disguise of a valet, directs his course towards a frontier covered with traitors and deserters, and evidently meditates a return into our country, with a force capable of imposing his own despotic laws.

Whether ought his flights to be considered as his own act, or the act of those who fled with him? Was it a spontaneous resolution of his own, or was it inspired into him by others? The alternative is immaterial; whether fool or hypocrite, idiot or traitor, he has proved himself equally unworthy of the important functions that had been delegated to him.

In every sense that the question can be considered, the reciprocal obligation which subsisted between us is dissolved. He holds no longer any authority. We owe him no longer obedience. We see in him no more than an indifferent person; we can regard him only as Louis Capet.

The history of France presents little else than a long series of public calamity, which takes its source from the vices of the Kings; we have been the wretched victims that have never ceased to suffer either for them or by them. The catalogue of their oppressions was complete, but to complete the sum of their crimes, treason yet was wanting. Now the only vacancy is filled up, the dreadful list is full; the system is exhausted; there are no remaining errors for them to commit; their reign is consequently at an end.

What kind of office must that be in a government which requires neither experience nor ability to execute? that may be abandoned to the desperate chance of birth, that may be filled with an idiot, a madman, a tyrant, with equal effect as by the good, the virtuous, and the wise? An office of this nature is a mere nonentity: it is a place of show, not of use. Let France then, arrived at the age of reason, no longer be deluded by the sound of words, and let her deliberately examine, if a King, however insignificant and contemptible in himself, may not at the same time be extremely dangerous.

The thirty millions which it costs to support a King in the éclat of stupid oriental luxury, presents us with an easy method of reducing taxes, which reduction would at once release the people, and stop the progress of political corruption. The grandeur of nations consists, not, as Kings pretend, in the splendor of thrones, but in a conspicuous sense of their own dignity, and in a just disdain of those barbarous follies and crimes which, under the sanction of royalty, have hitherto desolated Europe.

As to the personal safety of Louis Capet, it is so much the more confirmed, as France will not stoop to degrade herself by a spirit of revenge against a wretch who has dishonoured himself. In defending a just and glorious cause, it is not possible to degrade it, and the universal tranquillity which prevails is an undeniable proof that a free people know how to respect themselves.

Thomas Paine. Achille Duchâtelet.

[July 1, 1791.]

72. 'MATTERS COMING TO A CRISIS'

J. B. Holroyd, first Earl of Sheffield, passes through Paris on his way to visit his friend Gibbon at Lausanne, and sends on this letter describing his impressions. After the failure of the flight to Varennes, due largely to the breakdown of military arrangements under his command, the Marquis de Bouillé wrote to the Assembly (June 26), taking all the blame for the affair upon himself.

. . . I CAME here last night. I have already had an opportunity of good intelligence. Matters of the highest consequence are *this moment* in agitation. They are determined to get rid of the King, but how, is not so easy a business. Many of his enemies are sorry he was retaken, because they know not what to do with him (a Council will be appointed). I believe they would be glad to let him go, if they did not fear the Parisian mobility. The judges agree that the Gardes de Corps, who acted as couriers, cannot be tried. They will be suffered to depart whenever it will be safe. As to the Queen, when I said I was surprised they did not send her home (that is to the Pais Autrichiennes) to avoid mischief to her Person, and also to divert a disagreeable demand, I was told there is no doubt that she will be allowed to go if she pleases. De Buillé has emitted an invitation to Officers and Soldiers to join him. His letter to the National Assembly might well have been enough for a Captain of Grenadiers, but it does not smell of the grand Politician. I understand that scarce a General Officer remains with the Army on the Austrian border towards ——, and that numbers, even whole corps of officers, have deserted, but this I know not with any precision. I think we may go from hence in 4 or 5 days. Matters are coming to a Crisis. . . .

Lord Sheffield to Edward Gibbon.

[July 5, 1791.]

73. ARMY ALLEGIANCE

In view of the part played by Bouillé's troops in the flight to Varennes, the Assembly exacted a fresh oath of loyalty from the army. Lieut.-Colonel Keating, M.P. for Co. Kildare, published Travels through France, Spain and Morocco, *in* 1816-17.

I ARRIVED here on Saturday last. Since the capture of the King, or rather since his flight, they have been more strict about passports than before; that is all the difference I have yet been able to discover, except an increased scarcity of money, between the country as it is now and when I was last here. The day after my arrival the new oath was tendered and accepted by those officers of the army who were *democratically* inclined; those of a contrary opinion were obliged to make their escape the day before; of the Regiment de Dillon twelve men were absent; of the Regiment of Cavalry there were but eight officers out of near forty that swore. The other three regiments all swore. The form was, to use the arms put into their hands for the defence of the New Constitution, to die rather than suffer foreign invasion, to obey no orders but such as were given in consequence of decrees of the National Assembly, and much more to the same purpose, without ever mentioning the King's name. To the above oath the Swiss regiment was allowed to add, 'Sans préjudice à ce que nous devons à notre Souverain et à la capitulation.' The ceremony lasted nearly two hours. Old Rochambeau was the first who took the oath; he is here as 'Commandant des troupes de ligne du Département du Nord. . . .'

We are obliged here to take a passport for the purpose of taking even a morning ride, so strict are they at present.

As I do not find any inconvenience that a stranger can experience in his progress through this country, if he does not make a fool of himself by sporting opinions counter to the revolution, I shall set out from hence for Paris on Monday next. . . .

Lieut.-Colonel Keating to Dr. Arnold.

[Lille, July 6, 1791.]

74. VOLTAIRE'S FUNERAL

(1)

When Voltaire died, on May 30, 1778, the Archbishop of Paris refused him Christian burial, and he was hurriedly interred at Scellières, before the Bishop of Troyes could object. On May 30, 1791, the Assembly decreed that his remains should be brought to Paris, and publicly interred in the Panthéon. The recent flight of the King turned the ceremony of July 15 into an almost republican demonstration. Henry Temple, second Viscount Palmerston, Lord of the Admiralty and of the Treasury, was fond of travel, and wrote a Diary *in* France *during July and August, 1791, which was first published in* The Despatches of Earl Gower *(1885).*

THIS afternoon the procession of Voltaire took place though the weather was very unfavourable as it was found inconvenient to defer it. It was very long, but a great part of it consisted of very shabby, ill-dressed people whose appearance was made worse by the mud and dirt they had collected. Great quantities of National Guards attended; but in disorder and without arms, except such as were on duty. Deputations of different orders of people and among others the Academy. A figure of Voltaire, very like him, in a gown was carried first sitting in an elbow chair, and afterwards came the coffin on a very fine triumphal car drawn by twelve beautiful grey horses four abreast. The coffin was covered and over it a waxen figure was laid on a bed. After having made a great circuit round the town they came to the house of the Marquis de Villette, who is married to Voltaire's niece and where he died. There the figures stopped, a kind of hymn was sung, Madame Villette and her child came down, mounted the car and embraced the figure and then with several other ladies followed it on foot during the remainder of the procession, to the new Church of St. Geneviève where it is to be deposited.

Lord Palmerston.

[July 11, 1791.]

(2)

Jean Calas was the Protestant victim of the Parlement of Toulouse (1762), whose rehabilitation was one of Voltaire's greatest strokes against intolerance and injustice.

My father took me, on the preceding evening, to the place of the Bastille, where the remains of this illustrious writer . . . were placed on a pedestal raised on the ruins of the very prison in which he had once been confined. The following day, the procession that accompanied his sarcophagus to the Pantheon, was as numerous as the mass of mourners who followed the mortal remains of Mirabeau. The whole was *got up* in theatrical style. All the actors and actresses, singers and dancers, of the different theatres, were grouped round a statue of the philosopher, in the various costumes of his *dramatis personae*. Zaïre was walking next to Mahomet, Julius Caesar arm-in-arm with Oedipus, and Brutus with the widow of Malabar; while another group represented Calas and his family. One of the most singular objects in the procession was a portable press, which worked off various hand-bills, as the *cortège* proceeded, which were scattered amongst the people.

J. G. Millingen.

(3)

Ferney, now called Ferney-Voltaire, is the small village a few miles from Geneva, just across the French frontier, where Voltaire lived, and played at Providence, for the last 20 years of his life. That Beaumarchais should provide almost royal horses for the funeral was quite in character; for he was one of the richest men in Paris, his house and garden were among the sights of the city, and he was doing all he could to keep himself popular.

I attended the pageant of the poet of Ferney, but it was spoilt in great measure by a wet day, and owed much of its failure of success to the badness of the weather. The people were a little out of humour with the rain. The women said the *Bon Dieu* was aristocrate . . . I cannot, however, praise the triumphal car; as a machine *a l'antique*, it was incorrectly conceived, as a piece of modern production, it was heavy and clumsy. The horses, twelve in number, were beautiful in the extreme; they were white, and eight of them came from the stables of Monsieur, the King's brother, and four from Beaumarchais. The figure of Voltaire lying upon its back on the car produced but a sorry effect, especially, when, on account of the unevenness of the pavement, it could not be kept steady; the right arm too was dislocated by the repeated joltings of the carriage, and hung down like the arm of a malefactor broken upon the wheel. The show, nevertheless, gave universal satisfaction, and did not arrive at the cloister, where the body was to be interred, till after nine o'clock at night: I say the body, but more properly what was left of the body.

Stephen Weston.
[July, 1791.]

75. FEDERATION, 1791

Contrast the enthusiasm with which the fête of July 14 was celebrated a year ago (v. No. 45). It is now banned by most of the 'patriot' press, and followed (July 16, 17) by republican demonstrations, the second of which leads to the Massacre of the Champ de Mars.

JULY 14. This was the anniversary of the Federation and was again celebrated in the Champ de Mars. Mr. Pelham and I got an order to go into the École militaire, which commands the whole scene. There were by all accounts considerably fewer troops than last year and the bridge over the Seine and the triumphal arch were not there, but the weather was fine and the concourse of people on that account was greater than before. The procession as it entered passed before the École militaire, but the fine object was the general coup d'oeil of the whole multitude when collected. So many troops and such a number of people were I dare say never assembled before in a place so formed to shew them to advantage without a possibility of any considerable inconvenience from the crowd. The area is 900 yards long and about half that extent in breadth. The great altar, which is a building raised high from the ground to which four ample flights of steps in a circular form lead up, and on which altogether I doubt not but 2000 persons might stand, was in the middle. The École militaire, a very handsome building, is at one end; the other extends nearly to the

Seine. The whole area except in front of the École militaire is surrounded by a bank of a breadth and size proportionable to the place, sloping inwards down to the area, on which last year there were benches placed. This year the people stood. The numbers it would contain cannot be estimated. The people of Paris were pouring out to it the whole morning and yet it was not half full, though at a little distance it appeared to the eye of a spectator tolerably well covered. The troops which consisted of large detachments of the Gardes Nationales of Paris and all the neighbourhood I should suppose might amount to 20,000: They made no great figure in the area but they kept the people out. The procession consisted besides of great bodies of troops which marched with them, of detachments from all the great bodies of people concerned in all the departments of the government, the Courts of Justice, the Academies and various Societies of the Capital. The National Assembly who last year attended in a body sent this year a deputation of 24 members. The whole procession marched to the altar where were already placed about 60 priests, all in their white robes of ceremony; and as candles could not be used four fires were kept burning at the corners in vases raised on vast tripods in antique forms. The whole altar was now a cluster of people; and the banners which every Corps carried before them formed a circle completely round it. The Mass attended with musick took up some considerable time and afterwards the banners were carried in procession round the altar for a great while and every one in its turn was presented and had a long ribbon with the national colours tied to it. This closed the business, and those who had formed the procession marched back as it happened without much order. A little before the end the people contrived to get into the area which they appeared to fill and by that means presented a new scene which was curious in a different way.

Lord Palmerston.

76. SINCE VARENNES

Francis Moore, of the British Embassy, sends his views on the dangerous situation created by the flight to Varennes, and by the growth of republicanism. From Selections from the letters and correspondence of Sir James Bland Burges, Bart. (1885).

THE more I consider the effects of the King's flight, the more I see reason to regret that rash measure, which, even had he succeeded in effecting his escape, would not, in my opinion, have been equally advantageous either to himself or to his country, as his remaining quietly at Paris; for although his situation before the 21st ult. was very lamentable, it afforded considerable grounds to hope for an amendment. His resignation to the decrees of the National Assembly, the apparent indifference with which he saw himself stripped of his former power and splendour, and above all, the voluntary visit he had paid to the Assembly to protest his attachment to the constitution and declare himself its defender, had acquired him the good will and confidence of the nation; and had he continued to observe the same moderation, and allowed the Assembly to have finished (what they would have been pleased to call) the constitution, after the first effervescence of liberty, or rather licence, had subsided, the influence of a civil list of thirty millions would have gradually acquired a sufficient share of power to the monarch, whereas, by the fatal step of his *evasion*, he has laid the foundation of infinite misery to his country. He has irretrievably forfeited whatever hold he had of the confidence and affection of the people, and, at the same time, encouraged the Jacobins entirely to throw off the mask, and boldly to bring forward their wild republican doctrines, even in the National Assembly, where, although there is hitherto a great majority in favour of the present constitution, yet there is too much reason to apprehend that these Bedlamites (amongst whom it cannot be denied there are men of considerable ability, and who are employing incredible industry to acquire proselytes, by disseminating in all departments, and indeed throughout all Europe, the most licentious publications) will acquire the ascendancy in the next; and indeed, even supposing this should not be the case, and the next Assembly should prove no less favourable to monarchy than the present, the King will not now, I fear, be able to acquire that degree of influence, which I am inclined to think he might have done had he not attempted his escape.

In the Champ de Mars yesterday the greatest order was preserved which, considering the prodigious concourse of people, surprised me a good deal. I was very much gratified with this scene, and the more so as I went along with their joy, and felt that it was a natural and proper occasion of national exultations. This was far from being my sentiment last Monday when the procession of Voltaire took place. I then could not help being struck with the absurdity and frivolity of expending 10,000 pounds sterling in so unworthy a manner; and that at a time when the public finances are in so bad a state, and when the most important objects are in discussion; not to mention the indecency and impolicy of shewing so much respect to the memory of a man who had employed the greatest part of his time and talents in turning religion into contempt and ridicule.

Francis Moore to Mr. Burges.
[July 15, 1791.]

77. THE CHAMP DE MARS MASSACRE
(1)

On July 16 a manifesto calling for the King's deposition, and his replacement 'by constitutional means,' was read out at the 'altar of the country' on the Champ de Mars. On the 17th, at the same place, a fresh petition, demanding the establishment of 'a new Executive Power,' was signed by over 6000 persons; it was this meeting which was 'massacred' by the National Guard. Palmerston's account avoids the usual exaggerations.

JULY 17TH. This morning early there were gatherings of people in the Champ de Mars, and very unfortunately two men were discovered to have got into the great cavity under the Autel de la Patrie where they had carried their dinner and seemed to have proposed passing the whole day. They were discovered by boring holes through the steps and sides of the place; and the only conjecture that seems to have any probability with regard to their intentions, is that they thought they should see what might happen without being crowded, and that they should have a good prospect of the women's legs who might come up the steps. One of them is said to have been an invalid with a wooden leg, but a young man. This frolick however cost them very dear for the mob immediately decided that they were placed there to blow up with powder the altar with all the zealous friends of the *Patrie*, and seized and carried them before some little inferior magistrates of the Quarter. But finding these doubtful and undecided what they should do, they took them away again and executed them themselves with many circumstances of inhumanity. The Municipality of Paris, having had information the day before that a large body of people were to meet early at the ruins of the Bastile and from thence proceed to the Champ de Mars, had met early at the Hôtel de Ville and their chief attention had been directed to the quarter of the Bastile. There however nothing passed nor was any mob assembled. When they received the first information of the murder at the Champ de Mars, they immediately sent some of their body with a battalion of Guards to act as the occasion should require. The accounts they received from these Commissioners were unsatisfactory and at length they returned to inform their brethren of the very disorderly state of affairs. That they had met the mob carrying the heads of the two men (which is a favourite amusement) on poles, that one of the bearers had been seized but afterwards rescued, that a man had attempted to shoot Monsieur de la Fayette, but had been prevented, that the man had been seized but released at the desire of Monsieur de la Fayette, that on proceeding to the altar they had found a number of persons signing petitions against the Decree of the 15th, that the National Guard had been repeatedly insulted and driven away, that on the Commissioners presenting themselves to remonstrate they had been very ill received, but that the mob had insisted on sending 12 persons on their part as deputies to the Hôtel de Ville who were waiting without. The Municipality who had determined immediately before the arrival of their Commissioners to hang out the drapeau rouge which, accompanied with a proclamation is an establishment of martial law, and to proceed in a body accompanied with a very strong force to the Champ de Mars, agreed, however, to stop in order to hear what the mob ambassadors had to offer. These, however, on the sight of the drapeau rouge and of the troops and cannon prepared had stepped off and were probably gone back to apprize their friends. The expedition now proceeded. It was seven in the evening when they reached the Champ de Mars—in all the environs of which they found great crowds of persons who appeared as spectators. The bank, or glacis, as it is called, on each side the opening through which they were to enter was covered with people who began to insult them by calling out, à bas les bayonettes, à bas le drapeau rouge. The Mayor made a stop just in the entrance, and was proceeding to have the usual proclamations made when they were interrupted by a volley of stones from the bank and a pistol fired at the Mayor, which narrowly missed him and wounded a soldier just behind him. On this the troops without waiting for orders, as it seems, began to fire but probably in the air as it does not appear that any-one was killed by the first discharge though it was a pretty considerable one. The firing was stopped and the march continued into the Champ de Mars. The altar in the middle was now deserted so that the allied corps of civil and military continued their course between it and the bank which was now covered with people who had resumed their courage on finding no one killed, and renewed their attacks with stones and pistols. A more serious fire then took place from the troops and the cavalry began to charge with their swords, by which some execution was done. It is difficult to know the exact numbers that suffered, but the most probable accounts say about 16 killed and as many wounded who remained behind. Several of the troops were wounded with stones etc. and three were killed who are said to have been single when attacked. A complete dispersion now took place, the mob all flying into the town where they threaten the most violent revenge with fire and sword, that the National Assembly shall be driven out and Monsieur de la Fayette not suffered to live another day. Their fire however spent itself very much during their running, and the people of Paris were so little disposed to be inflamed by them that (proper guards being posted in various parts of the town) the remainder of the evening and night passed off with the utmost tranquillity.

Lord Palmerston.

(2)

As a result of the events of July 16–17, although the Jacobin Club, under Robespierre's leadership, disowned the petition of the 17th, the more moderate members seceded, and claimed to carry on the true succession in a Société des Amis de la Constitution séante aux Feuillants, *meeting in the Bernardine (nicknamed* Feuillant) *convent close by.*

A considerable number of suspicious foreigners have been taken up to-day but none, as your Lordship may easily imagine, are English: the most conspicuous is one Ephraim a Jew, supposed to be employed by the King of Prussia; cyphers were found in his possession but, as he declares he is employed about a commercial treaty, he may have made use of them without an improper design. Although I am convinced that none of the many English who are here are in the least personally concerned in the politics of this country, I endeavour to persuade them to use all possible caution in words as well as action, the more so as an opinion is gone abroad that both Government and Opposition in England have tampered with the democratic party here. The members of the Jacobins who are deputies, except Mr Roberspierre Mr Buzot and Mr. Pethion, have quitted that club and have composed another at the feuillants. They have also written addresses to all the provincial societies connected with the club of the Jacobins in order to prevent the bad effects which the addresses sent by that club may otherwise have in the provinces.

·　·　·　·　·　·

The chief advantage that Government has obtained by the coalition with the formerly popular party is more visible in the metropolis than it can be expected to be in the provinces, the strong [Forts de la Halle] men of the market and the suburb of St Anthony and the most wealthy bankers here appear to be still at their command, and, feeling secure of the National Guard, they have exerted the public force in a manner in which they otherwise could not have ventured to act.

Though the rage of republicanism may be overcome, it will be difficult to conquer the disgust the King's conduct has inspired.

[July 22.] As long as the red flag continues to be displayed at the Hotel de Ville we may expect to feel the effects of that energy which military law has given to Government. A wonderful change has taken place since the disturbance of the 17th compelled the majority of the Assembly to be sensible of its power. It is calculated that two hundred people have been imprisoned since that event, upon suspicion of fomenting sedition by writing or by other means. Danton is fled and Mr Robespierre the great *Denonciateur* and by office *Accusateur publique* is about to be *denoncé* himself. Ephraim the Jew is set at liberty; but a woman of the name of Etta Palm, who used to assume the title of Baronne d'Aelders, is confined upon the same suspicion.

Some addresses are arrived in favor of the decree of the 15th: the strongest of which is that from Rouen; there can be no doubt that the country at large approves of that decree but it will be wise in the Assembly to hasten the business that remains for them to finish and to make way for their successors for in a short time *tempus abire tibi* will be told them from all quarters; and their resemblance to the Long Parliament begins to be a common topic.

Lord Gower.

78. THE LUXEMBOURG GARDENS

The Luxembourg district of Paris—dominated by the buildings of St. Sulpice and other ecclesiastical establishments—was a centre of clericalism; and it was here that anti-clerical Sectionists, a year later, started the September massacres by a slaughter of priests. The Tuileries gardens were closed to the public from May to July (cp. No. 93).

As it is not possible to get into the Thuilleries, and as the Palais Roïal, like other good things, fatigues without satiating, I now and then pay a visit to the Luxemburgh gardens, where France is as she was in the plenitude of the old system, in bag and sword, and hat of three corners. Here you are sure to meet the disappointed band, and the whole tribe of the counter-revolutionists: it is here only that they hold up their heads, and display their orders. Clergy, Nobility, Monks of all colours, and Friars of all sizes: every order knows its place, and falls naturally into the rank to which it belongs—the Clergy excommunicate in the Alley des Chartreux, the Nobles and the Military plan their battles in the alley of the Carmes, and figure to the last with their ribands of red and blue.

Besides these, you have the discontented regiment of foreigners and outlaws, who having done every possible mischief to their own country, by serving against it, by plotting and countermining it, retire to this place in search of a little chance society, which it is impossible for them to find in their own neighbourhood.

Stephen Weston.
[August, 1791.]

79. KING AND CONSTITUTION

William Windham was at this time (aet. 21), M.P. for Norwich; later he became Secretary for War under Pitt and Grenville. The Vicomte de Noailles represented Nemours in the States-General, and was one of the leaders of the liberal nobles. Titles of nobility were abolished on June 19, 1790: hence the ci-devant. The President of the Assembly on Sept. 14, was the lawyer J. G. Thouret, deputy for the Commons of Rouen.

I MAY now just mention the little event that took place yesterday of the King's acceptance of the constitution. By the extreme friendly activity of Noailles (ci-devant vicomte) I got a place in the Assembly and was present at the whole ceremony. There was great respect and great applause, but the nature of the proceeding was necessarily humiliating and some circumstances in the conduct of it rendered it still more so. Before the King appeared, two very splendid chairs were placed, one of which I was surprised to see occupied by the president, who pronounced from thence—he and the King being for some time the only persons sitting—a long lecture, in which, besides the objection on account of its length, there was somewhat too much of 'la nation,' and somewhat too little of 'le roi.' The principle of this equality between King and president was, no doubt, that the president represented the nation: but that principle followed up should have put the King upon the footstool, with the president's foot on his neck: for there is no doubt, to me at least, in theory as well as in their practice, that the nation, rightly understood, is all in all. It would have been much better, in my mind, if, being bound in courtesy to remit much, they had carried their courtesy a little further, and remitted all. I hope that we shall be the people to keep up a little of the 'vieille cour' in our manners, while we lose nothing of the solid advantages and privileges that the new system can promise.

W. Windham.
[Sept. 15, 1791.]

80.   THE NEW ASSEMBLY

The last meeting of the Constituent Assembly was on Sept. 30, the first of the Legislative Assembly, elected under the Constitution of 1791, on Oct. 1. When the deputies dispersed on the 30th, Pétion, deputy for Chartres, and Robespierre, for Arras, were 'chaired' by the Paris crowd. The first dealings between the King and the new Assembly were unfortunate: offended by the way in which he received a deputation on Oct. 4, they passed a number of resolutions as to his reception in the House on the 7th, derogatory to his position.

His most Christian Majesty went on Friday last to the National Assembly and closed the business of that Assembly by a speech, a printed copy of which I inclose. In returning from thence he had the satisfaction of receiving the applause of the spectators, and of hearing a frequent repetition of *Vive le Roy*, but the very people who were heard to cry *Vive le Roy* the most hastened from thence to offer civic crowns to Mr Pethion and Mr Robertspierre, the chief fautors of republicanism in the last Assembly, and whom they chose to style *les Héros de la Constitution*.

The new Assembly has not yet given any proofs of its wisdom; of its rashness and ignorance it gave a convincing one last Wednesday: it shewed an absurd disposition to quarrel with the King about trifles, while he, on the other hand, was shewn a decided intention not to quarrel with them if he can possibly avoid it. Their rashness disgusted even the crowds in the Palais Royal, and an alarm occasioned by a fall of the public funds brought them to resipiscence; the next day they annulled their decree, and the majesty of the King of the French remains not less degraded than it was at the expiration of the Corps Constituant. For the particulars of the debate of Wednesday, I must refer to the Logographe: it seems to augur that the fanaticism of liberty will be prevalent, but it may have proceeded from an impatient desire, in those members who took the lead in it, of taking the first opportunity of shewing their importance and of proving what they might be capable of doing if not prevented.

Lord Gower.
[Oct. 7, 1791].

81. THE KING'S POSITION

For a time, after his reinstatement, the King was popular; but soon the arming of emigrant aristocrats at Coblentz and other places on the Rhine frontier, following the Declaration of Pillnitz (Aug. 27) by the Emperor Leopold and the King of Prussia, led to the Decree on emigration (Nov. 9); and the King's refusal to sanction this brought on a fresh crisis.

PARIS, since our arrival, has been as quiet as any large city can be, and as amusing as I found it last year. The King has been to the opera and the play in a private box, without decorations or ornaments. He is become extremely popular.

145

The minds of people seem to be much more settled since the finishing of the constitution, there is not nearly so much of politics talked in the cafés, nor are there the meetings and mobs in the Palais Royal. One hears nothing of the army on the Rhine, and the letters and declarations laughed at and their authenticity doubted. . . .

The King made his speech on Friday; we were present. When the chair (placed by the side of the President's) was brought in, *it* was exceedingly applauded, and the King himself received with violent applause, and stopped by it frequently in the midst of his speech. He came in attended by a deputation of the Assembly and his ministers, read his speech in a distinct, clear voice, was answered by the President, and then retired.

On Sunday evening I was at his mass. When it was over a man got upon a bench and cried out very loud, 'Je demande justice à votre majesté, je n'ai pas du pain à manger.' The King looked exceedingly red and alarmed, but collected himself, and bid him hold his tongue and go away. Everybody seemed to be on the King's side, and the man was carried away. He keeps a Court, rides out, and goes hunting without interruption. These circumstances would seem to shew that if the King manages well, he may gain popularity and confidence, and, if he was well advised, might in time bring about some changes beneficial to all. . . . James is in love with the Queen, and vows he will go every day to see her pass to mass. . . .

There seem to be fewer carriages and fewer fine people about this year than there were last. The fact is that almost all the nobility have left the country. Since the passage has been left open the emigrations have been amazing.

The New Assembly consists of very few of the ancient gentry; but there are several very sensible men amongst them. The most of them write their speeches, and read them, which is wise at first, as they are unused to speaking, but they are extremely disorderly for want of rules to preserve regularity and deference to some authority.

C. B. Wollaston   [Oct. 12, 1791.]

82. PARIS PILGRIMAGE

For Wordsworth's first visit to France, v. No. 46. In the autumn of 1791
he spent some little time in Paris, and stayed on 15 or 16 months at Orleans,
Blois, and (again) Paris. This extract belongs to the end of November, 1791.
For his return visit to Paris, v. No. 106(2).

THROUGH Paris lay my readiest course, and there
Sojourning a few days, I visited,
In haste, each spot of old or recent fame,
The latter chiefly; from the field of Mars
Down to the suburbs of St. Antony,
And from Mount Martyr southward to the Dome
Of Geneviève. In both her clamorous Halls,
The National Synod and the Jacobins,
I saw the Revolutionary Power
Toss like a ship at anchor, rocked by storms;
The Arcades I traversed, in the Palace huge
Of Orleans; coasted round and round the line
Of Tavern, Brothel, Gaming-house, and Shop,
Great rendezvous of worst and best, the walk
Of all who had a purpose, or had not;
I stared and listened, with a stranger's ears,
To Hawkers and Haranguers, hubbub wild!
And hissing Factionists with ardent eyes,
In knots, or pairs, or single. Not a look
Hope takes, a Doubt or Fear is forced to wear,
But seemed there present; and I scanned them all,
Watched every gesture uncontrollable
Of anger, and vexation, and despite,
All side by side, and struggling face to face,
With gaiety and dissolute idleness.
Where silent zephyrs sported with the dust
Of the Bastille, I sat in the open sun,
And from the rubbish gathered up a stone,
And pocketed the relic, in the guise
Of an enthusiast. . . .

William Wordsworth.
['The Prelude.']

83. GOODBYE TO THE QUEEN

For Mrs. Swinburne and her son, v. No. 20.

WHEN I had obtained my passports for myself and maid, I asked to take leave of the queen, and the interview was granted, which is a great favour, for she sees no one. She received me graciously, even kindly, and the manner in which she spoke of my son was calculated to set my heart at ease concerning him. She wished me every happiness. '*Vous allez dans votre heureuse famille,*' said she, '*dans un pays tranquille, où la calomnie et la cruauté ne vous poursuivront pas! Je dois vous porter envie.*' I ventured a few words of consolation, hinting that times were now improving, and that her popularity and happiness would be restored. She shook her head. We were alone. I know not how I was worked up to it, or had courage to make the proposal; but I did so— that if she thought herself in danger, my services were at her command, and that she could come with me to England in the disguise of my maid, whom I could easily dispose of, by sending her under some pretext to her friends at St. Germain. She thanked me, and smiled faintly, but said nothing would induce her to leave her family. She added that she had refused other offers of the same sort. 'Besides,' and she looked round, '*si je voulais, cela ne se pourroit pas; il y a trop d'espions.*' I took leave of her with regret and affection.

Mrs. Swinburne.
[London, Dec. 1, 1791.]

84. BECKFORD IN PARIS

The author of Vathek *was at this time living in Paris in his usual elaborate style. His difficulties in getting away 18 months later are described in No. 112.*

A THICK cloud hangs over Paris at this moment, fraught with some confounded crackers. I expect an eruption every minute. The assembly know not which way to turn themselves, and publick credit is at the lowest ebb. . . . Notwithstanding the confusion of the moment, all my baggage,

plate, books, horses, carriages, etc. have been admitted
duty free, and I must own nothing can exceed the civilities
I meet with from the nation; but there is no living in
comfort with a sword suspended over one's head by a
thread. I take the dear nation itself to be in that disagreeable
predicament. . . . I have a short stumpy pen, and write
more from the fist than the fingers, and make sad blots; no
wonder! Two or three Deputies are chattering at one end
of my room, and swilling tea, and observing that, since the
introduction of this English beverage, *un ne pense plus
librement*, etc., etc., a deel of French stuff.

William Beckford to Sir W. Hamilton.

[Dec. 15, 1791].

85. THE GARDE AND THE MOB

*Edward Jerningham, the poet and dramatist, had a brother Charles, who
held a commission in the French army. Monsr. de Brienne, Cardinal Archbishop of Sens (1788), had taken the civil oath, and still resided in his Paris
hôtel.*

OF an event that happened the other night I was an eye
witness: the mob pass'd our window on their way to the
Hotel de Brienne, three doors off: there they assembled
with Flambeaus without appearing to have any settled
resolution about destroying the house, for they stood at
least a quarter of an hour opposite the Hotel without
committing any violence. During this suspence the French
Gardes pass'd our Door, and surprising the rioters, they fell
upon them in a most inhuman manner, Beating their heads
with the Musket and applying the point of the Bayonet to
several. One poor wretch, escaping the tumult drop'd at
our door. My brother supplied him with Linen and everything requisite for the dressing of his wound, which, however, the Surgeon declar'd to be Mortal; the bayonet had
run so far into his stomach. When the battle was over,
Monsr. de Brienne (to remove a little the odium from his
name) order'd the man to be convey'd to his house,
where he died four hours after. By the means of the flam-

beaux I saw the military execution perfectly. The poor rioters made very little resistance, and they should have been taken prisoners and not treated as if they had opposed Arms to Arms.

Edward Jerningham the elder.

[Paris, early in 1792.]

86. A LETTER TO ROBESPIERRE

The text of this letter comes from Papiers inédits trouvés chez Robespierre, *etc.* (1828), *but the signature, there given as 'Theeman Shephen,' has been corrected from the catalogue of a sale of autographs in* 1874. *Alger* (Englishmen in the French Revolution, *p.* 54) *identifies (Mrs.)* Freeman Shepherd *with Harriet Augusta Freeman, who was a boarder at the English Benedictine nunnery, and translated Mercier's* Paris de l'An. 2440 (*London,* 1797). *A month after this letter she presented* 200 francs *to the Assembly, through Beurnonville, for the purchase of shoes for the volunteers. For Robespierre's address, cp. No.* 125.

MONSIEUR,

Je n'aime pas la dissimulation; je ne la pratique jamais en aucune occasion envers personne, et je n'endure pas qu'on la pratique envers moi. Vous en avez usé, Monsieur, vis-à-vis de moi. Vous m'avez trompée: vous m'avez fait accroire que vous acceptiez, pour le bien de la chose publique, ma petite offrande, et vous ne l'avez pas acceptée. Les comptes de recette et de déboursement que mes banquiers viennent, selon leur annuelle coutume, de me transmettre, en font preuve. Mon illusion a été bien douce et agréable, et mon réveil en est d'autant plus pénible. Vous êtes obligé, Monsieur, en honneur, ainsi que par pitié, de m'en dédommager par des réalités. Si la date de cet ordre faisait un obstacle à sa négociation, veuillez me le renvoyer, et j'en ferai un autre, revêtu de toutes les formalités requises pour son immédiate acceptation. Vous avez contracté, Monsieur, l'obligation de l'accepter et de vous en faire payer, en venant ici m'assurer de l'usage que vous comptez en faire. Ne méprisez pas aussi les Anglais; ne traitez pas avec cette humiliante dépréciation *la bégayante aspiration de bonne volonté*, envers la cause commune de tous les peuples, d'une *Anglaise*.

Les Français étaient autrefois célèbres par leur complaisance pour le sexe le plus faible, et le plus sensible par là même aux injures. Malheur à nous, si la révolution nous ôte ce précieux privilège! Mais je réclame un plus juste droit: ne faites pas à autrui ce que vous ne voudriez pas qu'on vous fît.

Dans la plus persévérante détermination de chercher satisfaction jusqu' à ce que je l'obtienne,

J'ai l'honneur d'être, Monsieur, votre vindicative servante,

Freeman Shepherd.

(à M. Robespierre, ancien député de l'assemblée constituante, maison de M. Dupley, menuisier, rue Saint-Honoré, vis-à-vis celle Saint-Florentin, à Paris.

12 Janvier, 1792.)

87. SIGHT-SEEING IN PARIS

William Hunter 'of the Inner Temple' left London on Feb. 14, spent a week in Paris, and travelled on to Lyon and Marseille, where he embarked for Smyrna. His Travels through France, *etc. were published in 1803.*

ANXIOUS to behold the place of the King's confinement, our first walk was to the palace of the Thuilleries. We stopped to examine the wing next the river, and our conductor began his observations by pointing out to us the four places, at one of which, it is conjectured, the unfortunate Louis made his escape, when he fled from his capital. Three of them are now strongly barricaded, and the other is blocked up. Since that fatal period, some national guards have been constantly stationed at the windows of his apartment, who, as if they gloried in insulting the feelings of a fallen monarch, seemed emulous of rendering themselves as conspicuous as possible.

·   ·   ·   ·   ·

The whole city is split into parties, and, at the corner of every principal street, the glaring letters of some inflammatory handbill invite the eye. All the coffee-houses are crowded with pretended politicians, who, according to their various prejudices, vent the noxious torrents of their fury; and groups of hirelings, half intoxicated, are everywhere bawling out their national airs. Even at the theatres, places which were instituted for sober relaxation and rational amusement, the boisterous voice of faction intrudes itself, and cannot be silenced. The aristocratical party, however, has lately, after a severe struggle, evidently gained ground, and is now sufficiently respectable to venture to avow itself.

. . . . .

The *Place Victoire*, where Louis the XIVth was, by the vanity of his subjects, for so many years, crowned with laurels which he never gained, is crowded every morning with brokers and Jews, whose business is to buy up specie with assignats. They are said to be employed by some eminent Paris bankers, who are unwilling that their names should be made public. . . . The statue of the King, with all the fulsome emblems which surrounded it, has been removed, and a single pyramidical pillar erected in its place, on which are to be recorded the triumphs of the new constitution.

William Hunter.
[Feb., 1792.]

88. 'THE ACCURSED REVOLUTION'

After his military service in Nova Scotia (1784–91), Cobbett married, came to England, and stayed in London during the spring of 1792; then crossed to France, studied the French language and literature at St. Omer, and was moving to Paris when alarmed by the events of August. In October he sailed again for America.

I ARRIVED in France in March 1792, and continued there till the beginning of September following, the six happiest months of my life. I should be the most ungrateful monster that ever existed, were I to speak ill of the French people in general. I went to that country full of all those prejudices that Englishmen suck in with their mother's milk against the French, and against their religion: a few weeks convinced me that I had been deceived with respect to both. I met everywhere with civility, and even hospitality, in a degree that I had never been accustomed to. I found the people among whom I lived, excepting those who were already blasted with the principles of the accursed revolution, honest, pious, and kind to excess. People may say what they please about the misery of the French peasantry under the old government: I have conversed with thousands of them, not ten among whom did not regret the change. . . . I did intend to stay in France till the spring of 1793, as well to perfect myself in the language, as to pass the winter at Paris. But I perceived the storm gathering; I saw that a war with England was inevitable; and it was not difficult to see what would be the fate of Englishmen in that country, where the rulers had laid aside even the appearance of justice and mercy. I wished, however, to see Paris, and had actually hired a coach to go thither: I was even on the way, when I heard at Abbeville that the King was dethroned, and his guards murdered. This intelligence made me turn off towards Havre-le-Grace, whence I embarked for America.

William Cobbett.

89. AN ENGLISH FRIEND OF THE QUEEN

For Quintin Craufurd, v. No. 68 (5). The first extract belongs to the time of Fersen's visit, there mentioned. The ring that Craufurd gives the Queen in the third extract is apparently the one whose impression she used later, when it was no longer safe to write, as her last message to Fersen (v. Söderhjelm, Fersen et Marie Antoinette, p. 323). Craufurd wrote in French, and I have shrunk from the attempt to translate into English this moving account by (perhaps) the last Englishman to see the Queen alive.

DEC. 1791. A six heures du soir, nous mîmes pied à terre au Carrouzel, traversâmes la cour des Tuileries, et entrâmes par une porte du château qui conduisait aux appartemens de la reine. Madame Thibaut, l'une de ses femmes, fidèle et fort attachée à sa majesté, me mena chez elle. Je l'ai vue souvent, et de la même manière, jusqu'à mon départ de Paris. Quelquefois, et peu après m'avoir parlé de choses qui ne pouvaient que l'intéresser vivement, je la retrouvais chez madame la princesse de Lamballe, qui demeurait au château, au pavillon de Flore: sa physiognomie, son ton, son maintien, tout était calme; rien ne se ressentait des sombres penseés dont elle venait de m'entretenir.

. . . . . .

Au commencement de 1792, autant que je m'en souviens, vers le fin du mois de janvier, sa majesté me manda de venir la trouver. Elle paraissait fortement affectée, me fit asseoir, et, après un moment de silence, me dit: 'Vous savez que le parti jacobin désire de me voir séparée du roi; ils ont résolu de me faire arrêter! J'ai été instruite ce matin que ce projet sera proposé ce soir à l'assemblée, et que le discours qui doit être prononcé à cette occasion par Condorcet, à été lu hier dans le comité secret des Jacobins. Si cette mesure est adoptée, comme je n'en puis douter, elle sera promptement exécutée. J'ai passé une partie de la journée à examiner mes papiers, pour m'assurer de n'y rien laisser qui puisse compromettre personne. Ensuite j'ai prié ma soeur de passer chez moi pour lui recommander mes enfans, et pour lui faire promettre de rester auprès d'eux et auprès du roi. Elle fut tellement agitée qu'elle se trouva mal. La scène était au-dessus de mes forces.' . . . En prononçant ces derniers mots, elle laissa couler quelques larmes, les seules que je lui ai vu verser. Elle me remit un paquet contenant des papiers qu'elle désirait qui fussent conservés, et que je lui rendis dans la suite .. . . La reine ne croyait pas que les jacobins osassent jamais attenter aux jours du roi; elle disait souvent que le gros de la nation ne souffrirait jamais qu'on fît violence à sa personne; mais elle paraissait intimement persuadée qu'elle-même serait victime de la haine de ce parti.

. . . . . .

Peu de jours avant mon départ de Paris, la reine, remarquant une pierre gravée que j'avais au doigt, me demanda si j'y étais attaché. Je lui repondis que non, que je l'avais achetée à Rome. 'Dans ce cas, je vous le demande: j'aurai peut-être besoin de vous écrire, et s'il arrivait que je crusse ne pas devoir le faire de ma main, le cachet vous servira d'indication.' Cette pierre représentait une aigle portant dans son bec une couronne d'olivier. Sur quelques mots que ce symbole me suggéra elle secoua la tête en disant, 'Je ne me fais pas illusion, il n'y a plus de bonheur pour moi. . . .' Et après un moment de silence: 'Le seul espoir qui me reste, c'est que mon fils pourra un jour être heureux; car le roi a été trop avili pour qu'il puisse jamais bien gouverner la nation.'

. . . . .

Le 14 avril 1792, j'allai le soir prendre congé de la reine. Elle me reçut dans son cabinet à l'entresol. Vers neuf heures, je la quittai. Elle me fit sortir par une pièce étroite où il y avait des livres, et qui conduisait à un corridor fort peu éclairé. Elle m'ouvrit elle-même la porte, s'arrêta encore pour me parler; mais, entendant quelqu'un marcher dans le corridor, elle me pria de me retirer, et ferma la porte. Il était tout simple, dans les circonstances où elle se trouvait, que je fusse frappé de l'idée que je la voyais pour la dernière fois, et cette sombre pensée me rendit un moment immobile. Tiré de ma stupeur par l'approche de celui qui marchait, je quittai la château, et retournai chez moi. Dans l'obscurité de la nuit, au milieu d'idées confuses, son aspect, ses derniers regards en la quittant, se présentèrent sans cesse à mon imagination et s'y présentent encore.

Quintin Craufurd.

90. DEFEAT

The war of 1792 opened disastrously. On April 2, Theobald Dillon's army, marching from Lille to Tournai, and the Duc de Biron's, advancing from Quiévrain on Mons, broke and fled, and Dillon was murdered by his own men. The ex-Marquis de Grave, who had replaced Narbonne as Minister of War on March 9, resigned on May 8.

By the most authentic accounts of Mr. Dillon's catastrophe it appears that the destruction of his little army was occasioned by his own imprudence. Totally unprepared for an engagement which he was instructed not to risk, he had ventured so near the enemy that he was attacked while his horses were grazing. The suspicion of treachery which was the cause of his cruel death as well as that of some officers under his command is entirely done away, and the horrors committed by his worse than cannibal soldiers are attributed even by the Jacobins to the discourses and writings by which the minds of the soldiers have been perverted within the last three years.

This is at least one step gained, and it is to be hoped for the sake of this country that they will at last discover that even in civil society, subordination, good-order and morals are necessary for its well-being.

With regard to Mr. de Biron's affair before Mons, we must wait for the particulars of it in his next dispatch; it appears by what we know of it at present that he shewed more abilities and more of the experienced officer than Mr Dillon; he however seems with the instructions of Mr Dumouriez to have imbibed too much of his impetuosity. Till he had left Quievrain all appeared prosperous. A small body of Houlans abandoned that town upon his approach, which gave him an opportunity of erecting the tree of liberty in the enemies' territory, and his troops that of getting drunk and dancing to the tune of *ça ira*. The next day however when he arrived near Mons he discovered that General Beaulieu had occupied the high ground near the town which he fondly imagined would have been left for him to possess, and on that account the town could not be taken by the force which he had with him. He determined therefore to rest his army for a few hours and then to retreat, having at that time learnt the fate of Mr. Dillon. At five o'clock p.m. he had a slight skirmish with the enemy. At ten the regiment *de la Reine Dragons* retreated crying out they were betrayed; Mr. de Biron followed them and brought back the greater number; upon his return finding the whole army in confusion, he immediately began the retreat, which he effected without much loss, till he arrived at Quievrain from whence the Houlans had driven the French garrison: he retook the place after an obstinate resistance but was obliged to abandon it immediately. His whole army was completely routed, and fled in the greatest confusion to Valenciennes, where he narrowly escaped the fate of Mr. Dillon, leaving their baggage, tents, artillery and military stores.

The news of these two total defeats which arrived within the space of a few hours, stunned the Jacobins; Mr. de Grave proposed the establishment of courts martial to try military offences without the intervention of a jury; this however was not sufficently relished to be immediately adopted, and the only proof that the Assembly has given as yet of its disposition to suppress licence is the *Décret d'Accusation,* which was past yesterday against the authors of the periodical papers called *l'ami du roy* and *l'ami du peuple.* It is probable that the present Ministry will not be able to withstand the shock.

Lord Gower.

[May 4, 1792.]

91. THE MOB IN THE TUILERIES

On June 20, the anniversary of the Tennis Court Oath, a crowd of demonstrators, after marching through the Manège, broke into the Tuileries; and for some hours the King and the royal family were at the mercy of the mob.

THE late attempt of the Jacobins to intimidate His Most Christian Majesty has failed entirely and has served only to impress more strongly on the minds of those who wish for order and good government an abhorrence of their principles and practices. The majesty of the throne was sullied, but it gave the King a happy opportunity of displaying an extraordinary degree of calmness and courage, which may be of infinite service. The circumstance of his having applied the hand of a grenadier to his heart, saying 'feel here if there are any signs of fear' is perfectly true.

157

As your Lordship will see in the Logographe the several accounts which the députies gave the National Assembly of the transactions in the palace, I shall not enter into a detail of them, I shall, however, inform your Lordship of all the particulars not mentioned by them, which have come to my knowledge. The King, finding the mob determined to force the door of the ante-chamber of his apartment, ordered his attendants to withdraw, and placed himself in the recess of one of the windows, where, attended by a few grenadiers, he suffered the mob to approach him, accepted from them a red cap with tricolor ribands, which he wore during the whole time that they remained in the palace, and, upon their expressing a wish that he should drink to the health of the nation, His Majesty condescended to comply with their request, and drunk the remains of some wine in a cup, out of which a grenadier had previously drunk. During this time the Queen and the Dauphin with their attendants were in the council chamber guarded by a table from the too near approach of the mob. It is singular considering that the populace was in every part of the royal apartment except the King's private bedchamber, that no other mischief should have been done except taking away the locks, and breaking the panels of the doors.

The admission of the mob is entirely to be attributed to the infamous conduct of the municipal officers: the commander of the National Guard had in his pocket an order from the administrators of the department to oppose force by force, but the orders of the Municipality were wanting.

Lord Gower.

[June 22, 1792.]

92. THE QUEEN AT THE OPERA

Grace Dalrymple, wife of Sir John Elliott, and mistress of the Prince of Wales, wrote an account of her life in Paris during the Revolution, at the request of George III, for his own reading. The Jacobins (says Paroy) cried Pas de maîtresses! pas de maîtres!

AFTER the 20th of June, the people who wished well to the

King and Queen were desirous that her Majesty should
sometimes appear in public, accompanied by the Dauphin,
a most interesting, beautiful child, and her charming
daughter, Madame Royale. In consequence of this she went
to the Comédie Italienne with her children, Madame
Elizabeth, the King's sister, and Madame Tourzelle,
governess to the royal children. This was the very last time
on which her Majesty appeared in public. I was there in
my own box, nearly opposite the Queen's; and as she was
so much more interesting than the play, I never took my
eyes off her and her family. The opera which was given was
Les Evénemens Imprévus, and Madame Dugazon played the
soubrette. Her Majesty, from her first entering the house,
seemed distressed. She was overcome even by the applause,
and I saw her several times wipe the tears from her eyes.

The little Dauphin, who sat on her knee the whole night,
seemed anxious to know the cause of his unfortunate
mother's tears. She seemed to soothe him, and the audience
appeared well disposed, and to feel for the cruel situation
of their beautiful Queen. In one of the acts a duet is sung
by the *soubrette* and the *valet*, where Madame Dugazon says:
'Ah! comme j'aime ma maîtresse.' As she looked particularly
at the Queen at the moment she said this, some Jacobins,
who had come into the playhouse, leapt upon the stage, and
if the actors had not hid Madame Dugazon, they would
have murdered her. They hurried the poor Queen and
family out of the house, and it was all the Guards could do
to get them safe into their carriages.

Grace Elliott.

[July, 1792.]

93. 'AT THE EVE OF A GREAT CRISIS'

*June 20 could only be a prelude to a trial of arms between the Tuileries
and the Hôtel de Ville. On the 28th Lafayette arrived from the front
to denounce the Jacobins before the Assembly, and to offer the Court his
aid; it was refused. On July 7, the Department of Paris suspended Pétion*
(Maire) *and Manuel* (Procureur de la Commune) *for their conduct on*

June 20: they were reinstated by the Assembly. On the 10th the Ministers resigned. On the 11th the Assembly proclaimed 'la Patrie est en danger.' During the last week of July thousands of volunteers enrolled for service in the army, and fédérés—*delegates of the National Guard—came in from all parts of the country to the capital, where they were given hospitality by the 'patriots.' The Marseillais arrived on the 30th. J. G. D. d'Eprémesnil, deputy for the Paris nobility, was nearly lynched in the Tuileries Gardens, which (after being closed since May) were reopened to the public at the end of July: but a tricolor ribbon (in place of sentinels) kept the crowd away from the palace.*

[JULY 6TH.] We are at the eve of a great crisis. The two contending parties must soon make the experiment which has the greatest force: in the mean time both sides shew signs of fear. His Most Christian Majesty expects the event with that courage which religion is known to inspire, but his Ministers seem to act without any well concerted or fixed plan. Mr de la Fayette's conduct during his stay in Paris was not sufficiently bold and energetic to affect the Jacobins with that degree of fear which it was intended to have produced, and it has only served to make them more active in sending for the assistance of their friends from all parts of the kingdom. Those friends are accordingly arriving from all quarters, from Marseilles, from Bordeaux, from Brest, and their arrival is legalized by a decree of the National Assembly which has received the royal sanction. Their stay in Paris according to that decree, for which I refer your Lordship to the Logographe No. 276, is indeed to be of short duration, but it will be long enough to answer any sinister purpose. On the other hand it may be doubted that Mr de la Fayette will be able, if he should think it necessary, to bring his army to the assistance of the metropolis. In this awful state of suspense, the inhabitants of Paris are waiting for the celebration of the fourteenth, at which the King and the National Assembly will assist.

[July 13th.] The solemn declaration of the Assembly that the country is in danger has had very little effect at least in the metropolis where the minds of the inhabitants are entirely occupied with providing lodgings for the *Fédérés* as they improperly call those who are arriving for the approaching ceremony, and with the *arrêté* of the administration of the department which has suspended the Mayor and *Procureur de la Commune* on account of their improper conduct with regard to the proceedings on the twentieth of last month. This sentence after some days' consideration has been confirmed by the King, and to-day the National Assembly has taken off the suspension of Mr Pethion, and has postponed their decision on Mr Manuel until they shall have heard his defence.

The number of people from the provinces as yet arrived, is not so great as was expected; great care is taken to provide accommodation for them by the Jacobins, lest they should be influenced by the Feuillants. Mr de Narbonne and indeed almost all the principal general officers in the armies of the Maréchal de Luckner and Mr de la Fayette are here.

The ceremony in the Champ de Mars will be similar to that at the federation in the year 1790. The Assembly will walk in procession, but the King will go in his carriage.

[July 20th.] From want of resolution on one part and from a regularly conducted system on the other, the situation of His Most Christian Majesty becomes daily more and more perilous. I have reason to believe, that the resignation of the present ministers, is to be attributed, when it came to the point, to a refusal to retreat from Paris. Notwithstanding which, from the present posture of affairs, I shall not be surprized if I have to inform your Lordship of His Most Christian Majesty's arrival at Rouen where he will find a great majority of the inhabitants ready to support his cause.

The Jacobins finding that the three regiments of regular troops in this town, were not sufficiently indisciplined to be relied upon by them, have contrived that they should be sent to the frontiers. There remains one regiment of Swiss which it will be difficult to dispose of in the same manner, owing to the treaty with the cantons, and to the sentiments of the private soldiers, as well as of the officers of that regiment. '

[August 3rd.] Since the cruel ill-treatment which Mr D'Epresménil experienced on the *Terrace des Feuillants* the populace who frequent that part of the garden of the Thuilleries have contented themselves with uttering imprecations against the royal family and those who are styled *aristocrates*: that they should have refrained from approaching the palace or even putting their feet on any other part of the garden which is separated from the terrace only by ribands which they themselves have placed there, is a singular circumstance, and carries the appearance of a sentiment worthy of a free people, but it may be accounted for on other principles: it being the interest of their leaders that they should not at this moment offer violence to the royal family. They may have had the good policy to form this silken separation which strengthened by opinion is stronger than one of stone or iron, for whoever should venture to pass those limits would be regarded by the rest as an Austrian or an *aristocrate* and treated accordingly.

Lord Gower.

94. TRAVELLING TO PARIS

Dr. John Moore, physician and man of letters (1729–1802), *was an experienced traveller, who published several books about his adventures on the continent. His* Journal *during a residence in France* (1793) *is a valuable account of the state of Paris from August to December,* 1792.

WE met many carriages with people flying from Paris: wherever we stopped, or had any opportunity of conversing with them, they gave an alarming account of the state of that city, and were surprised at our thinking of going there at this time. They all seemed to be impressed with the notion that an important event is about to happen.

One man said, that certain people had been of late engaged in a conspiracy which would break out *on the ninth of this month*. We could not help smiling at the notion of a conspiracy which was so well known beforehand, and considered his apprehensions as groundless.

I asked, however, of a genteel looking man who had just arrived at this place in the Diligence, whether he thought there was any danger in being at Paris? 'Pas le moindre,' answered he. They talk, said I, of dethroning the King. 'Tant pis pour lui,' said the man; 'mais cela ne vous regarde pas.' To hear a Frenchman talk with so much indifference of dethroning a King, however petty the Monarch might be, was what I did not expect; but to hear him speak with the same indifference of dethroning his own King, that, I confess, astonished me. I remember the time when the most dreadful convulsion of nature would have been considered in France as of less importance, and would have occasioned less alarm.

John Moore.
[Clermont, Aug. 6, 1792.]

95. 'A TRIP TO PARIS'

This is the title under which Richard Twiss, F.R.S., traveller and writer, published anonymously a vivid account of his experiences in Paris in the summer of 1792. The book contains a good deal of rumour or second-hand information; but the author generally says when this is so.

IN every one of the towns between Calais and Paris a full-grown tree (generally a poplar) has been planted in the market place, with many of its boughs and leaves; these last being withered, it makes but a dismal appearance; on the top of this tree or pole is a red woollen or cotton night-cap, which is called the *Cap of Liberty*, with streamers about the pole, or red, blue and white ribbands. I saw several statues of saints, both within and without the churches (and in Paris likewise) with similar caps, and several crucifixes with the national cockade of ribbands tied to the left arm of the image on the cross, but not one with the cockade in its proper place; the reason of which I know not.

.   .   .   .   .

The churches in Paris are not much frequented on the week-days, at present; I found a few old women on their knees in some of them, hearing mass; and, at the same time, at the other end of one of these churches commissaries were sitting and entering the names of volunteers for the army. The iron rails in the churches which part the choir from the nave, and also those which encompass chapels and tombs, are all ordered to be converted into heads for pikes.

· · · · ·

Hitherto cockades of silk had been worn, the *aristocrats* wore such as were of a paler blue and red than those worn by the *democrats*, and the former were even distinguished by their carriages, on which a cloud was painted upon the arms, which entirely obliterated them (of these I saw above thirty in the evening *promenade* in the *Bois de Boulogne*), but on the 30th of July, every person was compelled by the people to wear a linen cockade, without any distinction in the red and blue colours.

· · · · ·

I went once to Versailles; there is hardly anything in the palace but the bare walls, a very few of the looking-glasses, tapestry, and large pictures remaining, as it has now been near two years uninhabited. I crossed the great canal on foot; there was not a drop of water in it.

· · · · ·

I went several times to the National Assembly; the *Tribunes*, or *Galleries* (of which there are three) entered warmly, by applauses and by murmurs and hisses, into the affairs which were treated of.

· · · · ·

All the coats of arms which formerly decorated the gates of *Hôtels* are taken away, and even seals are at present engraven with cyphers only. The *Chevaliers de St. Louis* still continue to wear the cross, or the ribband, at the button-hole; all other orders of knighthood are abolished. No liveries are worn by servants, that badge of slavery is likewise abolished; and also all corporation companies, as well as every other monopolizing society, and there are no longer any *Royal* tobacco or salt shops.

· · · · ·

Books of all sorts are printed without any *approbation* or *privilege*. Many are exposed on stalls, which are very improper for the public eye. One of them was called the *Private Life of the Queen*, in two volumes, with obscene prints. The book itself is contemptible and disgusting, and might as well have been called, the *Woman of Pleasure.* Of books of this sort I saw above thirty, with plates. Another was a subject not fit even to be mentioned. I read a small pamphlet, entitled '*Le Christ-Roi,* or a Parallel of the Sufferings of Louis XVI etc.' I can say nothing in favor of it.

. . . . .

The common people are in general much better clothed than they were before the Revolution, which may be ascribed to their not being so grievously taxed as they were. . . . All those ornaments, which three years ago were worn of silver, are now of gold. All the women of lower class, even those who sit behind green-stalls, etc., wear gold earrings, with large drops, some of which cost two or three *louis,* and necklaces of the same. Many of the men wear plain gold ear-rings: those worn by officers and other gentlemen are usually as large as a half-crown piece. Even children of two years old have small gold drops in their ears. The general dress of the women is white linen and muslin gowns, large caps which cover all their hair, excepting just a small triangular piece over the forehead, pomatumed, or rather plaistered and powdered, without any hats; neither do they wear any stays, but only *corsets* (waistcoats or jumps). Tight lacing is not known here, nor yet high and narrow heeled shoes. Because many of the ladies *ci-devant* of quality have emigrated or ran away, and those which remain in Paris keep within doors, I saw no face that was painted, excepting on the stage. Most of the men wear coats made like great-coats, or in other words, long great-coats without any coat: this in fine weather and in the middle of summer made them appear to me like invalides. There is hardly any possibility of distinguishing the rank of either man or woman by their dress at present, or rather, there are no ranks to distinguish. The nation in general is much improved in cleanliness, and even in politeness. The French no longer look on every Englishman as a lord, but as their equal. There are no beggars to be seen about the streets in Paris, and when the chaise stopped for fresh horses, only two or three old and infirm people surrounded it and solicited charity, whereas formerly the beggars used to assemble in hundreds. I did not see a single pair of *sabots* (wooden-shoes) in France this time. The table of the peasants is also better supplied than it was before the revolution.

Before the 10th [of August] I saw several dancing parties of the *Poissardes* and *sansculottes* in the beer-houses, on the *Quai des Ormes* and the *Quai St. Paul*, and have played the favourite and animating air of *ça ira*, on the fiddle, to eight couple of dancers: the ceiling of these rooms (which open into the street) is not above ten feet high, and on this ceiling (which is generally white washed) are the numbers 1, 2, to 8, in black, and the same in red, which mark the places where the ladies and gentlemen are to stand. When the dance was concluded, I requested the ladies to salute me (*m' embrasser*) which they did, by gently touching my cheek with their lips.

I saw many thousands of these men [National Guard] from my windows, on the way to the *Tuileries*, early on *the* Friday morning [Aug. 10th]; their march was at the rate of perhaps five miles an hour, without running or looking aside; and this was the pace they used when they carried heads upon pikes, and when they were in pursuit of important business, rushing along the streets like a torrent, and attending wholly and solely to the object they had in view. On such occasions, when I saw them approaching, I turned into some cross street till they were passed, not that I had anything to apprehend, but the being swept along with the crowd, and perhaps trampled upon. I cannot express what I felt on seeing such immense bodies of men so vigorously actuated by the same principle. I also saw many thousands of volunteers going to join the armies at the frontiers, marching along the *Boulevarts*, almost at the same pace, accompanied as far as *Barriers*

by their women, who were carrying their muskets for them;
some with large sausages, pieces of cold meat, and loaves
of bread, stuck on the bayonets, and all laughing, or singing
ça ira.

Richard Twiss.
[July—Aug., 1792.]

96. THE FALL OF THE THRONE

(1)

'Brunswick's Manifesto'—the work of émigrés—*threatening vengeance on
Paris for any harm done to the King, was published in Paris on July 28. The
sections were now set on an insurrection to depose the King, and to summon a
national Convention: after several postponements, it was fixed for the night of
Aug. 9. The Carrousel was the court on the east side of the Tuileries. Bas (i.e.* à
bas*) les motions means 'No debating.'*

[AUGUST 9.] I had a good deal of conversation this evening
with a man of considerable understanding, who has lived
many years in this place, and is thought to have opportunities of knowing the true state of the public affairs: his
opinion is, that the Duke of Brunswick's Manifesto has been
of infinite prejudice to the King, because great pains have
been taken to make it believed that it was composed with his
knowledge and approbation. But this gentleman still
thinks, that not only the majority of the National Assembly,
but also of the most respectable citizens, and of the national
guards themselves, are enemies to the idea of dethroning the
King; and wish, *bona fide*, to maintain the Constitution to
which they have sworn; and that they disapprove of all
tumultuous assemblings of the people of the fauxbourgs,
with a view to force or terrify the King to withdraw his
veto from any decree of the Assembly, or on any other
account. They highly disapprove of that which took place on
the twentieth of last June, when the mob entered the
palace of the Tuileries, behaved in a very insolent manner,
and when the lives of the King and Queen were in imminent
danger.

It is imagined, however, that something of the same kind

167

is intended to-morrow by the inhabitants of the fauxbourgs, in conjunction with about twelve or fourteen hundred foederés, who lately arrived from Marseilles and from Brittany.

But the national guards being now aware of this intention, and having, no doubt, received instructions how to act, it is probable that the attempt will not be made; or, if it is, will prove abortive; in which case, like most unsuccessful insurrections, it will tend to strengthen, instead of weakening the hands of Government.

I am informed, that besides a complete battalion of Swiss, whose barracks are in the Carousal adjacent to the palace, a considerable number of disbanded officers, and other persons attached to the Court, sleep every night within the walls of the palace itself, which seems more than sufficient to prevent any effectual attempt from a disorderly multitude: and I should think it probable, that many of the citizens who were violent patriots at the beginning of the revolution are now tired of the disorderly state of affairs, and think, that supporting the King is the most likely way of obtaining that tranquillity which they have so much need of. They may also think, with great reason, that those who excite the populace in the suburbs, wish the ruin of the Constitution.

Between eleven and twelve at night, I was disturbed by a great noise in the streets from the beating of drums and repeated huzzas. The landlord informs me, that orders have been given to all the citizens to illuminate their windows; that there is reason to apprehend an attack on the Chateau of the Tuileries; that the drum has beat to arms, and that the national guards are all at the alarm posts of their respective departments. I went into the streets, which are all illuminated—the Pont Neuf is covered with soldiers under arms —a large party of the national guards are also in possession of the Pont Royal—nobody is allowed to pass: yet all seems to be conducted with so much regularity, that whatever mischief may have been intended, will, I hope, be prevented.

I was awaked about two in the morning by the sound of the tocsin, and am informed by the people of the hotel, who have not been in bed, that the inhabitants of the fauxbourgs St. Antoine, St. Marceau, St. Jacques, etc. are assembled; that they are joined by the foederés from Marseilles and Brittany, in the intention of marching to the Tuileries to require the King to withdraw his veto from the decree of the National Assembly against the priests who refuse the constitutional oath, and that for assembling an army of 20,000 men in the neighbourhood of Paris.

I hope they will be prevailed on to disperse without making an attempt so unconstitutional. If the King is not allowed the exercise of his veto when he judges it expedient, to give it him was a mockery.

[August 10.] Having fallen asleep about three, we were awakened at nine by the firing of cannon—and were told, that the Chateau was attacked. Soon after, we heard the cry of 'To arms, citizens, to arms! they slaughter your parents, your brethren, your sons!' and we saw men running half frantic through the streets, exclaiming in that manner. Lord Lauderdale, being still indisposed, could not go out; and my son remained at the hotel with him.

As soon as I was dressed I went into the streets; a party of the national guards, with a number of citizens armed, were marching towards the Tuileries—another body of men followed soon after, dragging several cannons along the Quai de Mazarin, where I was, to the Pont Royal. Some men flying from the Tuileries along this bridge, were killed by the national guards before they reached that end to which the cannon were advancing. Those cannon being mounted on the bridge, were repeatedly discharged against that part of the Chateau which looks to the Seine. Some women who stood near me on the Quai de Voltaire, as soon as they heard the first discharge, fell a-clapping their hands, and cried, Bravo! Bravo!

In the mean time there was some firing of musketry from the windows of the Louvre facing the river—a few people were killed and wounded on the keys. Those who were on the side next the Louvre had run from the key to the brink of the river, that they might be sheltered from the shot by the parapet. A party of national guards who marched along the Quai Mazarin, as often as they saw a group of people conversing together, called *Bas les motions*, and dispersed them—the officer at the same time advising all who were without arms to retire to their houses. A little after, as a body of pikemen hurried past, one of them in a very decisive style pointed me out as an aristocrate. Such an accusation in the streets of Paris, any time these four years, would have exposed a man to insult: in the present circumstances, when execution is generally the immediate consequence of accusation, it might have proved fatal; but the valet de place, who accompanied me, declared, that so far from being an aristocrate, or any thing like it, I was un Anglais. 'Bon!' cried the pikemen, and continued their course.

After this admonition I retired to the house of an acquaintance, in the Rue Jacob, from whence I went, a little after, to the Hotel de Moscovie. In the streets I met with great numbers of the national guards and foederés returning home, all of them with pieces of the red uniform of the Swiss guards who had been killed, stuck as trophies on the point of their bayonets.

John Moore.

(2)

When the attack began, P. L. Comte Roederer, procureur général syndic du Département de Paris advised the King to leave the Tuileries, and take refuge in the Assembly: soon after, Louis sent a written order to the Suisses to cease fire, and retire to their barracks. They tried to retreat through the streets or gardens, but were mostly massacred, as well as other armed defenders of the palace; and some 'aristocrats,' like the Comte de Clermont-Tonnerre, were murdered in the streets. The Marquis de Mandat, Commandant of the National Guard, had been entrusted by the Mayor (Pétion) with the defence of the Tuileries; but was summoned to the Hôtel de Ville on Aug. 9, deposed from his command, and murdered on his way to prison. N. F. Harmand, Baron d'Abancourt, deputy for the Commons of Château-Thierry in the States-General, had been Minister for War since the resignation of Dumouriez's Ministry in the middle of June.

[12 August.]

Early on Friday morning, the people having first taken possession of the arsenal moved towards the Thuilleries with a train of artillery: on their road they put to death several persons who had formed a false patrole. At ten o'clock the danger being imminent, the King with the royal family left the palace, and crossing the garden by the advice of the members of the department, took refuge in the National Assembly, in a room adjoining to which they have continued ever since. A short time after the action began between the people and the Swiss, who were left to guard the palace; the National Guards having either retired or gone over to the other side, a very sharp fire was kept up for near twenty minutes, when the Swiss were overpower'd and almost all killed at their posts or in their flight: the number of killed on both sides is not yet known, but cannot be less than fifteen hundred: several persons of distinction, among whom was Mr de Clermont Tonnerre were put to death in different parts of the town: the furniture of the palace was destroyed by the people, and the outbuildings adjoining to it are all burnt to the ground. The Assembly having first declared itself permanent, decreed, in the course of the day, that the executive power was withdrawn from the King, that his ministers had lost the confidence of the nation and that, for the present, the government should be trusted to a ministry named by themselves: that the primary assemblies should be convened for the twenty-sixth of this month, to which all *citoyens* should be admitted without distinction of rank or property in order to appoint a national convention to meet at Paris on the twentieth of September to decide ultimately upon the forfeiture of the Crown and the mode of establishing an executive power: that His Most Christian Majesty should be lodged in some place of safety and that the civil list should no longer be continued.

The Assembly has named for Ministers, Mr Danton *pour la Justice*, Mr le Brun *pour les Affaires Étrangères*, Mr Monge *pour la Marine*, Mr Servan *pour la Guerre*, Mr Clavière *pour les Contributions*, and Mr Roland *pour l'Intérieur*. Commissioners have also been named by the Assembly and sent to the several armies with very extensive powers.

The people of Paris on their side have named a new Common Council which has already broke the municipality except Messrs Péthion and Manuel.

Mr Mandat the late commander of the National Guard is I believe put to death, and they have given his place to Mr Santerre.

The people having begun to destroy the statues of Louis XIV and Louis XV, the Assembly by a decree ordered all the statues of Kings to be taken down.

The Assembly has ordered a Court Martial to be formed to inquire into the conduct of the few remaining Swiss officers and soldiers and has issued a decree of impeachment against Mr D'Abancourt, the late Minister of the War Department, for not having removed the Swiss soldiers from the capital.

Lord Gower.

(3)

A. J. Santerre, owner of a big brewery in the 'slummy' Faubourg St. Antoine, the eastern extension of the Rue Antoine, from the Bastille to the Barrière du Trône, had made himself popular by his charities during the hard winter of 1788-9, and was able to lead the 'East End' against the Tuileries on June 20, and Aug. 10. On Mandat's arrest he became Commandant of the National Guard.

[June, 1792.] The 20 June went to Paris where all the riff raff of the faubg. St. Antoin conducted by the famous Gl. Santerre a Brewer came to the Thuilleries and placed the red cape upon the King's head and Many other extravagante and abusive Language and indeede it might be called a ragged Regement. Some of those formidable wariors had a Stick with a blade of a Knife or Scessers tied to it for Armes and endeed 20 good fellows with sticks could have drove back Santerre with his formidable Army, however the gardes Nationale who was all under arms told me they had no orders to enterfere, so that the tumult went on and seemed to please the people to see the royalle family humbled.

[August.] But all seemed to prepaire for the great

catostrophe of the 10th August and Many people wished a Change and they talked of people come from Marsielles to attact the Thuilleries; this seemed a projected affaire and the Thuilleries was garded by the Suisse gardes and many more in Suisse dress was expecting to take part with the King. The night before we was nearly informed of what was to happen although non could emagin how it was to turn; the evening of the 9 by the fall of a Bottle from the wall which happened to cut my leg and render me lame so that I was forced to Sett upon our Terrasse which was opposite the Champs Elize and Thuilleries, where I could hear the first coup de Canon at the Thuilleries about 9 and then the other firing and tumult continued. I could see the people running to and fro in the Champs Elizee and the horror of the misacre increased and as the King left his gards and went to the Nationale Assembly, so that those poor wretches that had come to defend him being deserted by him was now left to be misacred by the rabble, whereas if the King had stopt there was the greatest part of the Sections was ready to defend him; but when they found he had gone to the assembly they all turned to the Mesacre of the poor Suiss gardes which could find no place of refuge as the Barierrs was shut. . . . Many of these anthrophages passed in the Street and stopt to show us parts of the Suisses they had misacred some of whom I knew and certainly before that would not have thought of any such thing. However the example seemed a rage and every one seemed to glory in what he had done and to Show even their furrie upon the dead body by cutting them or even tearing their clothes as monuments of triumph, so that this seemed as if the people were struck with a sort of Madness. . . . But it was impossible to describe all the acts of wanten horor that happened this day and the Mortification that the King met from those he had put his trust in. They condemned him and his familly to the prison of the Temple.

Thomas Blaikie.

(4)

The Loge du Logographe was a small box behind the President's seat in the Assembly, used by reporters.

[August 11.] I went this morning to see the places where the action of yesterday happened. The naked bodies of the Swiss, for they were already stripped, lay exposed on the ground. I saw a great number on the terrace, immediately before the palace of the Tuileries; some lying single in different parts of the gardens; and some in heaps, one above another, particularly near the terrace of the Feuillans.

The garden and adjacent courts were crowded with spectators, among whom there was a considerable proportion of women, whose curiosity it was evident was fully equal to their modesty.

The bodies of the national guards, of the citizens of the fauxbourgs, and of the foederés, have been already removed by their friends; those of the Swiss only lie exposed in this shocking manner. Of about 800 or 1000 of these, who were yesterday mustered in the Tuileries, I am told there are not 200 left alive.

Seeing a number of people going up the grand staircase of the palace, to see the ravage that was made in all the rooms by the action of yesterday, I intermingled with the crowd, and had ascended half way, when I heard the shrieks of some one above, and soon after the body of a man was carried down. I was told that he had been detected in the act of stealing some of the furniture belonging to the palace, and was instantly put to death by the people around him.

This expeditious method of executing justice removed all inclination of visiting the royal apartments: I descended to the terrace, and took another melancholy walk among the bodies of those whom I had seen two days before in all the pride of health and military pomp. In point of size and looks, I do not suppose there is a finer battalion of infantry in Europe than they formed at that time.

After they gave way, they were slaughtered by those who kept aloof while they resisted. Some were pursued through the streets, and dragged from the shops and houses whither they fled for shelter. About fifty or sixty who asked for quarter, were saved by the Marseillois: they were delivered to the national guards, and conducted by them to the Maison de Ville. While those unfortunate men were detained in the square, waiting for orders from the municipality into what prison they were to be confined, the multitude, enraged no doubt by the death of their friends and relations, and irritated at the sight of the wounded citizens who were carrying to their houses and to the hospitals, began to cry for vengeance on the prisoners; and at length, like a parcel of drunk savages, they burst through the ranks of the national guards, and butchered the defenceless Swiss in cold blood. I cannot deem the national guards guiltless. I have been told that they could not save the Swiss without killing the citizens: but such furies do not deserve the name of citizens, and were infinitely more criminal than the Swiss.

From the gardens of the Tuileries I walked through the centre gate of the palace into the court, and the Carousel, where the action first began. At the very beginning, a number of the crowd were killed and wounded at the bottom of the great stairs, by an unexpected fire from the top of the first flight of stairs. Some of the Swiss themselves, who were intermingled and conversing with the people, were killed by this fire. The bodies of the Swiss were lying in various parts of the area.

The barracks of the Swiss guards, which divide this large area from the Carousel, had been set on fire yesterday, and are still burning. Many of the bodies were thrown into the flames—I saw some half consumed.

Sick at the sight, I hurried from this scene of horror, and about mid-day I went to the National Assembly. While I waited at the door which enters to the Assembly from the garden of the Feuillans, for the gentleman who was to procure me admittance, a long procession advanced to the gate: it consisted of a number of persons, some in the uniform of the national guards, and some in the dress of citizens, each of whom held a man in a white waistcoat, but without a coat, by the hand. The latter were generally pale and dejected; and the men under whose protection they were, encouraged and supported them.

I was immediately informed that a considerable number of the Swiss were saved, and had been confined in the corps de garde of the post of the Feuillans: a mob, however, had begun to gather about the guardroom, and some horrid wretches among them cried aloud for the heads of those unhappy soldiers. On this, it was deemed the best means for their safety to conduct them to the bar of the Assembly, and demand its protection.

Lasource hastened to inform the Assembly of the danger in which the poor Swiss were, and to request its protection; while Gorsas remained at the door of the guardroom haranguing the mob, and using every means which humanity inspired, to prevent them from attacking the prisoners.

They were conducted accordingly from the guard-room to the Assembly door in the manner above mentioned, by some citizens, among whom was Lasource, and others of the deputies. I entered a little before the Swiss, and got a seat in the body of the house among the members.

The King, Queen, with their son and daughter, and the Princess Elizabeth, the Princess Lamballe, and three or four other attendants, had remained in the Loge du Logographe, yesterday, from nine in the morning till late at night. They had been then conducted to an adjacent committee-room, where they had remained all night, and returned to the same Loge in the morning, when the Assembly met. My eyes were naturally directed to the box in which they were. From the place in which I sat I could not see the King, but I had a full view of the Queen and the rest of the Royal Family. Her beauty is gone! No wonder. She seemed to listen with an undisturbed air to the speakers. Sometimes she whispered to her sister-in-law, and to Madame de Lamballe; once or twice she stood up, and, leaning forward, surveyed every part of the hall. A person near me remarked, that her face indicated rage and the most provoking arrogance. I perceived nothing of that nature; although the turn of the debate, as well as the remarks which were made by some of the members, must have appeared to her highly insolent and provoking. On the whole, her behaviour in this trying situation seemed full of propriety and dignified composure. I know not whether the height from which this unhappy Princess has fallen, and her present deplorable situation, may not make me view her with additional interest and partiality; but I am surprised to find that the edge of that rancour which has prevailed in this country against her, seems to be in no degree blunted by her misfortunes.

It was impossible to look at the Prince Royal without reflecting that his lot, which no doubt has been considered as the highest of all prizes, was now, of a sudden, and without any fault of his, changed into the most unfortunate that could be drawn in the lottery of life. At present he is too young to calculate the amount, or taste the bitterness of the calamity which has befallen him; and seemed to me to suffer more from being so long confined in such a narrow place, than from all that has happened besides, either to his parents or himself.

[August 13.] The public walks are crowded with men, women, and children of all conditions, with the most gay unconcerned countenances imaginable. A stranger just come to Paris, without having heard of the late transactions, and walking through the gardens of the Tuileries, Place de Louis XVI and Champs Elisées, would naturally imagine, from the frisky behaviour and cheerful faces of the company he meets, that this day was a continuation of a series of days appointed for dissipation, mirth, and enjoyment; he could not possibly imagine that the ground he is walking over was so largely covered with the bodies of slaughtered men; or that the gay lively people he saw were so lately overwhelmed with sorrow and dismay.

I drove to many places in Paris this morning. The epithet *royal*, which was formerly so profusely assumed and inscribed with pride and ostentation, is now carefully effaced from every shop, magazine, auberge, or hotel; all those also who were so vain of announcing over their doors that they were the tradesmen of the King or Queen, or in any way employed by them, have removed every word, emblem, or sign which could revive the remembrance of such a connection; and at present a taylor would rather advertise that he was breeches-maker to a sans culottes, than to a prince of the blood royal.

Above the great gate of the church of Notre Dame, are the figures in stone of twenty-six Kings of France, from Childebert the First to Philip August. I was told that in this general fury against kings, all those venerable personages had been hewn to pieces by the people. I had the curiosity to go to the cathedral on purpose, to see whether absurd zeal had been carried this length, and had the satisfaction of finding this royal society safe and uninjured by any hand but that of Time.

[August 16.] Having made it my business, ever since I have been in France, to take every opportunity of conversing with the people, I find a great alteration, I will not venture to say in their sentiments, but assuredly in their discourse.

Before the 10th of this month, many spoke in favour of the King, and justified his giving the veto to the two decrees of the National Assembly—one respecting a camp of 20,000 men in the neighbourhood of Paris, and the other regarding the priests who refused to take the oaths to the Constitution; they said, 'the King had a right, by the Constitution, to make use of this power of rejecting decrees at his discretion, and that none but seditious persons would attempt to force his consent.'

They blamed those, as such, who had excited the tumultuous procession of the inhabitants of the suburbs on the 20th of June; lamented that the executive power was not strong enough to punish them; hoped that this would soon be the case; and declared their belief that the King was calumniated by factious men who were enemies to the Constitution, while he sincerely wished to maintain it according to the oaths he had taken.

Some tradesmen who did duty as national guards have

acknowledged to me, that when called to arms on the night of the 9th, they considered that the purpose for which they were assembled, was to repel any attack on the palace, and defend the persons of the royal family; which duty it was their intention to perform, till they heard the general cry that the Swiss were massacring the people; and then they joined with the citizens against the Swiss, and those in the castle.

The truth, I have reason to believe, is, that few of the national guards took part in the action till the palace was forced, and the Swiss with all within it began to fly; and if the foederés and those from the suburbs had been dispersed, a great part of the national guards would have declared in that event, as they did in the other, for the victorious party.

Now every body seems to have the same sentiments, and hold the same language, namely, that the King was in correspondence with the emigrant princes, and betraying the country to the enemy. Certain papers have been found in the palace, which, it is said, make it very clear. On this subject I have not as yet been able to form a decided opinion; nor am I at all certain that the sentiments, which I hear announced by those who have surer grounds of judging, are conformable to their real opinion; for it is by no means safe to avow any way of thinking but one.

Great pains are taken to convince the people at large of the treachery of the court, and that a proscription was made, and a massacre intended, of the most distinguished patriots, in case the court had been victorious: this is not only insinuated in the journals, but pasted up in printed papers on the walls all over Paris.

In the mean time, in the gardens of the Tuileries, in the Place de Louis XV and Palais Royal, men are seen mounted on chairs haranguing to little circles which form around them: the continual theme of these orators, who are no doubt hired for the purpose, is the treachery of the King, and the profligacy of the Queen, whom they generally distinguish by the appellation of Monsieur and Madame Veto.

When I see such artful industry to enrage the people against the King and Queen, and hear of intended massacres without any proofs, so far from being convinced of the truth of what is so assiduously circulated, I rather dread that all these pains are taken to prepare the people's minds for measures which cannot yet be avowed.

John Moore.

97. PARIS SCENES

(1) JACOBIN CLUB

Many prominent members deserted the Jacobin Club during the Feuillant secession of July (v. No. 77 (2)); but by September the membership had risen again to 700 or 800. 'Mademoiselle Théroigne' de Méricourt was a foreign woman (born in Luxemburg in 1762) who, after playing a prominent part in the early scenes of the Revolution, returned to the Netherlands in 1790, was imprisoned by the Austrian government, interviewed by the Emperor Leopold, and allowed to return to Paris (perhaps in the hope that she would act as a spy) in Feb. 1792. She died in a Paris mad-house in 1817.

August 17.

THE hall in which the Jacobins meet, is fitted up nearly in the same style with that of the National Assembly. The tribune, or pulpit from which the members speak, is opposite to that in which the president is seated: there is a table for the secretaries and galleries for a large audience of both sexes, in the one as in the other. Men are appointed, who walk through the hall to command, or rather solicit, silence when the debate becomes turbulent at the club of Jacobins, in the same manner as the huissiers do at the National Assembly, and usually with as little effect: the bell of the president, and voices of the huissiers, are equally disregarded in stormy debates at both Assemblies.

I have been told that some of the most distinguished members in point of talent and character, have lately withdrawn from this society, and that it is not now on such a respectable footing as it has been. Roberspierre, who was a member of the Constituent Assembly, and of course cannot be of the present, has great sway in the club of

Jacobins, by which means his influence in the Assembly, and in the common council of Paris, is very considerable.

There was not, properly speaking, a debate at the Jacobins to-day, but rather a series of violent speeches against him. I understand indeed, that of late the speakers are generally of one opinion; for Roberspierre's partisans raise such a noise when any one attempts to utter sentiments opposite to what he is known to maintain, that the voice of the speaker is drowned, and he is obliged to yield the tribune to another orator whose doctrine is more palatable.

There were abundance of women in the galleries; but as there were none in the body of the hall where the members are seated, I was surprised to see one enter and take her seat among them: she was dressed in a kind of English riding-habit, but her jacket was the uniform of the national guards. On enquiry, I was informed that the name of this amazon is Mademoiselle Theroigne: she distinguished herself in the action of the 10th, by rallying those who fled, and attacking a second time at the head of the Marseillois.

She seems about one or two and thirty, is somewhat above the middle size of women, and has a smart martial air, which in a man would not be disagreeable.

I walked home about nine: the night was uncommonly dark; my way lay across the Carousel, along the Pont Royal to the fauxbourg St. Germain. I have frequently come the same way alone from the Caffé de Foy in the Palais Royal after it was dark. I never was attacked, nor have I heard of a single street robbery, or house-breaking, since I have been in Paris.

This seems to me very remarkable, in the ungovernable state in which Paris may be supposed to be since the 10th of this month.

(2) Champs Elysées

Mont-Martre was then just outside Paris: the Rue de Clichy led past it through the Barrière de Clichy to the Chemin de St. Denis, much as it does now. The Champs Elysées were inside; the Barrière de Chaillot standing on the site of the Arc de Triomphe.

August 19.

They talk of forming a fortified camp for 40,000 men near Paris, including Mont Martre, and all that side of the city which lies next to St. Denis; which looks as if they began to dread the approach of the Germans.

I saw no signs of this however at the Champs Elisées, through which I drove this evening.

All those extensive fields were crowded with company of one sort or other; an immense number of small booths were erected, where refreshments were sold, and which resounded with music and singing. Pantomimes and puppet-shews of various kinds are here exhibited, and in some parts they were dancing in the open fields. 'Are these people as happy as they seem?' said I to a Frenchman who was with me. 'Ils sont heureux comme des dieux, Monsieur,' replied he.

'Do you think the Duke of Brunswick never enters their thoughts?' said I. 'Soyez sûr, Monsieur,' resumed he, 'que Brunswick est précisément l'homme du monde au quel ils pensent le moins.'

One fellow, on a kind of stage, had a monkey who played a thousand tricks. When the man called him aristocrate, the monkey flew at his throat with every mark of rage; but when he called him un bon patriote, the monkey expressed satisfaction, and caressed his master.

I see a great many monkeys every day, who affect to be bons patriotes.

One has no great objection to those patriots who dance about like monkeys; but they who to the airs of the monkey join the disposition of tigers, and dance with heads upon pikes, are horrible.

(3) TEMPLE

The Temple, to which the royal family were transferred, under the care of the Commune, on Aug. 13, stood near the north-east angle, as the Bastille stood at the east angle of 'old' Paris. From the Temple, Louis, Marie Antoinette and Madame Elisabeth went to trial and execution; and there the Dauphin died.

August 25.

I went this morning to the Temple. Great misfortunes interest the mind like great virtues. I do not believe that, during the short stay I proposed to make in France, I should have thought of going to Versailles, had the Royal Family been living there in the same splendour I have seen them surrounded with on former occasions: but the cruel reverse they now experience, has seldom been absent from my thoughts since the 10th of this month; and although there was little chance of getting even a glimpse of them, I was attracted to the Temple merely because they are confined within its walls.

The ground which belongs to the Temple is surrounded by a high wall, on part of which are a kind of battlements which, I suppose, crowned the whole wall formerly. This wall also encloses a garden belonging to the principal body of the building; for a great many houses and separate buildings have been added, which are inhabited by trades-men who enjoy particular privileges, and before the revolution the whole was an asylum for debtors.

There were a great many of the national guards at the principal gate, and a party under arms in the inner court, when I arrived; but on being informed that there was a particular spot behind the building, from which I had a greater probability of having my curiosity gratified, I went there in company with two gentlemen and a valet de place.

We were told that the King and Queen frequently walked in the garden; and that the Prince and Princess Royal are seen there still oftener; that the King, who discovers less concern than the rest, sometimes asks questions of the workmen who are employed in the garden, and in repairing part of the building.

We stood on a sort of rising terrace, from whence we could over-look the wall. A person whom I accidentally met on the spot gave me this information, and pointed out two windows in the tower which he said belonged to the apartment of the King and Queen, and at which they were sometimes seen. While I stood looking at these windows, occasionally asking questions of our informer, one of the national guards, who was a sentinel near the place, came up, and, addressing me, said, Vous prolongez vos observations un peu trop, Monsieur: passez votre chemin, s'il vous plait.

Before I had time to speak, the valet de place said, Ces messieurs sont des étrangers—des Anglais.

The sentinel replied, Ici je ne connais personne, and then repeated what he had said.

Mais, Monsieur, pourquoi? resumed the valet.

Pourquoi! said the sentinel a little fiercely, parcequ'il le faut.

I checked the valet, and we did what the soldier required; for, to borrow an expression of Dr. Johnson, *the request was reasonable, and the argument cogent.*

John Moore.

98. INSURRECTIONAL COMMUNE

As soon as news of the fall of the throne reached England, Lord Gower was recalled: William Lindsay remained as chargé d'affaires, until the prison massacres in the first week of September. For six weeks after Aug. 10 the Legislative Assembly carried on under the fiction that its session of Aug. 9 had not yet ended, whilst the Executive was represented by a provisional Ministry. Real power lay with the Insurrectional Commune of Aug. 10. From this situation, the Elections to the Convention, and the approach of the Prussian army, issued the September Massacres.

[Aug. 27.] The situation of Paris is more quiet than could be expected after the late violent convulsion; and as the people are all armed and the Government extremely feeble, the present tranquillity of the town is a strong proof of how much pains must have been taken to instigate the multitude to the unwarrantable proceedings of the 20th of June and 10th of August. The Jacobins seem to have gone farther than they at first intended, and not to have foreseen that the mob, the instrument with which they overturned the old government, was likely soon to become formidable to themselves; the Assembly itself being now a good deal under the influence of the rabble; for though the six minis-ters form what is called a *conseil executif provisoire*, the real power is transferred to the Municipality and different sections of Paris. The Municipality has been entirely occu-pied since the 10th in collecting as much evidence and as many proofs as possible to inculpate the conduct of Their Most Christian Majesties. For this purpose every suspected house has been searched and seals put on all papers belonging to the emigrants or their relations; many hundred people connected with the court and the aristocracy have been thrown into prison, and two or three of the most obnoxious have been executed. It is generally thought that Her Most Christian Majesty will be brought to her trial in the course of a few days, and your Lordship must not be surprised at hearing the most disagreeable account on her subject; for she is regarded as the cause of all the late misfortunes and is held in such general detestation that hardly anybody will be bold enough not to find her guilty.

It being contrary to the Constitution to try the Most Christian King, the fate of that unfortunate monarch will probably be left undecided by the present Assembly; but the people will take effectual care that nothing shall divert the attention of the new Legislature from concluding the great business of the King immediately after it meets. It is supposed that His Majesty will at least be confined for life, his family excluded from the throne, and the new Government assume the form of a republic. The Primary Assemblies (where every individual except servants has a vote) met yesterday to choose the electors. These are to elect the deputies next Sunday and the Convention is to meet at Paris on the Tuesday sennight following for the dispatch of business. Almost all the members of the late and present Assemblies who have distinguished themselves by espousing the cause of the people in opposition to the court and the aristocracy are likely to obtain seats in the Convention National.

Your Lordship will be surprised that these measures should be carrying on at a time when a great and formidable army commanded by the ablest general in the world is penetrating the country; it is however equally true and unaccountable that the approach of the Duke of Brunswick does not excite that alarm which might be expected. The public declarations of His Serene Highness have only served to irritate, and nothing can exceed the unanimity and confidence which prevails through the country. As to any party which might second the views and facilitate the operations of the combined armies, I have reason to believe that if any does exist it is too insignificant both in numbers and power (except perhaps just on the frontier) to merit attention. It is thought that if the Duke of Brunswick winters in France, his army will be enervated and lose its discipline, and if he returns to the frontier he will be obliged to begin everything again on the opening of a second campaign. They say it is very possible he may penetrate to and conquer Paris, but in that case the Convention will remove to the south, where the enemy will find much difficulty in following them. I have reason to believe, my Lord, that these are the sentiments of the ablest people and of those who have at present the most influence in this country.

[August 30th.] The confusion in this unfortunate city increases daily; an insurrection of the inhabitants of the Fauxbourgs was expected yesterday evening, but the whole body of the National Guard being under arms all night in order to execute the Decree for searching private houses for arms etc. no material disturbance took place. The Assembly and the Municipality, jealous of each others' powers, are at variance, and the Jacobins have quarrelled among themselves. A decree having passed the day before yesterday that the barriers of Paris should be thrown open and a free communication be reestablished through the interiour of the kingdom, which has been interrupted since the 10th by the difficulty of obtaining passports and the impossibility of travelling without them, two or three of the leading demagogues who are afraid of not being elected to the Convention if the Assembly should change its present quarters, and who wish to exclude some of the moderate people such as Messrs Condorcet, Kersaint etc. from being re-elected, have made the people believe that the measure of opening the barriers is only a pretext to enable the Assembly and deputies to fly from Paris to the south and make a bargain with the enemy in case circumstances should render such a conduct necessary to their own safety. In this persuasion many of the Fédérés are averse to leave Paris to join the army notwithstanding the urgency of the moment. The Assembly may be regarded as in a sort of imprisonment and the Convention will soon be in a similar situation if it should meet in this capital. In order that your Lordship may be enabled to judge of the language, sentiments and conduct of the *men of the people* in this country I have the honour to inclose an account of a speech delivered a few days ago in the Jacobin Club. All the 83 departments have now sworn to adhere to the new order of things and support what is called Liberty and Equality.

W. Lindsay to Lord Grenville.

99. PROTESTANT PATRIOTISM

The Church of St. Louis du Louvre was on the south side of the space between the back of the Tuileries and the west front of the 'old' Louvre—then encumbered with buildings.

[SEPTEMBER 2.] I was this morning passing the church of Saint Louis du Louvre, and being told that it was now frequented by a Protestant congregation, I immediately joined them.

To behold an assembly of Protestants worshipping God according to the forms of their own religion, in a Roman catholic church, built on the spot where the massacre of St. Barthélemy began, and near that whence Charles IX fired, with his own hands, on his Protestant subjects, was not the least extraordinary thing I have had occasion to observe since I have been in France.

When I entered this church, I found it crowded with an audience of a very respectable and devout deportment.

The demeanour of the clergyman was of a piece with that of the audience. I enquired his name, and am sorry I have forgot it. His sermon was excellent, and gracefully delivered; he used more action than is common with English divines; but seemed free from affectation. He dwelt on the benevolent spirit of Christianity, and inculcated its precepts with a fervour that, I thought, proceeded from the heart. A patriotic form of prayer has been used in all the churches since the revolution; it refers to that event, and is affecting and well composed: this was the only thing the minister read. The King and Royal Family were included in it before the 10th of August: the only thing which displeased me during the service was, that, by order of the existing powers, they are now left out.

On the part of the wall of this church, where a saint formerly stood, is the following inscription:

Le devoir d'un citoyen:

Adorez	Dieu.
Respectez	la Nation.
Obeir	à la Loi.

Paix avec surveillance.
Liberté sans licence.
Egalité sans indécence.
C'est la véritable science.

The poetry of these lines is certainly not very admirable: it were much to be wished however, for the happiness of France, that she could obtain what is expressed in the second; as for *science*, she had no natural business among them, and must have been dragged in by her unruly relation *indécence*.

When I went into the street, people were hurrying up and down with rapid steps and anxious faces; groups were formed at every corner: one told in general that a courier had arrived with very bad news; another asserted that Verdun had been betrayed like Longwy, and that the enemy were advancing; others shook their heads and said, it was the traitors within Paris, and not the declared enemies on the frontiers that were to be feared.

John Moore.

100. THE PRISON MASSACRES
(1)

The massacres began at 3 p.m. on Sept. 2, and ended at 4 p.m. on the 4th. The first victims were some priests, being taken in carriages from the Mairie to the Abbaye (St. Germain-des-Prés), who were murdered outside the prison. The massacre of priests at the Carmes took place the same afternoon. The Princesse de Lamballe was among the victims at La Force. Mme de Tourzel and her daughter were imprisoned there, but were spared. The Princesse de Tarente was similarly 'acquitted' at the Abbaye. The total number of victims was from 1100 to 1400.

I HAD the honour to mention in my last letter that a courier arrived here yesterday afternoon with an account that the Prussians were some leagues on this side Verdun. Immediately on receiving this intelligence the National Assembly decreed that as universal an alarm as possible should be spread through the whole country in order that no time might be lost in preparing for the general defence; in consequence however of the fermentation excited in Paris by the sounding the Tocsin, firing the alarm guns and beating to arms, the people assembled in different parts of the town in a very tumultuous manner, and at about seven o'clock in the evening surrounded the church called l'Église des Carmes, where about 160 Priests *non sermentés*, and taken into custody since the 10th, were confined. These unfortunate people fell victims to the fury of the enraged populace and were massacred with circumstances of barbarity too shocking to describe. The mob went afterwards to the prison of the Abbaye, and having demanded of the jailors a list of the prisoners they put aside such as were confined only for debt, and pulled to pieces most of the others. The same cruelties were committed during the night and continue this morning in all the other prisons of the town. When they have satiated their vengeance, which is principally directed against the refractory Priests, and those who were concerned in the affair of the 10th, it is to be hoped the tumult will subside, but as the multitude are perfectly masters, everything is to be dreaded. The Assembly deputed some of its most popular and most eloquent members to endeavour to bring the people to reason and a sense of their duty. These gentlemen escaped being insulted but were not listened to. The Royal Family were all safe and well late last night. It is impossible to describe to your Lordship the confusion and consternation which at present prevails here. The Prussians are advancing rapidly, they have already cut off the communication between the armies of Messrs Luckner and Dumouriez; and intelligence is just arrived that a detachment of 2000 men lately sent from hence to reinforce Verdun is fallen into the enemy's hands.

P.S. It is confidently reported that Mesdames de Lamballe, de Tourzelle and de Tarente were among those who fell victims to the popular fury, and the number of people already massacred are said to amount to four thousand. I have received no answer from Mr Le Brun.

W. Lindsay to Lord Grenville.

[Sept. 3, 1792.]

(2)

In view of the massacre, Lindsay left Paris as soon as he could get a passport, and was back in London by Sept. 8. But two English witnesses remained behind —Dr. Moore till Dec. 4, and the spy,' Colonel George Monro, till Jan. 21, 1793. Monro's letters to Lord Grenville are printed in The Despatches of Earl Gower *(1885).*

4 September, 1792.

About one o'clock on Sunday fore-noon three signal guns were fired, the Tocsin was rung, and one of the Municipality on horseback proclaimed in different parts of the city, that the enemy was at the gates, Verdun was besieged, and could only hold out a few days. The inhabitants were therefore ordered to assemble in their respective sections, and from thence to march to the Champ de Mars, where they were to select an army of sixty thousand men.

The first part of this proclamation was put in execution, but the second was totally neglected; for I went to the Champ de Mars myself where I only saw M. Péthion, who on finding no one there returned home. During the time the officer of the Municipality was making the proclamation, two others attended at the bar of the National Assembly to acquaint them with the steps that had been taken by the direction of the Conseil de la Commune. The Assembly applauded their conduct, and immediately passed a decree, directing that those who refused their arms to those that wished to serve, or objected serving themselves, should be deemed traitors and worthy of death, that all horses of luxury should be seized for the use of the army, and that those who refused to obey the orders of the present executive power should be punished with death. It concluded by decreeing that twelve members of the National Assembly should be added to the other six that at present compose the executive power. As soon as these decrees were passed, the carriages and horses of gentlemen were seized in the streets (agreeable to the spirit of the decree). Their owners were obliged to walk home, and the horses in general were sent to the École Militaire, and the carriages were put under the care of different guards. The proceedings with the beating of drums, firing of cannon, and the marching up and down of armed men of course created no little agitation in the minds of the people. That however was nothing to the scene of horror that ensued soon after. A party at the instigation of some one or other declared they would not quit Paris, as long as the prisons were filled with Traitors (for they called those so, that were confined in the different Prisons and Churches), who might in the absence of such a number of Citizens rise and not only effect the release of His Majesty, but make an entire counter-revolution. To prevent this, a large body of sans-culottes attended by a number of Marseillais and Brestois, the hired assassins of a Party, proceeded to the Church de Carmes, rue de Vaugirard, where amidst the acclamations of a savage mob they massacred a number of refractory Priests, all the Vicaires de Saint Sulpice, the directors of the Seminaries, and the Doctors of the Sorbonne, with the *ci-devant* Archbishop of Arles, and a number of others, exceeding in all one hundred and seventy, including those that had been confined there since the tenth. After this they proceeded to the Abbaye, where they massacred a vast number of prisoners, amongst whom were also many respectable characters. These executioners increasing in number, different detachments were sent to the Châtelet, the prison de la Force, de Ste Pélagie, and the prisons of the Conciergerie. At all these places a most horrid massacre took place, none were exempted but debtors and many of these fell victims to the fury of the people. During this sad scene, the more humane, which were but few in number, hurried to the National Assembly to obtain their interference for stopping such melancholy outrages. They immediately decreed that six of their members should go and see if it was possible to prevent such cruelties. With difficulty these members arrived at the Abbaye; when there one of them got upon a chair to harangue the people, but neither he nor the others could make themselves heard, and with some risk, they made their escape. Many of the Municipality attended at the different prisons, and endeavoured to quell the fury of the people, but all in vain; they therefore proposed to the mob a plan of establishing a kind of Court of justice in the prisons, for the immediate trial of the remaining offenders. They caught at this, and two of the Municipality with a detachment of the mob, about two on Monday morning, began this strange Court of justice. The gaoler's list was called for, those that were confined for forging assignats, or theft, with the unhappy people that were any way suspected to be concerned in the affair of the 10th, were in general massacred; this form took place in nearly all the prisons in Paris. But early on Monday morning a detachment with seven pieces of cannon went to attack Bicêtre. It is reported that these wretches charged their cannon with small stones and such other things, and fired promiscuously among the prisoners. I cannot however vouch for this, they have however not finished their cruelties there yet, and it is now past six o'clock Tuesday evening. To be convinced of what I could not believe, I made a visit to the prison of the Abbaye about seven o'clock on Monday evening, for the slaughter had not ceased. This prison, which takes its name from an adjoining Abbaye, stands in a narrow street, which was at this time from a variety of lights, as light as day: a single file of men armed with swords, or piques, formed a lane of some length, commencing from the prison door. This body might consist of about fifty; these people were either Marseillais, Brestois, or the National Guards of Paris, and when I saw them seemed much fatigued with their horrid work. For besides the irregular massacre that continued till two o'clock on Monday morning, many of them delighted with their strange office continued their services when I left them, which was about nine on Monday evening.

Two of the Municipality were then in the prison with some of the mob distributing their justice. Those they found guilty were seemingly released, but only to be precipitated by the door on a number of piques, and then among the savage cries of *vive la nation*, to be hacked to pieces by those that had swords and were ready to receive them. After this their dead bodies were dragged by the arms or legs to the Abbaye, which is distant from the prison about two hundred yards; here they were laid up in heaps till carts could carry them away. The kennel was swimming with blood, and a bloody track was traced from the prison to the Abbaye door where they had dragged these unfortunate people.

I was fortunate enough to be present when five men were acquitted. Such a circumstance, a by-stander told me, had not happened in the operations of this horrid tribunal; and these inconsistent murderers seemed nearly as much pleased at the acquittal of a prisoner as they were at his condemnation. The Governor of the Invalides happened to be one of those I saw acquitted, the street rung with acclamations of joy, but the old man was so feeble with fear, and suspense, and so overcome with the caresses of his daughter, who was attending to know his fate, that they both sunk lifeless into the arms of some of the spectators, who carried them to the Hospital des Invalides. The same congratulations attended the others that were acquitted and the same those that were condemned. Nothing can exceed the inconsistency of these people. After the general massacre of Sunday night many of the dead bodies were laid on the Pont-neuf to be claimed, a person in the action of stealing a handkerchief from one of the corpses was hacked to pieces on the spot, by the same people who had been guilty of so much cruelty and injustice.

One of the Municipality was fortunate enough for that night to save some of the women, but many of these underwent the same mock trial next day; and the Princess Lamballe, after having been butchered in the most shocking manner, had her head severed from her body, which these monsters carried about, while others dragged her body through many of the streets. It is even said they attempted to carry it to the Queen, but the Guards would not permit that. Mademoiselle de Tourzelles was also reported to have been murdered, but I understand that she and Madame de Ste Brice were saved from the fury of the people, and carried *à la section des droits de l'homme*. Many other women of family were killed and others escaped. Major Bauchman of the Swiss Guards was beheaded on the Place de Carouzel early on Monday morning. Mr Montmorin, Governor of Fontainebleau and nephew of Mr Montmorin late Minister, who was killed at the Abbaye, had been regularly tried and acquitted on Friday, but not being released was also massacred at the Conciergerie. Monsieur d'Affry was acquitted by the people and escaped. In all it is supposed they have murdered four thousand, some say seven, but I think that exaggerated.

By what I can understand it was late on Sunday evening before Mr Péthion took any steps to prevent the progress of this unexampled outrage, and the National Guards of course made no opposition to such irregularities. The Mayor however at last sent to the Temple the Commandant General of the National Guards, and I am happy to inform you that in the midst of all this confusion, though there was a crowd in the street, yet the court of the Temple was quiet. The Section du Marais has sworn not to permit any violence to be exercised against the prisoners in that place, and the National Assembly have also appointed six of their

members as a safe-guard to the sacred persons of Their
Majesties, and a number of the Municipality also attend. A
motion was made last week to confine Their Majesties in
separate apartments; that right was however found to rest
with the Municipality, and I have the pleasure of saying
that Their Most Christian Majesties still enjoy the comfort
of being together, and were, not an hour ago, in perfect
good health.

I ask pardon for giving such a detailed account of such
uncommon barbarity, which I am sure must be as disagreeable for you to read as it is for me to commit such acts
to paper, but they ought to be particularized to the eternal
disgrace of a people who pretend to be the most civilized
among the nations of Europe.

George Monro to Lord Grenville.

[Sept. 4, 1792].

101. INVASION AND ELECTIONS

*The elections for the new Convention began in Paris on the same day as the
prison massacres, Sept. 2, and ended on the 19th. Meanwhile, since the fall of
Verdun on Sept. 2, Dumouriez had delayed the Prussians' advance by holding
the passes of the Argonne; but it was not till the 20th that the enemy was
finally stopped at Valmy, and forced to retreat. Monro's narrative is one of
the best accounts we have of the situation in Paris during these critical weeks.*

WEDNESDAY [Sept. 5] half past 2 o'clock. On Tuesday a
report was circulated that the National Assembly meant to
replace His Most Christian Majesty on the throne, or invite
his Royal Highness the Duke of York to occupy his place.
The Ministre de la Guerre complained much of the evil
occasioned by such reports, which only tended to agitate
the minds of the people: the Assembly on this decreed that
some of their members should be sent to the different
sections to contradict such reports, and soon after Messrs.
Dubayet et Larivière made a motion which they all swore
to that no stranger should ever give laws to France, and
that no King should ever sully their liberty.

While such proceedings were carrying on in the National

Assembly, a Mons. Moras in the Club of the Jacobins was inciting them in the strongest language to address the National Assembly for the immediate trial of His Most Christian Majesty, and avowedly persuading them to establish a republican Government. As this motion, though received with approbation was not seconded, I had the satisfaction of seeing it dropped.

On Monday the address of a Monsieur Mossy, a citizen of Marseilles, to the electors, on the approaching National Convention was read in the same club: this man follows the same steps as Mr. Moras, but with greater insolence recommends it strongly to the electors to make choice of no one to represent them that will not insist upon the prompt punishment of Their Majesties, and in strong language he likewise directs them to stipulate with their representatives that they will adopt no Government but a Republic.

Nothing else material has happened in either of these two houses, if you except an account of plots and risings in different parts of the country, many of which I am afraid are imaginary; and different detachments of armed citizens, who were going to the army, that had the honour of marching through the hall of the Assembly: as also their decreeing that all the gold and silver belonging to the Royal Palaces, or the Hôtels of the Emigrants, should without loss of time be sent to the Mint for the purpose of being made into money. I must likewise add they have passed a decree, that the Municipality, the Conseil General, les Corps administratifs, and the commandant of the National Guard etc. with all the citizens of France are invited to take an oath to defend the lives and property of the people, *et la liberté, l'égalité*. Extraordinary couriers have also been sent into the different departments to *cherish the spirits et échauffer les cœurs* of all the inhabitants. Such things, with an account that the Russians are marching twenty-two thousand men to their frontiers, and that with a fleet they have in the Black Sea they mean to attack their coasts, formed the chief of their proceedings till Wednesday morning. In the mean time the different sections of Paris have been forming and are still forming their respective quotas for the army. This has created a good deal of inconvenience to the inhabitants, and of course some discontent. I however cannot but observe on the whole, that the party is strong in opposing the combined powers; but they are all conscious, that undisciplined troops can make no stand against such as they have to oppose; and I have no doubt, were a Prussian army once to appear before Paris, that many of the King's friends, who are either quiet or concealed citizens that want peace, and a vast number of people that are averse to the Jacobin principles, would readily declare themselves for the Royal party. Twelve of the National Assembly are directed to attend daily some works they have begun to throw up on the heights round Paris; of these and the citizens that are gone and are still going I shall be able to give you a better account in my next. I cannot help adding that, notwithstanding a tolerable unanimity, there exists a general complaint of some kind or other. The Ministers of every department are complaining of being unable to carry on the routine of their different offices for the interference of people who are ignorant of the nature of them; in short they all wish to be directors, but except the poor people that have been compelled to go to the army none wish to be actors, and, from what I can see and hear, they want a confidence in their army, which is not a little increased by the loss of Verdun.

[September 6th.] Had a supply of gunpowder not been obtained from Rouen they would have been badly off for that, and shot, although they have now also got some of that, with cannon, howitzers, and some firelocks from Rochefort. The inhabitants are giving in their iron pots to supply the place of shot, and are depriving the dead of their coffins to make musquet balls; and it has even already been proposed to kill all the dogs in the capital as so many useless mouths, but notwithstanding the cruelties they have committed, yet they revolted at this act of barbarity.

[Saturday, Sep. 8th.] Mr. Payne is chosen one of the Deputies for the Départment de l'Oise, and Mr. Robespierre

197

one of those for Paris, Mr. Péthion for the Département d'Eure et Loire, and Messrs. Grégoire et Chabot for the Département de Loire et Cher. The elections go on very fast, and I am sorry to find that the principles of the Jacobins have extended much into the interior part of the country. Two hundred of the Swiss Guards who escaped the affair of the 10th and the late massacre, have consented to be incorporated in the National Guards, in order to save their lives. The Marseillais still remain in Paris. They consist of about four hundred, and there is not the smallest doubt but they are Genoese assassins, hired for the purpose. We are also in daily expectation of five thousand of the National Guards of Bourdeaux, who are little better. I can assure you as a fact that many of the citizens are in daily fear of a general pillage, and sooner or later it will certainly take place. The National Assembly have directed the Mayor to make a report of the state of the city every day, but his report is not to be attended to, for the police of the city is entirely annihilated. The other evening in the Palais Royal which was always bad but is now intolerable, a poor man happened to say that sending all these citizens to the army was sending them to be butchered. He had scarcely pronounced the word, when he was killed by the blows of a hundred swords and clubs.

[Sep. 9th.] The number of men, for I cannot call them troops, that have left this for the army is prodigious. Exclusive of the adjacent villages, Paris alone has sent seventy thousand, and they are still enrolling; many of whom, as the Hôtel I live in joins that of L'Hôtel de la Guerre I had an opportunity of seeing, and I am convinced as a military man that they must tend more to create confusion in a regular army than to be of any advantage to it. As the Duke of Brunswick of course has good intelligence, he knows this. I have heard to-day that the multitude of people that are besides this either at or going to Chalons is beyond belief. As not half of these can however be armed or clothed, and none of them scarcely disciplined, they must therefore be so many useless mouths. Indeed General

Luckner and the Ministre de la Guerre are aware of this and have made several applications to the Assembly to prevent people going that have not arms.

The cause among the lower order of people is more popular than I imagined, I cannot therefore help thinking the Duke of Brunswick ought to get before Paris as quick as he can. There has been a report flying about to-day, that Thionville is taken, and that Metz is besieged, but I cannot vouch it as a fact, as it comes from no authority. Horses and waggons have been impressed in vast numbers to-day to carry provisions, camp equipage, and other things to the army. I don't know how they mean that Paris should stand a siege, for they seem to be carrying most things out of it. A quantity of assignats were again burnt on Friday, but neither gold nor silver nor yet even copper is scarcely to be seen. The National Assembly from the multiplicity of complaints that were made have put a stop to their taking any more of the coffins of the dead, and have given directions that the prison de Châtelet should be taken down, which will add much to the beauty and health of that part of the town.

Doctor Priestly, it is announced to the Assembly this day, has been elected one of the Députés for the Département of the Somme.

[Friday, 14th to Monday Sept. 17th, 1792.] The want of police has got nearly to the height I expected it would; the blackguards of Paris have begun this day to stop people publicly in the streets, and take their watches and buckles from them; they have even taken the ladies' rings from their fingers, and from their ears: my traiteur was obliged to bring me metal spoons for fear of the others being taken; a general pillage as I said before will at last take place. The Mayor has exerted himself a little in this business, and the people have assisted in protecting themselves. One woman killed one of these villains with her scissors. I myself never move out but with pistols in my pocket, as I find them more necessary here than in Turkey.

[Sept. 20th to the 22nd.] The National Convention met agreeably to order on the 20th, but did little else that evening than mention the authority they were assembled by, name Mr. Péthion for their president, Messrs. Camus, Vergniaud, Brissot, Rabaut, and Lasource for their secretaries and call over the names of three hundred and seventy-one members which was all that were then present, and which after some little conversation was agreed to be a majority.

Next day after some little ceremony between them and the National Assembly, as the hall of the Tuileries was not quite finished they adjourned to that of the Assembly; their coming there was announced some time before by a deputation from the Convention, of which number was Philip Joseph Egalité *ci-devant* Duke of Orleans, so that everything was ready for their proceeding immediately to business which was done by Mr. Manuel moving that the president of the Convention should be lodged in the palace of the Tuileries and every time he opened the sitting, the members should rise, that they might never forget their rights, nor the respect due to the Sovereignty of the people. The previous question was passed upon this motion without any opposition; and after a variety of other debates, some wishing to declare all the powers of the old government null and to reappoint them, others opposed this, and the debate turned chiefly upon the Sovereignty of the people and the attention that ought to be paid to their wishes in forming a new constitution, and that they should almost individually sanction such an act. Upon this Mr. Danton after resigning his place of Ministre de la justice, said it was impossible to have any constitution, but that which was accepted by a majority of the people in the Assemblées primaires; and that all persons and property of whatever kind should be put under the safeguard of the people. This was passed, and they also decreed that all laws that were not repealed, and the powers that were not suspended, were still provisionally to exist, and that all taxes and public contributions should be collected as before. The

Convention was then going to adjourn for an hour or two when Mr. d'Herbois, one of the members for Paris, said there was a declaration they could not dispense making that night, which was the abolition of Royalty; this after a very short conversation was unanimously agreed to, and on Saturday the suppression of every attribute of Royalty wherever it might be, and the destruction of everything that recalled the idea of such a government was decreed; the seal was to be changed and to bear a Roman fasces surmounted with a cap of Liberty, and the exergue La République Française, and all public deeds were in future to be dated from the first year of the Republic.

George Monro to Lord Grenville.

102. A REPUBLICAN BONFIRE

For John Owen at an earlier stage of his journey, v. No. 67.

THE procession, of which I spoke in my last, now found me in the number of its train. I lost no time in mixing with the crowd, and informing myself of their plan and intentions. It appeared, that the portraits of their Kings, and all the books, records, and registers which regarded the establishment of royalty, were already carried to the place of rendezvous; and the ceremony of consuming these upon a funeral pile, was to be conducted in the presence of the national military. The guard, which composed a numerous body, marched to the ground, distant about half a league from the city, in detachments representing the quota which every district furnished. When arrived at the field, they were drawn up into a circle of considerable compass, in the centre of which was a pile of wood surrounded by pointed cannon; *bonnet rouges* were hoisted upon different standards, and streamers at regular intervals proclaimed 'La Liberté ou la mort.' A signal-gun being fired, the torch was applied; and almost instantaneously the whole pile was seen in a blaze. The portraits and books were then thrown upon the raging materials; and the name of the royal victim loudly pronounced, as each was severally consumed. The first volume of smoke which ascended into the air, excited the shouts and triumphs of the exulting spectators. The soldiers placed their hats upon their bayonets, and raised them as signals of applause. The populace adopted the same expedient; and all who had canes, hoisted their hats with expressions of furious joy. This ceremony, if such it may be called, was renewed upon every sacrifice which the flames received; but when the name of Louis Quatorze was announced, the shouts of the populace were beyond measure furious. The ashes of his portrait mounted amidst the groans and curses of forty thousand spectators.

John Owen.
[Lyons, Sept. 9, 1792.]

103. 'TO THE PEOPLE OF FRANCE'
For Paine's visits to France, v. No. 70. This letter is printed in An
Impartial Sketch of the Life of Thomas Paine (*London*), 1792.

Paris, Sept. 25,
First year of the Republic.

FELLOW CITIZENS !

I receive, with affectionate gratitude, the honour which the late National Assembly has conferred on me, by adopting me a Citizen of France; and the additional honour of being elected by my fellow citizens a Member of the National Convention. Happily impressed, as I am, by those testimonies of respect shown towards me as an individual, I feel my felicity increased by seeing the barrier broken down that divided patriotism by spots of earth, and limited citizenship to the soil, like vegetation.

I came not to enjoy repose. Convinced that the cause of France is the cause of all mankind, and that liberty cannot be purchased by a wish, I gladly share with you the dangers and honours necessary to success.

I am well aware that the moment of any great change, such as that accomplished on the 10th of August, is unavoidably the moment of terror and confusion. . . . But let us now look calmly and confidentially forward, and success is certain. It is no longer the paltry cause of Kings, or of this or of that individual, that calls France and her armies into action. It is the great cause of all. It is the establishment of a new era, that shall blot despotism from the earth, and fix, on the lasting principles of peace and citizenship, the great Republic of Man. . . .

The public cause has hitherto suffered from the contradictions contained in the Constitution of the former Constituent Assembly. Those contradictions have served to divide the opinions of individuals at home, and to obscure the great principles of the Revolution in other countries. But when those contradictions shall be removed, and the Constitution be made conformable to the declaration of Rights; when the bagatelles of monarchy, royalty, regency, and hereditary succession, shall be exposed, with all their absurdities, a new ray of light will be thrown over the world, and the Revolution will derive new strength from being universally understood.

The scene that now opens itself to France extends far beyond the boundaries of her own dominions. Every nation is becoming her colleague, and every court is become her enemy. It is now the cause of all nations, against the cause of all courts. . . .

In entering on this great scene, greater than any nation has yet been called to act in, let us say to the agitated mind, be calm. Let us punish by instructing, rather than by revenge. Let us begin the new era by a greatness of friendship, and hail the approach of union and success.

Your Fellow Citizen,
THOMAS PAINE.

104. POLITICAL CHARACTERS

At this time (October, 1792) the contest between the Jacobins (or Montagnards) and Girondins was already distracting the Convention. Robespierre, Danton, and Marat were leading members of the former party, Roland and Dumouriez of the latter.

(1) Dumouriez

[October 13.] I went this morning to the Conventional Assembly, and was admitted into the box where, on the 11th of August, I had seen the unfortunate family, now prisoners in the temple, seated.

The hall and galleries were uncommonly crowded, because Dumouriez, who arrived in Paris last night, was expected to come to the Assembly this day.

The forenoon was spent in debates in which Buzot, Vergniaud, and some other of the most distinguished members of the Convention took part. About one o'clock I saw one of the huissiers go to the President, and I heard him acquaint him, that Dumouriez attended in the adjoining room.

The President, however, did not interrupt the debate, which continued for at least an hour after this information was given. It was known to some in the Assembly, that Dumouriez was waiting to be called in; several members thinking the President was ignorant of that circumstance went up and whispered him—he signified by a nod that he already knew it, and allowed the debate to continue.

It struck me as singular, that a General who in such critical circumstances had rendered the most important services to his country, and was just returned victorious, should be treated with such coolness—I have no doubt it was done on purpose, and, in the republican spirit, intended as a hint to the General not to overvalue his importance.

At last, however, the President read a letter from General Dumouriez, in which he informs the Convention, that he desires to pay his duty to them, and waits their orders. A member moved that he should be admitted directly; and the General, attended by several officers, appeared at the bar, amidst the applause of the Assembly, and the acclamations of the galleries. He is considerably below the middle size, of a sharp and intelligent countenance, and seems rather above 50 years of age.

He was dressed in the uniform of a General Officer, blue and gold lace; he is said to be a great deal less attentive to dress than is usual in France; but in any dress I should know him to be a Frenchman. He possesses the peculiar vivacity of air and manner that distinguishes the natives of this country. I understand that he is remarkably entertaining and agreeable in conversation; that though he has indulged in pleasure, and yielded to dissipation, yet he is capable of the most indefatigable exertion, both of body and mind, when the importance of the object requires it; that he has always been fonder of pleasure than of money, and ever ready to sacrifice both for renown. His enemies, who allow that he possesses great acuteness of mind, and the most unshaken courage, throw doubts upon his steadiness in other respects. His military talents have been sufficiently evinced in the course of the last memorable campaign: without the singular circumstances which raised him to command, and drew them into action, the man who with inferior force baffled the attempts of the most renowned Generals of the age, would have remained undistinguished and subordinate to those on whom birth without talents, or age which has not profited by experience, so often devolves the command of armies.

(2) MARAT

[October 17.] I never was more surprised in my life than when Marat, having ascended the tribune at the Jacobins, began to repeat these assertions. The man's audacity is equal to any thing, but what I thought full as wonderful was the degree of patience, and even approbation, with which he was heard. The house was crowded, and it contains a very numerous audience. When Marat is in the tribune, he holds his head as high as he can, and endeavours to assume an air of dignity. He can make nothing of that; but amidst all the exclamations and signs of hatred and disgust which I have seen manifested against him, the look of self approbation which he wears is wonderful—so far from ever having the appearance of fear, or of deference, he seems to me always to contemplate the Assembly from the tribune, either with the eyes of menace, or contempt.

He speaks in a hollow croaking voice, with affected solemnity, which in such a diminutive figure would often produce laughter, were it not suppressed by horror at the character and sentiments of the man.

(3) ROBESPIERRE

[October 26.] Robespierre is a man of small size, and a disagreeable countenance, which announces more fire than understanding; in his calmest moments, he conceals with difficulty the hatred and malignity which is said to exist in his heart, and which his features are admirably formed to express. He distinguished himself in the Constituent Assembly by the violence of his speeches, and much more since, in the Jacobin society, by the violence of his measures. His eloquence is employed in invectives against tyrants and aristocrates, and in declamations in praise of Liberty. His speeches are barren in argument, sometimes fertile in the flowers of fancy.

Robespierre is considered as an enthusiast rather than a hypocrite: some people think him both, which is not without example; but, to me, he seems to be too much of the first to be a great deal of the second.

He has always refused every office of emolument: his passion is popularity, not avarice; and he is allowed, even by those who detest many parts of his character, and are his enemies, to be incorruptible by money.

(4) ROLAND AND DANTON

Roland is not supposed to possess all the energy of character that belongs to Danton; in many other respects they differ. Roland is believed to be a thorough republican: Danton, it is thought, does not lay much stress on the form of government, and would have no objection to monarchy, provided the monarch were a creature of his own; for I do not find that it is suspected that he aspires to reign in person.

Roland and Danton were often in opposition with each

other when joined in the same administration. Roland struggled with all his might against the usurpations of the General Council of the Commune of Paris after the 10th of August: Danton favoured and abetted them. Roland exclaimed against the massacres in September, did every thing he could to put an end to them; and on that account was himself in imminent danger. Danton, though he was then minister of justice, is accused of having been criminally passive on that very pressing occasion. Roland uses his whole influence to bring the authors of those savage scenes to justice; Danton uses his to stifle all investigation of that nature.

In external appearance and manner, those two men differ as in all the rest; Roland is about sixty years of age, tall, thin, of a mild countenance and pale complexion. His dress, every time I have seen him, has been the same, a drab-coloured suit lined with green silk, his grey hair hanging loose.

Danton is not so tall, but much broader than Roland; his form is coarse, and uncommonly robust: Roland's manner is unassuming and modest—that of Danton fierce and bois-terous; he speaks with the voice of a Stentor, declaims on the blessings of freedom with the arrogance of a tyrant, and invites to union and friendship with the frown of an enemy.

John Moore.

105. WILL THE KING BE TRIED?

The Girondins *were so called because their best speakers were* Vergniaud, *Guadet, Gensonné, and other deputies from the Gironde Department: the Jacobins, because they were led by Parisian deputies, prominent members of the Jacobin Club. The first great struggle between these parties arose on the question of the King's trial.*

THE Trial of Charles the First of England, translated into French from the State Trials, is to be found of late on all the booksellers' tables around the hall of the Convention. An abridgement of the same is cried by the hawkers of pam-phlets in the Palais Royal and the various entries to the

National Assembly: the conversation is now greatly turned to that subject, and to the expected process of Lewis XVI. I never believed, however, that there was a serious intention in the Convention to bring the King to trial, and still less did I think it probable that it would be in their contemplation to bring him to the scaffold; an idea which I cannot entertain without horror. Besides, however devoid of principle some of them may be, I could not conceive that they would commit such an act of cruelty and injustice, without any of the motives which incite wicked men to deeds of such atrocity. Their personal interest evidently dictates the preservation of the King's life, and it seemed unlikely that any member of the Convention, one only excepted, could be actuated by personal enmity: they are almost all of the middle or inferior ranks of life; none of them have ever had opportunities for that kind of intercourse with the King, which usually generates either personal friendship or hatred: they may like or dislike, respect or despise his general conduct and character; but I could see none of the usual sources of personal hatred either good or bad, especially as, with respect to the exercise of authority, the whole reign of Lewis XVI has been a reign of moderation. He has always manifested a desire to meet the wishes of his subjects; and perhaps his aversion to every measure which had the appearance of being violent, with too great a disposition to *grant*, have deprived him of the power of *refusing*, and reduced him to the state he is in. I am persuaded that none of his ancestors had so just a claim to the epithets which the public and historians have affixed to their names, as the unfortunate Lewis XVI has to that of *Louis le trop bon*...

These considerations were sufficient hitherto to induce me to believe that there was no serious intention in the Convention to bring the King to a trial. But I now begin to fear that a process in some shape or other will very soon be brought on, and when once begun, there is no knowing what may be the issue in a town so much in the power of the populace, and of *such* a populace as that which Paris contains at present.

Will the King be Tried?

I am led to this alteration of opinion from having very lately heard a number of citizens, whom I thought of a different opinion, declare their conviction that the King was betraying the country. The rancorous activity of his enemies has at length persuaded them, that, instead of another Henry IV between whom and Lewis XVI they formerly found a resemblance, they actually had another Lewis XI or Charles IX on the throne.

Besides, whether the King ought or ought not to be judged, is not merely considered as a matter of justice or even of expediency, but, most unfortunately, it has become a party question, in which passion may have more weight than either. Danton's party knows that the Girondists wish to save the King, which is reason sufficient with the former to do every thing in their power to promote his trial and condemnation, and to represent the opposition of the other party as a proof of their being aristocrates and royalists in their hearts.

Marat, who is the great agent of Danton and Robespierre, declares that it is highly unjust, and would be a shameful deviation from the flattering tenet of egalité, after having condemned M. de la Porte and other inferior criminals, to pass over the greatest criminal of all.

Finally, I have been impressed with fears respecting the fate of the King from a variety of circumstances, too minute to be mentioned, which have struck me very lately. It is certainly horrid and disgraceful to human nature, but I am afraid that the populace of this city have heard so much of a grand example that ought to be exhibited to Europe, and their imaginations have dwelt so long on the idea of a King being tried for his life, and afterwards led to execution, that they cannot with patience bear the thoughts of being disappointed of such an extraordinary spectacle.

John Moore.

[Oct. 31, 1792.]

106. LOUVET AND ROBESPIERRE
(1)

The personal quarrels in the Convention came to a head in Louvet's accusation of Robespierre. J. B. Louvet de Couvray, a man of 32, had made a name five years before, as the author of the mildly scandalous Aventures du chevalier de Faublas, *and more recently by his* Emilie de Valmont, *a propagandist novel in favour of divorce and the marriage of clergy. Politically a Girondin, and a protégé of Roland, he had a personal grudge against Robespierre, who he thought had excluded him from the Brissotin Ministry in the spring of 1792.*

November 3.

Having heard that a debate of importance was expected, I went to the Conventional Assembly two days ago earlier than usual.

Roland was to present a memorial respecting the state of Paris. When he appeared, contrary to custom, they postponed the business then transacting, to attend to him. He began by saying, that if the strength of his voice was equal to that of his mind, he should himself read the address which he held in his hand; but as his breast was delicate, he begged that one of the secretaries might be allowed to read it for him.—Lanjuinais ascended the tribune, and read.

In this memorial were stated all the usurpations and acts of despotism which had been committed by the Commune since the tenth of August, many of which were unknown to the generality of the deputies, and seemed to fill them with equal surprise and indignation. With this memorial Roland presented a letter addressed to the Minister of Justice, in which information is given, ' that expressions of the most alarming tendency had been used by certain persons of late; that it had been even insinuated that the business begun in September had not been completed; that the whole cabal of Roland and Brissot should be cut off; that there was a scheme for this purpose; that Vergniaud, Guadet, Buzot, La Source, and others displeased the real patriots; and that *Robespierre* was the properest person for conducting the government in the present emergency.'

'Ah the villain!' one of the members called aloud, as soon as this name was pronounced.

There was such an uproar in the Assembly for some time after Roland's memorial had been read, that no person in particular could be distinctly heard: the noise was mostly occasioned by expressions of rage against Robespierre, and partly by a cry that the memorial should be printed, and sent to all the departments and all the municipalities in France.

Robespierre ascended the tribune: the cry against him was so violent that his voice could not be distinguished: he at last was heard to say, that he wished to justify himself from the calumnies of the Minister. He was interrupted by a new cry to close the discussion: he then said he wished to speak against the printing of the memorial.

This was also refused by a pretty universal exclamation; but on its being observed, that they could not decree a proposition without hearing those who wished to speak against it, he was allowed to proceed. He began with a few sentences concerning the printing the paper, and immediately deviated into an eulogium on his own conduct. Guadet, the President, reminded him of the question.

'I have no need of your admonitions,' said Robespierre; 'I know very well on what I have to speak.'

'He thinks himself already Dictator,' exclaimed a member.

'Robespierre, speak against the printing,' said the President.

Robespierre then resumed, and declaimed on every thing except against the printing.

His voice was again drowned by an outcry against his wanderings. The President strove to procure silence, that Robespierre might be heard; which he no sooner was, than he accused the President of encouraging the clamour against him.

No accusation could be more unjust or more injudicious than this, because it was false, and because every body present was witness to its falsehood. The President had done all in his power that Robespierre might be heard, and had actually broken three bells by ringing to procure him silence.

The President then said, 'Robespierre, vous voyez les efforts que je fais pour ramener le silence—mais je vous pardonne une calomnie de plus.'

Robespierre resumed, and continued to speak of himself a considerable time in the most flattering terms.

Many people prefer speaking of themselves to any other topic of discourse, as well as Robespierre; but in him this propensity is irresistible. Praise acts as a cordial on the spirits of most people, but it is the praise they receive from others which has that effect: what is peculiar to Robespierre is, that he seems as much enlivened by the eulogies he bestows on himself, as others are by the applause of their fellow-citizens.

The panegyric he pronounced on his own virtues evidently raised his spirits, and inspired him with a courage which at last precipitated him into rashness. 'A system of calumny is established,' said he with a lofty voice, 'and against whom is it directed? against a zealous patriot. Yet who is there among you who dares rise and accuse me to my face?'

'Moi,' exclaimed a voice from one end of the hall. There was a profound silence; in the midst of which, a thin, lank, pale-faced man stalked along the hall like a spectre; and being come directly opposite to the tribune, he fixed Robespierre, and said, 'Oui, Robespierre, c'est moi qui t'accuse.'

It was Jean-Baptiste Louvet.

Robespierre was confounded: he stood motionless, and turned pale; he could not have seemed more alarmed had a bleeding head spoken to him from a charger.

John Moore.

[Nov. 3, 1792.]

(2)

Wordsworth's second visit to France ended with a stay in Paris from the third week in October to the end of December, 1792. Louvet's speech denouncing Robespierre was delivered in the Assembly on Oct. 29.

. . . To Paris I returned,
And ranged, with ardour heretofore unfelt,
The spacious city, and in progress passed
The prison where the unhappy Monarch lay,
Associate with his children and his wife
In bondage; and the palace, lately stormed
With roar of cannon by a furious host.
I crossed the square (an empty area then!)
Of the Carrousel, where so late had lain
The dead, upon the dying heaped, and gazed
On this and other spots . . .
   With early morning towards the Palace-walks
Of Orleans eagerly I turned; as yet
The streets were still; not so those long Arcades;
There, 'mid a peal of ill-matched sounds and cries,
That greeted me on entering, I could hear
Shrill voices from the hawkers in the throng,
Bawling, 'Denunciation of the Crimes
Of Maximilian Robespierre'; the hand,
Prompt as the voice, held forth a printed speech,
The same that had been recently pronounced,
When Robespierre, not ignorant for what mark
Some words of indirect reproof had been
Intended, rose in hardihood, and dared
The man who had an ill surmise of him
To bring his charge in oppenness: whereat,
When a dead pause ensued, and no one stirred,
In silence of all present, from his seat
Louvet walked single through the avenue,
And took his station in the Tribune, saying,
' I, Robespierre, accuse thee ! '

William Wordsworth
[' The Prelude '.]

107. REPUBLICAN MANNERS

J. L. David, the famous painter, and Jacobin deputy for Paris in the Convention, became the 'producer' of revolutionary functions, and the designer of official uniforms.

IT is not surprising, that a people of great sensibility, and naturally versatile, should fly from one extreme to another; yet one would hardly have expected that Republican manners would have been much to the taste of the French nation.

There is however in Paris at present, a great affection of that plainness in dress, and simplicity of expression, which are supposed to belong to Republicans. I have sometimes been in company, since I came last to Paris, with a young man, of one of the first families in France, who, contrary to the wishes and example of his relations, is a violent democrate. He came into the box where I was last night at the playhouse; he was in boots, his hair cropt, and his whole dress slovenly: on this being taken notice of, he said, 'That he was accustoming himself to appear like a Republican.' It reminded me of a lady, who being reproached with having a very ugly man for her lover, said, *C'est pour m'accoutumer à la laideur de mon mari.*

They begin to *tutoyer* each other, that is, to use in conversation the singular pronoun *tu*, instead of the plural *vous*, as the Romans did, and the Quakers do. They have substituted the name Citoyen, for Monsieur, when talking to or of any person; but more frequently, particularly in the National Assembly, they pronounce the name simply, as Buzot, Guadet, Vergniaud. It has even been proposed in some of the Journals, that the custom of taking off the hat and bowing the head should be abolished, as remains of the ancient slavery, and unbecoming the independent spirit of free men; instead of which they are desired, on meeting their acquaintance in the street, to place their right hand to their heart as a sign of cordiality.

David, the celebrated painter, who is a Member of the Convention and a zealous Republican, has sketched some designs for a republican dress, which he seems eager to have introduced; it resembles the old Spanish dress, consisting of a jacket with tight trowsers, a coat without sleeves above the jacket, a short cloak, which may either hang loose from the left shoulder or be drawn over both: a belt to which two pistols and sword may be attached, a round hat and feather, are also part of this dress, according to the sketches of David; in which full as much attention is paid to picturesque effect as to conveniency. This artist is using all his influence, I understand, to engage his friends to adopt it, and is in hopes that the Municipality of Paris will appear in it at a public feast, or rejoicing, which is expected soon. I said to the person who gave me this account, 'that I was surprised that David, who was so great a patriot, should be so anxious about an object of this kind.'

He answered, 'that David had been a painter before he was a patriot.'

Part of this dress is already adopted by many; but I have only seen one person in public completely equipped with the whole; and as he had managed it, his appearance was rather fantastical. His jacket and trowsers were blue; his coat, through which the blue sleeves appeared, was white with a scarlet cape; his round hat was amply supplied with plumage; he had two pistols stuck in his belt, and a very formidable sabre at his side: he is a tall man, and of a very warlike figure; I took him for a Major of Dragoons at least: on enquiry I find he is a miniature painter.

John Moore.
[Sept. 28, 1792.]

108. SCENES FROM THE FRONT

An anonymous booklet called A Tour through the Theatre of War in the Months of November and December, 1792, and January, 1793 (*London,* 1793) *contains 'a variety of curious, entertaining and military anecdotes,' some of which had already appeared as letters in the author's* Diary. *The victory of Jemappes (April 6) had enabled Dumouriez to free Belgium from the Austrians. Early next year the declaration of war against England and Holland (Feb.* 1) *encouraged him to invade Holland: but on March 16 he was heavily defeated at Neerwinden; and on April* 5, *he deserted to the enemy* (*v. No.* 114).

(1) PICARDY VOLUNTEERS

WE came to Calais in time to see one battalion of this regiment [of volunteers from Picardy] march away, and to say truth, their appearance accorded well with the bloody purpose they had manifested the evening before [to lynch the aristocrats in the town prison]. There was no uniformity in their uniforms, nor anything like equality in their size. Their arms were rusty, their accoutrements dirty, and some of them in the common dress of peasants. But in their looks was much determination, and though only embodied a month before, they marched and performed a few military motions with tolerable precision. The native *allegresse* of the French was here exhibited in lively colours. Some were laughing; some were singing in the ranks; some had their ammunition bread stuck upon their bayonets, and some had fiddles tied to their knapsacks—*Vive l'égalité*—No regard to rank and dignity is here a check to the freedom of social intercourse. . . . Many of them chaunted the Marseilles hymn, and many of them bad the inhabitants of Calais farewel! *Adieu*, said they, *bons citoyens de Calais; nous allons voir s'il y a des ennemis*. At this moment an officer stepped up to us, who, by the ease and familiarity of his address, seemed a true Frenchman of former times. *Ces messieurs sont Anglais* ? said he, and without waiting for our answer, continued: 'I have much esteem for the English; they are a generous nation; they send us muskets and knapsacks.' The English, said I, have little claim to generosity on that account: they send you muskets for your money; a Jew or a Dutchman would do the same. *C'est égal*, said he. I thought, however, that one compliment deserved another, and so I began to praise the apparent confidence of the soldiers who had just marched away. 'Tis true, said he, the poor fellows have but just put on the military harness, and yet they are absolutely careless of life. All our volunteers are the same. Formerly a village was a scene of desolation, when the *subdelegué* wanted a man or two for the militia. But now myriads of men spring up armed out of the earth. Inspired by the word liberty, they fight with an ardour unheard of before. 'Tis a perfect rage. They go foaming at the mouth to the attack of a battery, with as much contempt of the enemy's fire, as if they had been fed all their lives upon bullets. But I am sorry to say, that a lamentable spirit of insubordination and cruelty prevails among them. It is a disgrace to the nation.

(2) A YOUNG BELGIAN PATRIOT

A little further on, as we were going slowly up a hill, I saw a young lad walking very lame, and losing his shoe[s] at every moment in the mud. As he did not call upon pestilence and the devil to run away [with] them, and the road into the bargain, I was sure he could not be a Frenchman, although he had the national uniform on his back. We asked him if he also would get up behind, and he joyfully accepted our offer. But as the weather was cold, and he seemed weakly, we soon after found means to make room for him in our carriage. I then asked him if he had been wounded. *Dieu merci*, he had only been cut down at the battle of Gemappe, and then wounded in the foot while lying on the ground, which was the reason of his walking so lame. I told him he was too young to run such hazards, and bear the fatigues of a military life. Too young! said he, with a proud smile, that ill concealed a little indignation, too young! why, I am now nineteen, and near three years ago was shot through the body in the Belgic war. He added, that at the beginning of the present campaign he had been ill of a fever; that he had been sent to the hospital at Maubeuge; that in the time of his convalescence, he had walked out with some of his comrades; that they had fallen in with a party of French, who were engaged with the enemy at Grisoelle; that he had taken up a dead man's musket to have his shot, *tout comme un autre*, and that a ball from the rifle gun of a Tyrolean chasseur had hit him in the neck. When I inquired into the motives of his taking up arms, he said he had been on the side of the patriots before, and had heard that they were up again, and so he had left his home at Namur, where he had a father, a mother, and a little sister *assez aimable*, and he would leave them again as soon as it should please God and the blessed Virgin to cure the lameness of his foot; for a patriot should always fight for his country, and should not mind a wound or two, or a

ANON.

little pain in a good cause. I am now going to Brussels,
said he, to see some relations I have there. Go where thou
wilt, said I to myself, thou art a brave youth, and not only a
patriot, but a philosopher, although I verily believe thou
dost not know the meaning of the word.

(3) DUMOURIEZ'S ARMY

The second day after leaving Brussels brought us to
Liége, where we found General Dumouriez and his army;
a gallant army and a noble chief. The patient fortitude with
which the soldiers endured the hardships of a winter
campaign, was equal to the active courage with which they
stormed the redoubts of Gemappe. Encamped in the middle
of the month of December in a cold northern latitude, they
only seemed to regret the vigour of the season, because it
prevented them from marching after the enemy. Yet these
troops, of a nation so generally branded with effeminacy,
were ill provided against the bleakness of the weather, and
the endless continuance of the rain. The National volunteers,
the chief strength of the army, were bare of clothes, and straw
was as scarce as it was necessary in the camp. The small
quantity they had was no sooner spread in the tents, than it
was completely drenched, and by a natural consequence it
soon after rotted; so that the soldier lay with half his body
in the water, and if he set his foot out of the tent, he sunk
up to his knees in the mud. This was their situation when
encamped; but what was it when the necessity of the service
required whole divisions of the army to sleep on their arms,
with no other cover than the inclement sky. Frequently,
when the rain was pouring in a torrent from heaven, and
lying stagnant on the saturated earth, some of them reposed
their weary limbs in the water, some slept erect, girt to a
tree, while others danced away the lingering hours; and not
unfrequently, after such a night as this, they have been seen
to march away laughing, and singing their patriotic songs.
Gaiety was ever the Frenchmen's birthright, but never was
it so strongly exhibited as since they have been animated
by the spirit of patriotism. This cheerfulness is always

218

accompanied by another characteristic of the nation; an uncommon degree of carelessness and disregard of danger. In the plains of Champaign, the two armies were often within sight, and almost within shot of each other. At such times, there stood the Prussians, menacing a charge, in regular array, with supported arms, and motionless as statues; and *here* were the French, dancing in rings around their fires, and broiling their meat on the points of their bayonets.

On a march, woe to the game that gets up before them; a hundred soldiers are sure to send after it the contents of their muskets, not without danger of shooting their comrades. Even the presence of the enemy is insufficient to correct this deviation from discipline. It once happened, as a battalion of volunteers was advancing to the attack, in the momentary expectation of receiving and returning the enemy's fire, that they trod up a solitary hare. As she ran along the line, she was saluted with a universal shout, and with a shot or two at least from every company she passed. The fugitive however escaped, it being no easy a matter to kill so small an animal with a single ball.

. . . It was predicted that endless dissensions and jealousies would embroil the regular troops with the national guards; but the fears were so ill founded, that it is impossible to conceive an army living in more universal harmony than that of Dumouriez. At public and private tables, nothing is more common than to see the shoulder-knot of a grenadier touching the epaulet of a colonel; nor does this vicinage seem to surprize either party. The one shows no haughtiness, the other no servility, and both interchange upon equal terms the salutation of *citizen*, or *comrade*. Though a stranger may be startled at it at first, his wonder diminishes when he finds that not a few of the common national volunteers are men of property, some of them possessing ten, twenty, and thirty thousand livres a year. . . . Many of the officers, many even of the superior ranks, have been raised from that of private soldier. In a ball or a drawing-room, they would, no doubt, make an awkward figure; but surely after a long apprenticeship to war, they are as fit to lead a company or a battalion into the fire, as a giddy and beardless boy, just broke loose from the military school.

Republican severity is by degrees removing that foppishness in dress and manners that sprung from the example of a frivolous court. The small sword, that formerly dangled at the side of the French officers and soldiers, has resigned its place to a weighty sabre. The three-cornered hat, that sheltered them neither from rain, sun, nor blows, is very generally changed into a helmet. Their hair, for the most part cut short, is in the state nature gave it; and many of their whiskers grow unchecked by the razor. The whole of their dress, in short, bespeaks more attention to utility than show. Some of their new corps must however be excepted, particularly the legion of the celebrated St. George. This is a body of seven hundred men, composed of creoles, negroes and mulattoes, and is dressed and accoutred in the richest and most brilliant manner.

Anon.

109. THE KING'S TRIAL
(1)

F. D. Tronchet, a lawyer of 67, was deputy for the Third Estate of Paris in the States-General. C. G. Malesherbes, 72, had been an enlightened Minister de la Maison du Roi et des provinces (1774–6). *Monro does not mention R. de Sèze, who 'led' Louis' defence before the Convention.*

[DECEMBER 17TH.] The trial of His most Christian Majesty was to have come on last Friday, but after much confusion and violent debates it is now delayed till the 26th inst. Messrs. Tronchet and Malesherbes are to be his counsel; many have offered and only one named Target has refused; on his refusal the King fixed on the above two: the gratitude of the one and the propriety of the other's letter make me take the liberty of enclosing them. Ladies ambitious of defending their Sovereign's cause have even offered their services and were anxious to obtain that honour.

The National Convention have decreed that His Majesty

should again be permitted to communicate with the Royal family, but with that barbarity that has marked the whole of this Revolution, add that he shall not see them all together; if he sees the Royal children first, they are not to be seen afterwards by Her Majesty or Madame Elizabeth, but in the presence of some of the Municipality. The absurd reason they assign for this cruelty is that no messages may pass between the Royal family by means of the children; they are all in perfect health, and I am happy to find people more interested about them than they were.

Robespierre's party is still strong; Rolland's is strengthening with Brissot's, and Péthion within these few days has considerably altered his tone. Ministers I understand have been privately threatened by Robespierre's party, and Marat is suspected to be on the eve of deserting it: Chambon, the present Mayor, is reputed to be a moderate man and averse to the proceedings of the Municipality. Rolland and Brissot's party are certainly struggling to save the king in order to humble Robespierre's party, and I myself from everything I can learn have not the smallest doubt but they will succeed.

[December 27th.] His Most Christian Majesty made his appearance yesterday at the bar of the National Convention. He left the Temple about nine o'clock, and as he went as fast as the coachman could drive, he arrived at the Convention in about ten minutes. He appeared to me perfectly composed and in good health; his appearance and address had again a very great effect upon the people. He left the Convention about twelve o'clock, and returned to the Temple in the same style he left it, no disturbance of any kind happened, and everything at this moment is perfectly quiet. After His Majesty and his Council retired, the debates that ensued in the Convention were attended with the most extreme violence and confusion. A motion was made by Monsieur Manuel to suspend any farther proceedings on the business before them till the opinion of the eighty-four Departments was taken upon it. This was opposed by Robespierre's party, and increased the confusion. The president attempted to take the voice of the members on the motion, but eighteen or twenty of Robespierre's party flew from their seats, and with their fists clenched threatened the president in the most violent manner. Similar scenes continued till near five o'clock, when they adjourned and are to continue the same business to-morrow. The King makes no farther defence, so that the Convention have only to decide whether he is guilty or not, and what shall be his punishment. This I am confident embarrasses them much, and I have every reason to hope if he is not massacred his life will be saved, which I most fervently pray to the Almighty may be the case.

[December 31st.] The debates respecting the fate of His Most Christian Majesty have been carried on with still more indecency and violence since I had the honour of writing you on the 27th inst. Their debate on this business had scarcely begun on Thursday, when after a variety of opinions Monsieur St. Just proposed putting His Majesty to death without waiting for the opinion of the different Departments (for the referring his fate to them had been proposed by many). This unjust, and inhuman proposal gained universal applause from the Tribunes, which was even encouraged by some of the Deputies; the majority however resented this savage conduct, and the remainder of the day from 12 o'clock till six in the evening in the midst of this melancholy transaction which occupies even the mind of the most thoughtless, was spent in debating whether applauding on this occasion should be permitted or not. After blows, and the most scandalous behaviour that can possibly be conceived, it was decreed that applauding should be permitted, but that one of the members should be reprimanded for having encouraged it.

The debates since that have been carried on with a little more decency, though the bloodthirsty party of Robespierre exert every nerve to excite the Convention and the people to terminate the days of their unfortunate monarch: whether this will take place or not is however yet undecided. A majority of the Convention is clearly for sparing his life, and should it be referred to the Departments most of them are decidedly in his favour; much however is to be dreaded from the populace of Paris, whom Robespierre's party is exciting to the most execrable and most horrid act.

George Monro to Lord Grenville.

(2)

The indictment of the King was drawn up on Dec. 11. On the 27th he was questioned before the Convention.

I watched the King with the minutest attention, and I observed, that in looking around the Assembly, he happened to cast his eyes on the standards which had been taken from the Austrians and Prussians, and gave a sudden start, scarcely perceptible to any but a close observer, and from which he recovered himself in an instant. A wooden chair was brought, and Barrère invited him to be seated. He then read the whole of the charges, during which the King fixed his eyes upon him, but seemingly not with attention. From this circumstance, I did flatter myself (and there were many members of the Convention who also wished it) that like Charles the First, he would either deny the competency of the tribunal to try him, or have appealed to the people; but he adopted neither the one nor the other. To every charge he answered directly, without premeditation, and with such skilful propriety, that the audience were astonished; and this gave rise to an idle report, that Péthion had contrived to furnish him with a copy in the Temple. . . .

When he was accused of shedding the blood of Frenchmen, he raised his voice with all the consciousness of innocence, and in a very strong tone of indignation, replied, 'No, sir! I have never shed the blood of Frenchmen.' His spirit was evidently wounded at this charge, and I perceived a tear trickle down his cheek: but as if unwilling to give his enemies an opportunity of discovering any weakness in his conduct, he instantaneously wiped it away with his hand, and then gently rubbed his forehead, to denote that he was oppressed with heat. . . .

The King was plainly dressed in an olive silk coat, and looked remarkably well; Barrère the president wore a dark mixture, a scarlet waistcoat, and a lead coloured pair of kerseymore breeches, with white silk stockings. Péthion was elegantly dressed in black, as well as several of his party; Robespierre was also dressed in black; Orleans was habited in blue, and the majority of the members looked like blackguards; Legendre wore no neck cloth, and had his collar open à la Brutus. . . .

H. R. Yorke.

(3)

Paine's French was not good enough for a speech in the Convention; so he circulated this interesting suggestion in print. (See Conway's Life of Paine, *ii. 4).*

Let those United States be the guard and the asylum of Louis Capet. There, in the future, remote from the miseries and crimes of royalty, he may learn, from the constant presence of public prosperity, that the true system of government consists, not in monarchs, but in fair, equal, and honorable representation. In recalling this circumstance, and submitting this proposal, I consider myself a citizen of both countries. I submit it as an American who feels the debt of gratitude he owes to every Frenchman. I submit it as a man who, albeit an adversary of Kings, forgets not that they are subject to human frailties. I support my proposal as a citizen of the French Republic, because it appears to be the best and most politic measure that can be adopted. As far as my experience in public life extends, I have ever observed that the great mass of people are always just, both in their intentions and their object; but the true method of attaining such purpose does not always appear at once. The English nation had groaned under the Stuart despotism. Hence Charles I was executed; but Charles II was restored to all the powers his father had lost. Forty years later the same family tried to reestablish their oppression; the nation banished the whole race from its territories. The remedy was effectual; the Stuart family sank into obscurity, merged itself in the masses, and is now extinct.

Thomas Paine.

[Jan. 15, 1793.]

(4)

After the King's appearance before the Assembly (Dec. 26), a series of debates followed, till, on Jan. 14, it was determined to come at once to the vote. On the 15th, 707 deputies (all who were present) declared 'Louis Capet guilty of conspiracy against the safety of the state,' and a majority of 68 out of 711 decided against the 'appeal to the people,' which might have saved his life. On the 16th–17th (the voting went on all night), out of 721 votes cast, 366 (a majority of 5), were for death; when, on a recount, there were added to the majority the votes of those who had wished the execution of sentence to be delayed, it was 53. Finally, on the 19th, this suggestion of a surcis was put separately, and was lost by 70 votes.

I am sorry it has fallen to my lot to be the messenger of the most disagreeable intelligence, that I, or any one else was perhaps ever obliged to communicate. The National Convention after sitting near thirty-four hours on Thursday night, voted that the punishment of death should be inflicted upon His Most Christian Majesty. This unjust, and iniquitous judgment was carried by a majority of rather more than a hundred; fifty of this number, though they voted for death, differed in opinion from the rest in respect to the time it should be inflicted; some thinking it should not be put in execution till the war was finished, and others proposing it should be postponed, till the voice of the people was taken: Péthion and many of the leading members voted for death with these restrictions.

The sudden turn the opinions of the majority of the National Convention took, after what I at different times have had the honour of communicating to you can be more easily imagined than described; the King's friends were confounded, and amazement was strongly painted in the face of most men I had an opportunity of speaking to: few of the members who went to the National Convention on Thursday morning with a positive resolution voted as they intended; this sudden change in their sentiments can therefore only be imputed to fear or some such other base principle: that there was however some reason for this must be allowed, for, notwithstanding a report made to the Convention to the contrary, the mob had become very alarming, and had even threatened some of the members, particularly Mr. Villete, whom they threatened to massacre if he did not vote for the death of His Majesty.

If this was not the cause of such a sudden change in opinion it can then only be imputed to political views, which had for their object England and Spain making some proposals to save the life of His Majesty. For this reason they came suddenly to the resolution of passing sentence of death upon him, in hopes if possible to intimidate these two nations, whom they naturally suppose much interested for the life of the King. For this reason also, it is supposed death will not yet be inflicted upon him, in order to give these nations an opportunity of making proposals if they wish it: but should either of them declare war it is said His Majesty will immediately be put to death. This opinion Mr. Somers had from some of the members of the Comité de défense général; I however think it my duty to remark that this worthy and well informed gentleman is so much attached to His Royal Master, that on this occasion he may perhaps have thrown out such a hint in hope it might at least be tried by one of these powers in order if possible to save the life of the King. I am however myself really much afraid if His Majesty is not already dead he can scarcely be saved. The day I left Paris there were some thousands of armed men parading in different parts of the city ready to commit any sort of riot, and threatening destruction should the King not be put to death.

I cannot express the horror that was painted even in the countenance of every individual in the National Convention where the very worst of the very worst of mankind are assembled, when Égalité gave his vote for the death of His King and relation; Manuel in a very proper and spirited manner attacked him upon it. This execrable branch of the

House of Bourbon has had a remittance of more than twenty thousand livres sent him lately from England; this in some manner contributes to the payment of the assassins he and Robespierre have now in pay.

The King is perfectly reconciled to his fate, the situation of Her Majesty, Madame Elizabeth, and the Princess Royal is melancholy indeed. The last mentioned of this Royal Family has for some time past been unwell, and the indelicate conversation that took place in the Convention upon the Queen applying for her physician is not to be described. The Dauphin is perfectly well and universally beloved by all ranks of people. Should they attempt to put the King to death horrid scenes will then happen in Paris, indeed every one's mind is already prepared for it, and in order to intimidate the Royal party nothing but proscriptions and massacres are held out by Robespierre's party. One list is said to contain the names of more than forty thousand people. Many of the members of the National Convention I have spoke with never expect to escape, and fear possesses the mind of the strongest.

George Monro to Lord Grenville.

[Jan. 21, 1793.]

110. THE KING'S EXECUTION
(1)

The King was executed in what is now the Place de la Concorde on Jan. 21, 1793.

On the day of the execution, every shop was closed; a deadly stillness reigned throughout the streets, although throngs of curious people were threading their way, in mournful silence, towards the Boulevards, and the quarters through which the dismal *cortège* was to proceed towards the place of execution—the Place Louis XV—then called Place de la Révolution, where the guillotine was erected.

Although no apprehension could be entertained of any popular outbreak, or bold attempt of the Royalists, with a sufficient force, to rescue their King, yet measures were taken by the Republicans that seemed to indicate the fear of some *coup-de-main* to snatch their victim from their fangs. Every street leading to the Boulevards was occupied by troops, posted by Santerre, and cannon planted in different stations, by which the sad procession was to pass.

With my faithful Coté, whose democratic energies were now damped by the solemnity of the day, and who, notwithstanding his endeavours to appear indifferent, was every now and then sobbing and wiping off a falling tear, I went to the corner of the Rue Michaudière, and took up my position before the Bains Chinois. . .

The morning was bitterly cold and misty. The approach of the column was announced by a thundering roll of drums —it appeared to me that there must have been more than a hundred drummers; while now and then a flourish of trumpets added to the solemnity of the gloomy music of this unmelodious death-march. Thousands of National Guards and *fédérés*, followed by the populace of the Faubourgs, armed with pikes, and two brigades of field-pieces, preceded the immediate escort of the condemned monarch. The carriage he was in was nearly concealed by the mounted gendarmes that surrounded it, so that I could not catch a glimpse of his person. Santerre, with a numerous staff, followed, and the march was closed by hosts of soldiers belonging to the National Guard and the line, in marching order.

Notwithstanding the general excitement kept up by the Republican party, both by the distribution of money and liquor, a dead silence prevailed. Not a cry was heard during the progress of the funereal procession to the place of execution. One might have thought that the freezing atmosphere of the day had benumbed every tongue.

J. G. Millingen.

(2)

Henry Essex Edgeworth de Firmont (from a family estate at Firmount, near Edgeworthstown) left Ireland at the age of 4, was trained for the Catholic priesthood at Toulouse and Paris, and settled in the capital as spiritual director of the Irish colony there. In Feb. 1791, he became confessor to

Madame Elisabeth; and it was she who recommended him to the King. He stayed on in France, at risk of his life, till 1796. It is to be noticed that he does not mention the famous words, 'Son of St. Louis, rise to heaven': in fact, he never used them: they were invented by a royalist journal.

The unfortunate Louis XVI, foreseeing to what lengths the malice of his enemies was likely to go, and resolved to be prepared at all events, cast his eyes upon me, to assist him in his last moments, if condemned to die. He would not make any application to the ruling party, nor even mention my name without my consent. The message he sent me was touching beyond expression, and worded in a manner which I shall never forget. A King, though in chains, had a right to command, but he commanded not. My attendance was requested merely *as a pledge of my attachment for him, and as a favour, which he hoped I would not refuse. But as the service was likely to be attended with some danger for me, he dared not to insist, and only prayed (in case I deemed the danger to be too great) to point out to him a clergyman worthy of his confidence, but less known than I was myself, leaving the person absolutely to my choice.* . . . Being obliged to take my party upon the spot, I resolved to comply with what appeared to be at that moment the call of Almighty God; and committing to His providence all the rest, I made answer to the most unfortunate of Kings, that whether he lived or died, I would be his friend to the last. . . .

The King finding himself seated in the carriage, where he could neither speak to me nor be spoken to without witness, kept a profound silence. I presented him with my breviary, the only book I had with me, and he seemed to accept it with pleasure: he appeared anxious that I should point out to him the psalms that were most suited to his situation, and he recited them attentively with me. The gend'armes, without speaking, seemed astonished and confounded at the tranquil piety of their monarch, to whom they doubtless never had before approached so near.

The procession lasted almost two hours; the streets were lined with citizens, all armed, some with pikes and some with guns, and the carriage was surrounded by a body of troops, formed of the most desperate people of Paris. As another precaution, they had placed before the horses a number of drums, intended to drown any noise or murmur in favour of the King; but how could they be heard? Nobody appeared either at the doors or windows, and in the street nothing was to be seen, but armed citizens— citizens, all rushing towards the commission of a crime, which perhaps they detested in their hearts.

The carriage proceeded thus in silence to the Place de Louis XV, and stopped in the middle of a large space that had been left round the scaffold: this space was surrounded with cannon, and beyond, an armed multitude extended as far as the eye could reach. As soon as the King perceived that the carriage stopped, he turned and whispered to me, 'We are arrived, if I mistake not.' My silence answered that we were. One of the guards came to open the carriage door, and the gend'armes would have jumped out, but the King stopped them, and leaning his arm on my knee, ' Gentlemen,' said he, with the tone of majesty, 'I recommend to you this good man; take care that after my death no insult be offered to him—I charge you to prevent it.' . . . As soon as the King had left the carriage, three guards surrounded him, and would have taken off his clothes, but he repulsed them with haughtiness: he undressed himself, untied his neckcloth, opened his shirt, and arranged it himself. The guards, whom the determined countenance of the King had for a moment disconcerted, seemed to recover their audacity. They surrounded him again, and would have seized his hands. 'What are you attempting?' said the King, drawing back his hands. 'To bind you,' answered the wretches. 'To bind *me*,' said the King, with an indignant air. 'No! I shall never consent to that: do what you have been ordered, but you shall never bind me. . . .'

The path leading to the scaffold was extremely rough and difficult to pass; the King was obliged to lean on my arm, and from the slowness with which he proceeded, I feared for a moment that his courage might fail; but what was my astonishment, when arrived at the last step, I felt that he suddenly let go my arm, and I saw him cross with a firm foot the breadth of the whole scaffold; silence, by his look alone, fifteen or twenty drums that were placed opposite to me; and in a voice so loud, that it must have been heard at the Pont Tournant, I heard him pronounce distinctly these memorable words: *I die innocent of all the crimes laid to my charge; I pardon those who have occasioned my death; and I pray to God that the blood you are going to shed may never be visited on France.*

He was proceeding, when a man on horseback, in the national uniform, and with a ferocious cry, ordered the drums to beat. Many voices were at the same time heard encouraging the executioners. They seemed reanimated themselves, in seizing with violence the most virtuous of Kings, they dragged him under the axe of the guillotine, which with one stroke severed his head from his body. All this passed in a moment. The youngest of the guards, who seemed about eighteen, immediately seized the head, and shewed it to the people as he walked round the scaffold; he accompanied this monstrous ceremony with the most atrocious and indecent gestures. At first an awful silence prevailed; at length some cries of 'Vive la République!' were heard. By degrees the voices multiplied, and in less than ten minutes this cry, a thousand times repeated, became the universal shout of the multitude, and every hat was in the air. . . .

The Abbé Edgeworth.

III   THE EMIGRATION

The chief times of emigration were July, 1789 (the Fall of the Bastille), June, 1791 (the flight to Varennes), and August, 1792 (the fall of the throne); its chief centres, Turin, Coblentz, and Brussels. These two extracts, from Lady Knight's Letters from France, 1776–95, and the correspondence of Sir James Bland Burges, give one side of English opinion about the emigrants.

(1) ROME

I HAVE a strong pity for the emigrants, but very slender faith in the generality of them. Ambition and avarice are the two leading passions of the French, consequently self-love governs them, and I should be ashamed to say how very few I know and have known that I do not think hate all other nations; nor do I believe anything can be more hurtful to the English nation than that the French should be so mixed in our society; they will undermine our national character.

Lady Knight.
[Rome, March, 1792.]

(2) BRUSSELS

The chief magistrate of Brussels, upon refusal of non-residence to a noble emigrant, concluded with this remark, *C'est vous, monsieur, et vos confrères, qui causent tous les malheurs de l'Europe.*

It seems to be the determination of all the German States, etc., not to grant any asylum to the emigrants; but obliging a man to carry a musket contrary to his inclination and perhaps *temperament physique*, shows a want of policy on the one hand, and liberality on the other. It is very certain that the emigrants in many cities act with the usual imprudence of Frenchmen. Frequenting gambling-houses, etc., *car il faut vivre*. Running in debt is natural enough, and money borrowed is to return four hundred (on getting back to France) for twenty-five. I made it a point of frequenting the *tables d'hôte* in the different towns I passed through, and it appears that three principles actuated the emigrants—*l'honneur, l'ambition, et la crainte*. Two-thirds emigrated from ambition, and the other third may be divided between honour and fear. All the emigrants acknowledge this, and, what is very flattering to an Englishman, they all speak in raptures of the generosity of the British nation. But a Frenchman will be a Frenchman as long as he lives, and though Great Britain acts a noble part in this present very interesting period, yet consequences must be attended to, and conclusions drawn. Fifty thousand emigrants know the geography and almost every inch of

the Low Countries, etc., ten thousand that of England.
Journals are kept, remarks made, etc. What forms and com-
pletes a good general is knowing the *local*. I do not
choose to prophecy, but if the emigrants are restored to
their possessions without France being dismembered, it
will be the worst day that Europe ever saw, and particularly
Great Britain.

F. Daniel to Mr. Burges.

[undated, but probably 1794.]

112. PASSPORTS

*For Beckford's residence in Paris, v. No. 84. Foreigners in France were
generally well treated, even after the outbreak of war, and no measures were
taken to imprison them, or to sequestrate their property, till August, 1793.
But many Englishmen and Dutchmen thought it best to leave the country on the
outbreak of war with England and Holland in February, 1793. The* Comité
de Salut Public *was set up on April 6.*

I HAVE been for more than these ten days past in a constant
course of solicitation in order to obtain my passports.
The laws are positive against their being granted to any
subjects of countries at war with France, and it was not
without the most perseverant exertion that I have [at] length
procured an exception in my favour. My application to my
section or parish was the first step—from thence—to the
Revolution Committee—then to the Committee of Surveillance or Police—who referred me to the Committee of
Publick Safety. After tedious, tumultuous, and desultory
debates at all these assemblies the business was brought before
the Maison Commune, ci-devant Hotel de Ville. Here I
found tenfold opposition—a thousand strangers, English,
Dutch, Spaniards, etc., had been applying for 6 weeks
past in vain. . . . Your letter of the 9th was produced, and
in consequence of its proving the risks that my fortune (?)
would run by a longer stay in this country—the passport
was issued. I am tired and jaded to death—all my anxieties
redoubled by the thought of those you endure upon my
acct.—but there was no remedy—not an hour's idle delay

—and I may think myself in luck to have obtained my passport at all.

William Beckford to Thomas Wildman.

[May 3, 1793.]

113. AN ENGLISH FAMILY IN FRANCE

From A narrative of the sufferings of an English family (1795)·
E. D. F. J. Duquesnoy, deputy for Pas-de-Calais, had demanded the expulsion of foreigners from France (March 15), and was sent (April 4) with Carnot and four others on a mission to the Northern Army, beginning with Dunkirk.

OUR Family had, from motives of economy, resided in France since the year 1785. We were settled very agreeably at St. Omer, in Artois, well acquainted with all the best French families, and had a most pleasant English Society. Mr W. was enjoying much better health in France than in England; and so much pleased were we with our situation, that, though War had been declared against England, yet the extraordinary tranquillity of the place, and the publication by the national Convention of a Decree promising protection to all Strangers resident in the Country, and inviting them to remain in it under safeguard of the Law, deluded us into a belief of security, and determined us not to think of returning to England, at least till the storm appeared approaching, when we foolishly thought we should always have time to fly. It was a cruel stroke to us, when, in May 1793 (I think it was), the Representants Duquesnoy and Carnot shut the Port of Calais, at a moment when the town was full of strangers from the interior of the Kingdom ready to embark, and absolutely forbade any English leaving the Country. The Seals were also put on the Post Office. This gave us a momentary alarm, which, however, soon subsided, and the only ill consequence we then felt was that the communication with our friends in England was stopped for a time; yet we doubted not that this would soon be arranged by the way of Ostend, as had been usual in all former Wars, as we were informed by several English who had lived in France in those days, and who had remained entirely unmolested. Our remittances were drawn for us with the same facility as formerly, and the change was high in favour of England, at this time about 80 for a pound sterling. The calm continued uninterrupted at St. Omer; and as all the English resident there were persons who had been established many years in France, and with reason respected by the Townspeople, whose interest it was to preserve us in the country, none of us had an idea of fear respecting our personal security. In the month of June was granted (or at least winked at) a power to the Committee Revolutionaire at Calais to grant Passports by way of Ostend. These Passports were obliged to be signed by the Commander-in-Chief at Dunkerque. Several persons of our acquaintance who wished to leave France profited from it. Things continued in this state till the end of the month of July, the Allied troops victorious, and the general opinion that the French would be beaten.

Anon.

114. DUMOURIEZ'S TREACHERY

Dumouriez was followed by some 1,000 men, but many of them deserted soon afterwards.

WE are now in an extraordinary crisis, and it is not altogether without some considerable faults here. Dumouriez, partly from having no fixed principles of his own, and partly from the continual persecution of the Jacobins, who act without either prudence or morality, has gone off to the Enemy, and taken a considerable part of the Army with him. The expedition to Holland has totally failed, and all Brabant is again in the hands of the Austrians.

You may suppose the consternation which such a sudden reverse of fortune has occasioned, but it has been without commotion. Dumouriez threatened to be in Paris in three weeks. It is now three weeks ago; he is still on the frontier near to Mons with the Enemy, who do not make any progress. But if France and the National Convention act prudently this project will not succeed. In the first place there is a popular disposition against it, and there is force sufficient to prevent it. In the next place, a great deal is to be taken into calculation with respect to the Enemy. There are now so many powers accidentally jumbled together as to render it exceedingly difficult to them to agree upon any common object. . . .

Had this revolution been conducted consistently with its principles, there was once a good prospect of extending liberty through the greatest part of Europe; but I now relinquish that hope. Should the Enemy by venturing into France put themselves again in· a condition of being captured, the hope will revive; but this is a risk that I do not wish to see tried, lest it should fail.

Thomas Paine to Jefferson.

[April 20, 1793.]

115. A LETTER TO DANTON

On April 13, Danton had proposed a decree disclaiming any intention on the part of the Republic to interfere with the internal affairs of other countries, and establishing the death ·penalty for anyone proposing a transaction with foreign powers which did not recognize the principles of liberty and equality on which the French republic was based. The first Maximum law, requiring a return of all stocks of grain in the country, and empowering the authorities to fix the price at which it could be sold, was passed on May 4. The Constitution, which the Convention had been summoned to create, was still hanging fire, and was not achieved until after the expulsion of the Girondin leaders from the Assembly on June 2. This letter is reprinted from Conway's Life of Paine, *ii. 51.*

Paris, May 6th, 2nd year of the Republic [1793].

CITOYEN DANTON.

As you read English, I write this letter to you without passing it through the hands of a translator. I am exceedingly disturbed at the distractions, jealousies, discontents, and uneasiness that reign among us, and which, if they continue, will bring ruin and disgrace on the Republic. When I left America in the year 1787, it was my intention to return the year following, but the French Revolution, and the prospect it afforded of extending the principles of liberty and fraternity throughout the greater part of Europe, have induced me to prolong my stay upwards of six years. I now despair of seeing the great object of European liberty accomplished, and my despair arises, not from the intrigues of aristocracy and priestcraft, but from the tumultuous misconduct with which the internal affairs of the present revolution is conducted.

All that now can be hoped for is limited to France only, and I agree with your motion of not interfering in the government of any foreign country, nor permitting any foreign country to interfere in the Government of France. This decree was necessary as a preliminary toward terminating the war. But while these internal contentions continue, while the hope remains to the enemy of seeing the Republic fall to pieces, while not only the representatives of the departments but representation itself is publicly insulted, as it has lately been and now is by the people of Paris, or at least by the tribunes, the enemy will be encouraged to hang about the frontiers and await the issue of circumstances. . .

The danger every day increases of a rupture between Paris and the departments. The departments did not send their deputies to Paris to be insulted, and every insult shown to them is an insult to the departments that elected and sent them. I see but one effectual plan to prevent this rupture taking place, and that is to fix the residence of the Convention, and of the future Assemblies, at a distance from Paris.

I saw, during the American Revolution, the exceeding inconvenience that arose by having the government of Congress within the limits of any Municipal Jurisdiction. . . . In any one of the places where Congress resided, the municipal authority privately or openly opposed itself to the authority of Congress, and the people of each of those places expected more attention from Congress than their equal share with the other States amounted to. The same thing now takes place in France, but in a far greater excess.

I see also another embarrassing circumstance arising in Paris of which we have had full experience in America. I mean that of fixing the price of provisions. But if this measure is to be attempted, it ought to be done by the Municipality. The Convention has nothing to do with regulations of this kind; neither can they be carried into practice. The people of Paris may say they will not give more than a certain price for provisions, but as they cannot compel the country people to bring provisions to market, the consequence will be directly contrary to their expectations, as they will find dearness and famine instead of plenty and cheapness. They may force the price down upon the stock in hand, but after that the market will be empty.

There is also a circumstance to be taken into the account which is not much attended to. The assignats are not of the same value they were a year ago, and as the quantity increases the value of them will diminish. This gives the appearance of things being dear when they are not so in fact. . . .

As soon as a Constitution shall be established I shall return to America; and be the future prosperity of France ever so great, I shall enjoy no other part of it than the happiness of knowing it.

In the meantime I am distressed to see matters so badly conducted, and so little attention paid to moral principles. It is these things that injure the character of the Revolution, and discourage the progress of liberty all over the world. . .

There ought to be some regulation with respect to the spirit of denunciation that now prevails. If every individual is to indulge his private malignancy or his private ambition, to denounce at random and without any kind of proof, all confidence will be undermined and all authority be destroyed. Calumny is a species of Treachery that ought to be punished as well as any other kind of Treachery.

It is a private vice productive of public evils; because it is possible to irritate men into disaffection by continual calumny who never intended to be disaffected. It is therefore equally as necessary to guard against the evils of unfounded or malignant suspicion as against the evils of blind confidence. It is equally as necessary to protect the characters of public officers from calumny as it is to punish them for treachery or misconduct. . . .

I have written a letter to Marat of the same date as this, but not on the same subject. He may show it to you if he chuse.

Votre Ami,
Thomas Paine.

116. THE FALL OF THE GIRONDINS

On May 31—June 2, a popular insurrection forced the Assembly to put under arrest 27 leading deputies of the Girondin party. This fragment is from the Dropmore Papers. (*Hist. MSS. Comm. Rep.* 14.)

THIS city is in the greatest confusion. The cannon of alarm is just fired, and the tocsin rings everywhere. The minority, or *Maratists*, with the sections, want to murder the majority, and dissolve the Convention. . . Everything announces to-day the speedy dissolution of the Convention. The most sanguinary motives are making carnage and destruction hang suspended over the head of this guilty city. How I shall escape, Heaven only knows. I am afraid to go out this morning to acquire intelligence. The most hellish cries interrupt me every moment. . . . The Girondists have to-day all the power of the Convention in their hands, but Paris, with its sections and Jacobins, will in the end triumph. Blood and massacre will be the result of their success.

['Written in invisible ink between the lines of an ostensible letter on mercantile affairs. Without address or signature.' Paris, May 30, 1793.]

Anon.

117. MADAME ROLAND IN PRISON

Manon Phlipon, wife and inspirer of Roland de la Platière, the Girondin leader, was arrested during the insurrection of May 31—June 2, imprisoned in the Abbaye, St. Pélagie (Sept.–Oct.), and the Conciergerie, and executed on Nov. 8.

MADAME ROLAND was indeed possessed of the most distinguished talents, and a mind highly cultivated by the study of literature. I had been acquainted with her since I first come to France, and had always observed in her conversation the most ardent attachment to liberty, and the most enlarged sentiments of philanthropy: sentiments which she developed with an eloquence peculiar to herself, with a flow in power of expression which gave new graces and new energy to the French language. With these extraordinary endowments of mind she united all the warmth of a feeling heart, and all the charms of the most elegant manners. She was tall and well shaped, her air was dignified, and although more than thirty five years of age she was still handsome. Her countenance had an expression of uncommon sweetness, and her full dark eyes beamed with the brightest rays of intelligence. I visited her in the prison of St. Pelagie, where her soul, superior to circumstances, retained its accustomed serenity, and she conversed with the same animated cheerfulness in her little cell as she used to do in the hotel of the minister. She had provided herself with a few books, and I found her reading Plutarch. She told me she expected to die; and the look of placid resignation with which she spoke of it, convinced me that she was prepared to meet death with a firmness worthy of her exalted character. When I enquired after her daughter, an only child of thirteen years of age, she burst into tears; and at the overwhelming recollection of her husband and her child, the courage of the victim of liberty was lost in the feelings of the wife and the mother.

Helen Maria Williams.

[June, 1793.]

118. THE EXECUTIONER

The office of public executioner had been hereditary in the Sanson family for over a century. C. H. Sanson, who held the position from 1778 (he had done the work for his father since 1758) to 1795, was the fourth of his family to do so since 1684. He was assisted by his two brothers, and his elder son, till the latter's death (Aug. 27, 1792); and he was succeeded by his younger son, a captain of artillery (1795), and his grandson (1840).

I WENT into my chamber to write and sign a certificate for

them [two Englishmen], which I intended to take to the guard house to obtain their release. Just as I had finished it, a man came into my room, dressed in the Parisian uniform of a captain, and spoke to me in good English, and with a good address. He told me that two young men, English-men, were arrested and detained in the guard house, and that the section (meaning those who represented, and acted for the section) had sent him to ask me if I knew them, in which case they would be liberated. This matter being soon settled between us, he talked to me about the Revolu-tion, and something about the 'Rights of Man,' which he had read in English; and at parting offered me, in a polite and civil manner, his services. And who do you think the man was who offered me his services? It was no other than the public executioner, Samson, who guillotined the King, and all who were guillotined in Paris, and who lived in the same street with me.

Thomas Paine.
[July (?) 1793.]

119. LIFE UNDER THE TERROR

As a result of his 'Girondist' sympathies, which drove him into hiding during the summer of 1793, Paine was arrested on Dec. 31, and remained in prison till November, 1794.

I USED to find some relief by walking alone in the garden, after dark, and cursing with hearty good will the authors of that terrible system that had turned the character of the Revolution I had been proud to defend. I went but little to the Convention, and then only to make my appearance, because I found it impossible to join in their tremendous decrees, and useless and dangerous to oppose them. My having voted and spoken extensively, more so than any other member, against the execution of the King, had already fixed a mark upon me; neither dared any of my associates in the Convention to translate and speak in French for me anything I might have dared to have written. . . . Pen and ink were then of no use to me; no good could be done by writing, and no printer dared to print; and whatever I might have written, for my private amusement, as anecdotes of the times, would have been continually exposed to be examined, and tortured into any meaning that the rage of party might fix upon it. And as to softer subjects, my heart was in distress at the fate of my friends, and my harp hung upon the weeping willows.

As it was summer, we spent most of our time in the garden, and passed it away in those childish amusements that serve to keep reflection from the mind—such as marbles, Scotch hops, battledores, etc., at which we were all pretty expert. In this retired manner we remained about six or seven weeks, and our landlord went every evening into the city to bring us the news of the day and the evening journal.

Thomas Paine.

120. NATIONAL DEFENCE

Millingen's description is almost a mise-en-scène *of Carnot's famous decree of Aug. 23, 1793, mobilizing the nation.*

No words could describe the popular enthusiasm when a foreign invasion was expected. Every one flew to arms; pikes were fabricated by millions—every weapon that could arm a soldier—musket, pistol, fowling-piece, sword, or couteau de chasse, was deposited by the owner on the altar of the country in every section. Women, young and old, and little children, assembled by thousands in the churches, to make up linen for the army, and lint and bandages for the wounded; while every man who had two pairs of shoes, gave up one of them for the use of the volunteers proceeding to defend the frontiers. At the same time, leaden coffins were torn out of the vaults, the remains of the dead scattered in the streets, until the atmosphere was putrid, while the lead was cast into bullets, and little children were taught to make cartridges. The walls of the cellars of every house were regularly scraped, to be run into a lixivium for the extraction of saltpetre. The National Guard were drilled day and night, both in the manual and platoon exercise, and the use of artillery; while thousands flocked to the heights of Montmatre, Montrouge and other points covering the capital, on which field-works were thrown up. Thither they carried their humble meals in a basket, and worked from break of day until dark, with spade, mattock, and pick-axe. When exhausted with toil, they staggered to their distant homes, still singing the burthen of the *Marseillaise*.

J. G. Millingen.

121. ENGLISH NEGOTIATIONS

Sampson Perry, radical editor of the Argus, *fled to Paris at the end of 1792, and frequented the society of Helen Maria Williams, her companion J. H. Stone (who had acted as his Paris correspondent), and her Jacobin friends. Of these, Hérault de Séchelles, ex-aristocrat and friend of the Queen, deputy in the Legislative Assembly and the Convention, became a member of the first Committee of Public Safety (May 30, 1793), and was re-elected on to the second committee (July 10); but fell under suspicion of improper dealings with foreign powers, was arrested (March 17, 1794), and executed with the Dantonists.*

It is difficult to credit some of the details of Perry's story; for Stone and Miss Williams were both imprisoned in October, 1793, and after release, seem to have remained in Paris, or at Marly, until July, 1794, when they went to Switzerland.

THE Parisian newspapers having, about this time, made the persecution of the English ministry against free writers a frequent topic, I was particularly named, in some of them, as having been forced to take refuge in that city. To this notoriety, I impute the invitation I received from a lady, whom I mention with equal pleasure and gratitude, for the public spirit, the assistance she gave the cause of her country, and for the great solicitude she evinced to prevent, as much as lay in her power, the patriots of any nation from falling in the struggle of her own. This lady, notwithstanding her fortune was daily diminishing by the progress of the revolution, kept an open house every Sunday, for all those friends to the rights of mankind, who had distinguished themselves in any manner, or in any part of the world. . . . There were seldom fewer than twenty persons at this plain *civic dinner*; and those whom I most recollect at this time were Herault de Sechelles, Anacharsis Cloots, Chabot, Symon, Aristide Couthon, Saint André, Chales, Maribon Montaut, Massieu, Laignelot, Tallien, Breard, David, Julien de Toulouse, and Nioche. . . . Herault de Sechelles, as well as Couthon, had been, by the Convention, nominated a member of the committee of public safety. Herault was a man of talents, but inclined to *vanity*—a dangerous propensity in a revolution, one of the objects of which is, to establish a simplicity of manners. He could speak English; and as all hope of making up the difference with England was not extinguished, he was fixed on by the other members to take the *diplomatic part* upon himself. He called upon me a few days afterwards, paid many compliments to my nation, and, after a preface . . . he made no hesitation to say, that it was the desire of the committee to open a communication with England again, if it could be done consistently with the honour of France, and the views of the people. . . . He added, that he found, on coming into office, a project laid down by his predecessors for commencing such a treaty with the English opposition; but as two noblemen's names were most conspicuous in it, he was persuaded nothing could be done with it; such was the inveterate prejudice the whole country had against titles. He now entered into particulars. He said that the committee had fixed their expectations on Mr. Sheridan, as a man of talents, and zeal in the cause of philosophy and national good fellowship; that moreover, not being of the *privileged cast*, there would be no jealousy excited in the minds of the French against such a treaty, should it fail of its effect. He knew I had a female relation in France; he suggested, therefore, that the committee would give her and a friend passports, if I would consent to try the experiment. . . . But not to be too particular concerning this circumstance in this place, . . . I shall only observe that the result of the next conversation was my sending my friend and her companion to England with letters to Mr. Sheridan, and two others of some note in the opposition. . . . The letters, I am informed, were delivered . . . *Parties* at this time degenerated into *factions*; and whether it was suspected by his colleagues that Herault de Sechelles made an improper use of his authority as a member of the committee, I know not, but his influence declined soon after; insomuch that he was presently denounced, and a decree of accusation issued against him: one article in which was, that 'he had given information to the English injurious to the interests of France.' He was immediately imprisoned. . . .

Sampson Perry.

122. PARIS DURING THE TERROR

(1)

So few Englishmen remained in Paris and out of prison during 1794 that this letter has some value. It is from the Dropmore Papers (*cf. No. 116*).

ON my return from Havre de Grace I found yours of the 5th instant. I note the contents. I have been under the necessity to return here, as I could not get horses or any conveyance from Havre de Grace to go to Brest, and it [is] very expensive in this country at this time, more so than it is in England; and I never found the cold so much in England as I do here, and what the people will do for bread I cannot tell; there is not any to be got without you have a card from the section, saying how much you are to have. There is ten gentlemen in the house with me, besides the servant, and we are allowed four loaves for the house, which I suppose is about 12 pounds. However, we are much better off here than they are in the country. I find that there is many places that there is not any to be got. I shall leave this to-morrow morning, and I am told it will take me 16 days to go there; the road is so very bad, and no horses to be got, and some part of the road we must have a guard of soldiers, as I understand that there is 40 to 50 thousand men in arms in La Vendée, but not altogether in one body. You will hear from me at all opportunities till the latter part of March, when I shall sail for America.

Thomas Eldred to Sarah Eldred.
[Paris, Jan. 19, 1794.]

(2)

Archibald Hamilton Rowan (his third name came with property inherited from his grandfather), joined the 'United Irishmen,' and was imprisoned at Dublin in 1794. His Autobiography (ed. Drummond, 1840) describes his escape in a small boat to France, where he had lived in 1781–4, and his experiences there at a time when most British subjects were in prison. At first imprisoned at Brest, he was soon sent to Paris, and well treated, as a rebel against the British Government: ultimately he got away again, stayed with friends at Rouen and Havre, and in July, 1795, reached America.

'Mr. Sullivan' is probably Jean Baptiste O'Sullivan, one of Carrier's lieutenants at Nantes, and a witness at his trial. Prieur de la Marne and Jean Bon St. André were both members of the Committee of Public Safety. The 'decree acknowledging God' is that proposed by Robespierre in his speech of May 7, 1794. 'Citizen Herman' was head of the Commission des administrations civiles, police, et tribunaux, set up by the decree of April 1, 1794. The quarrels in the Committee that led to the fall of Robespierre, the execution of his supporters on the Paris Commune, and the anti-Jacobin reaction of Thermidor are here seen from a fresh angle.

On reading my letter, Mr. Sullivan happening to recollect the name, came into the prison, and finding I was the person he supposed, promised to write to the *Comité de Salut Public* for me; and by the return of the post, he got orders to Prieur de la Marne, who had replaced Jean Bon St. André at Brest, to liberate me, and send me and Sullivan to Paris; for which place we set out the next morning, in a *Berline à quatre chevaux*, with the tricolour flag flying from the roof as usual, as a representative of the nation, and at its expense. . . . As we passed along, in various demesnes we saw hanging on the trees, and on most of the substantial-looking houses, notices of *'Propriété Nationale à Vendre.'*

On our arrival at Orleans, the decree acknowledging God, and the immortality of the soul, which had just passed the Convention, was about to be promulgated by a great fête!

All the public functionaries, of every sort, civil and military, were assembled at the chief church, which was then opened for the public. About half way up the very handsome steeple of the church, a large board was placed, on which the words '*Le peuple François reconnoit l'Etre Suprême et l'Immortalité de l'Ame*' was blazoned in large gold letters, with a screen before it. At a signal the screen fell, amidst the firing of cannon and musketry, and bands of music playing, while the multitude responded, '*Vive Robespierre!*' who was supposed to be the framer of the decree.

We continued our route to Paris, where we arrived the same night and drove to the Committee of *Salut Public*.

I had been suffering under an attack of fever, which hung over me from the time I left Brest, and which rendered me almost incapable of answering the few questions put to me by Robespierre, who on seeing my situation, dismissed us, and ordered our attendance on the next morning. My fever had however, increased so much during the night, that I could not rise from my bed; and Monsieur Colon, the chief surgeon of the army, was ordered by the Committee to attend me. I was lodged in a superb suit of apartments, in the *Hotel de la Place République* (formerly Palais Royale) with orders to furnish me with every thing I could require, *au depens de la nation.* . . .

I can scarcely speak highly enough of the constant attendance of Monsieur Colon both day and night; nor his absolute refusal of the most trifling gratuity. In about six weeks I was sufficiently convalescent; and I waited on the *Comité de Salut Public.* Some few questions concerning the state of parties in Ireland and England were put to me, and I was then dismissed, and ordered to apply to Citizen Herman, Intendant of the Finance, for anything I should require. . .

I now took lodgings in the hotel in which my mother had lived, and where my eldest son was born. It was in the Rue Mousseau, and had been bought by, or given to a lock-smith, who had formerly been employed at Versailles. In this house I witnessed several of the inconveniencies of a revolutionary government. He was ordered to prepare carriages for four heavy guns. He had no plan or model given him, nor was it in his line of business; yet he was made responsible for the wood as well as the iron work. I saw one of these carriages rejected four times by the inspector, who could not even point out its faults. Another extortion practised upon housekeepers, was the searching for salt-petre. This was carried on by persons who demanded entrance into the cellars, and forced the proprietors to remove casks, bottles, wood, or any thing that came in their way. Unless well paid, they instantly commenced excavations; in this case, the owner of the house was obliged to pay, according to their very erroneous measurement, a certain sum per cubic foot for the earth removed, and as much more for that which they brought, as they said, to fill up the cavity.

The dissension between the members of the *Comité de Salut Public* now became serious. Callot, d'Herbois, Barrere, and their partizans, industriously heaped the odium of all the measures of severity upon Robespierre, hoping to screen themselves from enormities which were common to all such governments. In this they were seconded by all the enemies to the revolution; and their united efforts, on the 9th. Thermidor, brought Robespierre, Couthon, and St. Just, to the scaffold, rather than any excessive cruelty they had been guilty of, which was the order of the day, under the pretence of public good.

In two days after the execution of Robespierre, the whole commune of Paris, consisting of about sixty persons, were guillotined in less than one hour and a half, in the Place de la Revolution; and though I was standing above a hundred paces from the place of execution, the blood of the victims streamed under my feet. What surprised me was, as each head fell into the basket, the cry of the people was no other than a repetition of '*A bas le Maximum!*' which was caused by the privations imposed on the popu-lace by the vigorous exaction of that law which set certain prices upon all sorts of provisions, and which was attributed to Robespierre. The persons who now suffered were all of different trades; and many of them, indeed, had taken advantage of that law, and had abused it, by forcing the farmers and others who supplied the Paris market, to sell at the maximum price, and they retailed at an enormous advance to those who could afford to pay. I did not see Robespierre going to the guillotine; but have been informed that the crowd which attended the waggon in which he passed on that occasion, went so far as to thrust their umbrellas into the waggon against his body.

From this period everything bore a new face. Marat's bust and the *bonnet de liberté* were torn down and trampled upon in the theatres and other public places. The revolutionary committees, one of which was established in each of the forty-eight districts into which Paris was divided, were reduced to twelve. The armourers, and other workmen, who had been brought from Liege and other places to Paris, to work for the republic, were sent back to their different habitations. The meetings of the citizens in their sections, which took place every *Quintidi* and *Decadi*, were limited to *Decadi* only. The hour of meeting was changed from evening to noon; and the allowance which had been made by government of one day's labour to all citizens attending those meetings was discontinued. But the greatest alteration which now took place was that of dispersing the Jacobin Club. Several noted members of this society were imprisoned, while those who had been confined on suspicion of incivism, were released in great numbers.

It now became a measure of personal safety, to be able to declare that one had been imprisoned during Robespierre's tyranny. It was dangerous even to appear like a Jacobin, as several persons were murdered in the streets, by *La Jeunesse Parisienne*, merely because they wore long coats and short hair.

On my first arrival in Paris, there was an immense number of houses on which was painted in large letters, '*Propriété Nationale à vendre*'; and on almost all others, the words,'*Liberté, Egalité, Fraternité, ou la mort.*' After the death of Robespierre, the *three* last words were decided to be terrorist, and were expunged every where. At the time of the horrid explosion of the powder magazine in the *Plaine de Grenelle*, dismay appeared on the countenance of almost everyone. By this dreadful catastrophe seven hundred workmen lost their lives; and their widows were inscribed on the books of the section—(I lived in the *Section des Champs Elisées*) as having lost their husbands on that day, and being thrown on the republic for support. Every misfortune prior to this time had been laid on Pitt and Coburg; *now* the Jacobins were considered to be the evil genii of the French nation; so that this accident, and some fires which took place about this time in Paris, were attributed to them. I thought it a doubtful case whether the renewed Committee of *Salut Publique* would hold up against the Jacobin party; but the former was seconded by the Royalist party, who were duped into the idea that royalty would be well re-established the moment the Jacobins were effectually overthrown. The Royalists, however, by this coalition became ultimately victorious over both parties.

Archibald Hamilton Rowan.

123. TRIBUNAL AND GUILLOTINE

The Tribunal extraordinaire criminel, *reorganized by a Decree of Sept. 5, 1793, in four sections, and, called from October onwards* Tribunal révolutionnaire, *sat in the Palais de Justice. M. J. A. Herman and Dumas were the presiding judges.*

In the centre of the hall, under a statue of justice, holding scales in one hand, and a sword in the other, with the book of laws by her side, sat Dumas, the president, with the other judges. Under them were seated the public accuser, Fouquier-Tinville, and his scribes. Three coloured ostrich plumes waved over their turned up hats, *à la Henri IV*, and they wore a tri-coloured scarf. To the right were benches on which the accused were placed in several rows, and gendarmes, with carbines and fixed bayonets by their sides. To the left was the jury.

.   .   .   .   .

Never can I forget the mournful appearance of these funereal processions to the place of execution. The march was opened by a detachment of mounted gendarmes—the carts followed; they were the same carts as those that are used in Paris for carrying wood; four boards were placed across them for seats, and on each board sat two, and sometimes three victims; their hands were tied behind their backs, and the constant jolting of the cart made them nod their heads up and down, to the great amusement of the spectators. On the front of the cart stood Samson, the executioner, or one of his sons or assistants; gendarmes on foot marched by the side; then followed a hackney-coach, in which was the *Rapporteur* and his clerk, whose duty it was to witness the execution, and then return to Fouquier-Tinville, the *Accusateur Public*, to report the execution of what they called the law.

The process of execution was also a sad and heart-rending spectacle. In the middle of the Place de la Révolution was erected a guillotine, in front of a colossal statue of Liberty, represented seated on a rock, a Phrygian cap on her head, a spear in her hand, the other reposing on a shield. On one side of the scaffold were drawn out a sufficient number of carts, with large baskets painted red, to receive the heads and bodies of the victims. Those bearing the condemned moved on slowly to the foot of the guillotine; the culprits were led out in turn, and, if necessary, supported by two of the executioner's valets, as they were formerly called, but now denominated *élèves de l'Executeur des hautes oeuvres de la justice*; but their assistance was rarely required. Most of these unfortunates ascended the scaffold with a determined step —many of them looked up firmly on the menacing instrument of death, beholding for the last time the rays of the glorious sun, beaming on the polished axe; and I have seen some young men actually dance a few steps before they went up to be strapped to the perpendicular plane, which was then tilted to a horizontal plane in a moment, and ran on the grooves until the neck was secured and closed in by a moving board, when the head passed through

what was called, in derision, *la lunette republicaine*; the
weighty knife was then dropped with a heavy fall; and, with
incredible dexterity and rapidity, two executioners tossed
the body into the basket, while another threw the head after
it.

J. G. Millingen.

124. ENGLISH ADVICE TO ROBESPIERRE

*This letter, the writer of which was an English resident at Boulogne, is
taken from* Papiers inédits trouvés chez Robespierre (*ii.* 177). *It doubtless
influenced Robespierre's speech of Jan. 28, 1794, denouncing England.*

Au citoyen Maximilien Robespierre, député à la Convention nationale.

. . . Je suis bien convaincu qu'une voie est maintenant
ouverte par laquelle la vérité peut entrer triomphante dans
notre île. Il me reste à désirer que cette voie soit aplanée, et
gardée par une sagesse égale à celle qui a su la montrer.
Empêche, Robespierre, je te le conjure, qui on y jette les
pierres de la discorde. . . . Les épithètes injurieuses que
l'on prodigue à notre caractère national ou individuel,
ne sont-elles pas pourtant des obstacles non moins fatals
aux progrés de la vérité? Je ne m'arrête pas pour prouver
qu'elles sont injustes, quoique le fait que je t'envoie m'en
fournirait une belle occasion. Tu sais bien que tout peuple
est essentiellement bon, *même celui à qui j'appartiens*. Je ne
m'arrête pas même pour examiner si ces injures sont l'effet
d'une irritation patriotique de l'ignorance ou de la mal-
veillance; j'insiste seulement que les intérêts de l'humanité
demandent qu'elles soient bannies absolument de cette
discussion solennelle, et discréditées partout autant qu'il
soit possible.

Fais voir sa malheureuse servitude à l'Anglais, avec bien-
veillance, avec délicatesse; tandis qu'il apprend à regarder
son gouvernement comme un fardeau qui l'écrase, et ses
gouverneurs actuels comme des tigres qui le déchirent,
qu'on lui présente les républicains français comme ses

bienfaiteurs, comme ses frères. Ce n'est pas la calomnie qui
l'éclairera . . . Que la douce fraternité introduise la vérité
juisqu'a dans ses foyers. . . .

Salut et fraternité
N. S. J. Patterson
4 Pluv. An. II [Jan. 23, 1794].

125. ROBESPIERRE AT HOME

In the summer of 1791 *Robespierre moved from the rue Saintonge to* 366 *rue
St. Honoré, where, in a* 2-*storied house round a builder's yard, lived Maurice
Duplay, a* maître menuisier, *with his wife, his daughters Eléonore, Victoire,
and Elisabeth, his son Jacques-Maurice, and his nephew Simon, who had
lost a leg at the battle of Valmy. In a later note Millingen says it was chiefly
from the daughters that he derived his information about Robespierre: if this
interview took place in* 1794, *he was only* 12 *at the time. The two Albittes,
A. L. and J. L., both deputies in the Convention, were sons of F. A. Albitte,*
Sieur Dorival. *David Williams, a Unitarian Minister, spent the winter of*
1792 *in Paris, and became, like Paine, Girondist in sympathy.*

HE lived in an obscure house, No. 396, in the Rue St.
Honoré, at a carpenter's, of the name of Duplay, with
whose family he boarded. Strange to say, I observed, over
the street entrance, a wooden eagle, that looked like a figure-
head of a ship. A singular coincidence in the dwelling of a
man who, beyond a doubt, aimed at dictatorship. I was
ushered into a large room in the *rez-de-chaussée*, at the bottom
of a timber-yard, and was most kindly received by an
intelligent young man with a wooden leg, whom I thought
was his brother, but found to be a nephew of the landlord,
and Robespierre's secretary: I read to him my memorial,
but when he saw that it was in favour of an Englishman,
he shook his head, and frankly told me, that I had but little
prospect of succeeding in my application. He himself
ushered me into Robespierre's *cabinet*. He was reading at
the time, and wore a pair of green preservers: he raised his
head, and turning up his spectacles on his forehead, received
me most graciously. My introducer having stated that I was
*un petit ami de Dorival Albitte—un petit Anglais, Que veux-tu?
que demandes-tu?* was his brief and abrupt question. I referred

him to the contents of my memorial, on which he cast a mere glance, and then said, 'If it were in my power to liberate an Englishman, until England sues for peace, I would not do it—but why come to me? Why not apply to the Comité? Every one applies to me, as if I had an omnipotent power.' Here a strange twitching convulsed the muscles of his face. At this present moment I recollect the agitation of his countenance. He then added, 'Your brother is much safer where he is. I could not answer for the life of any Englishman were he free. All our miseries are the work of Pitt and his associates; and if blood is shed, at his door will it lie. Do you know, *enfant*, that the English here set a price on my head, and on the heads of every one of my colleagues? That assassins have been bribed with English gold—and by the Duke of York—to destroy me? The innocent ought not to suffer for the guilty, otherwise every Englishman in France should be sacrificed to public vengeance.'

I was astonished. After a short pause he added, ' Do you know that the English expected that this Duke of York would have succeeded the Capets? Do you know Thomas Paine and David Williams?' he continued, looking at me with an eagle eye; 'they are both traitors and hypocrites.'

He now rose, and paced up and down his room, absorbed in thought; he then suddenly stopped, and, taking me by the hand, said '*Adieu, mon petit, ne crains rien pour ton frère.*' He then turned off abruptly, and my guide led me out.

There was something singularly strange and fantastic in this extraordinary man, at least, so it appeared to me. He smiled with an affected look of kindness; but there was something sardonic and demoniac in his countenance, and deep marks of the small-pox added to the repulsive character of his physiognomy. He appeared to me like a bird of prey—a vulture; his forehead and temples were low and flattened; his eyes were of a fawn colour, and most disagreeable to look at; his dress was careful, and I recollect that he wore a frill and ruffles, that seemed to me of valuable lace. There were flowers in various parts of the room, and several cages, with singing-birds, were hanging on the walls and near the window, opening on a small garden. There was much of the *petit-maître* in his manner and appearance, strangely contrasting with the plebeian taste of the times.

On taking my leave, his secretary told me that he was certain Robespierre would be glad to see me, if ever I needed his assistance. I availed myself of this permission, and called upon him several times, although I only saw him once after my first introduction; indeed, it was very difficult to obtain access to his presence. On these occasions I never observed about the house those bands of ruffians by whom he was said to be guarded, although his door was crowded with wretched postulants who claimed his protection and influence.

J. G. Millingen.

126. DANTON AND BARÈRE

There is a well-known pencil sketch of Danton by David. A man who cultivated the tastes of the day, and an admirer of Rousseau, whilst Rousseau was admired, Barère may well have kept a 'cabinet' of natural history specimens.

THE only member of the Government I saw, whose brutality revolted me, was Danton. There was something inexpressibly savage and ferocious in his looks, and in his stentorian voice. His coarse shaggy hair gave him the appearance of a wild beast. To add to the fierceness of his repulsive countenance, he was deeply marked with the small-pox, and his eyes were unusually small, and sparkling in surrounding darkness, like the famous carbuncle. David, who looked upon him as a demi-God, attempted several times to delineate this horrid countenance, but in vain; exclaiming: *'Il serait plus facile de peindre l'éruption d'un volcan, que les traits de ce grand homme.'* . . .

This monster gave me but little consolation regarding my brother; and, after having cast a hasty glance on my petition, he vociferated: 'You may thank your stars, *petit malheureux*, that you and all your family have not been sacrificed to public indignation, to avenge the wrongs inflicted on us by your perfidious country!'

.   .   .   .   .

At this period, I also saw Barrère, to whom I had been introduced both by the Albittes and my old friend Dugazon, the comedian. He lived in the Rue St. Honoré, near the Place Vendôme, in an elegant apartment, the ante-chamber of which was ever crowded with petitioners, soliciting his assistance. He was a man of highly polished manners, possessing much suavity, and would have been thought of gentle disposition. He spoke English tolerably well. In his room was a collection of shells, and when he observed that I was looking at them with a curious eye, he said, 'As the son of a Dutchman, I suppose you must like shells'; and when he heard me remark on the beauty of some of his, he gave me some very valuable duplicates. He made the same observation as Robespierre on my brother's imprisonment and added 'that the English were much safer in a *maison de détention* than if they were at large in such troublesome times.'

J. G. Millingen.

127. THERMIDOR

On Sept. 13, 1794, His Majesty's ship Alexander *(74 guns) under Captain Bligh, left Portsmouth with three other ships and a convoy, bound for the Mediterranean. Chased by a French squadron of 9 sail off St. Vincent, and parted from her companions, the* Alexander, *after 2¼ hours' fighting, surrendered. The survivors, including Major Trench of the Marines, were taken on board* Le Marat, *Captain Le Franq, and landed at Brest. In* Letters *written in France to a Friend in London (1796), Major Trench describes his experiences at Quimper between Nov. 1794 and May, 1795.*

MY residence among the French is not yet six weeks old; and in this short space of time, wonderful has been the alteration of opinion. When we were taken, I was perpetually stunned with the exclamations of *Vive la Montagne! Vivent les Jacobins!* But suddenly, *La Montagne* is become the theme of execration, and the Jacobin club is cashiered.

I gained a confirmation of these events oddly enough. I had observed the disuse of these ridiculous cries for some days, and had overheard a conversation which had raised my suspicions. To ascertain their justness, I bade one of the boys call out as before. 'Ah!' said he, 'that is forbidden; *à présent il faut crier, au diable la Montagne! à bas les Jacobins!*' which he immediately ran along the deck exclaiming. The memory of Robespierre they have uniformly affected to hold in abhorrence; but if I may trust to a hint, which was imparted to me on board the prison-ship, very different was once the tone of Captain Le Franq, and all his officers. They now load the character of this extraordinary man, before whom, not six months since, they prostrated themselves like reptiles, with all the assassinations and misery which have overspread France during the last two years. To him alone, it seems, every crime which stains the national character is imputable.

Major Trench ["on board Le Marat, Brest-Water," Dec. 18, 1794].

128. THE REVOLUTION IN BRITTANY

Three out of these four extracts describe the state of religion in Brittany, after the Civil Constitution of the Clergy (Oct. 1790) had first been overlaid by Culte de l'Etre Suprême (May, 1794), and then replaced by the 'Disestablishment' law of Feb. 1795. The third extract is concerned with the Rising of the 12th Germinal (April 1) in Paris, and the character of the local Vigilance Committee.

(1) QUIMPER CATHEDRAL

[MARCH 2, 1795.] On leaving the representative, after presenting to him the Admiral's letter, as I was going out of the door, I heard the sound of an organ, proceeding from the cathedral, which was very near the house: I went in, and found mass celebrating in the presence of a congregation consisting chiefly of poor people from the country, with a few of the higher ranks, many more of whom, I was assured, would have been there, could they have believed themselves secure from reproach; but the return of religious

worship was yet too young for them to incur the risk—
they were all kneeling at their devotions, with great
appearance of fervency, while a fine grey-headed respectable-
looking priest, habited in his pontificals, officiated at the
altar. I walked the whole length of the church, through rows
of people on their knees, which formerly might have been
deemed disrespect in a heretic; but now I met with nothing
but courtesy and regard, all seeming conscious that the basis
of their persuasion and mine was the same, however we
might differ in external forms of adoration. Here I had leisure
to contemplate the scene of desolation which this venerable
temple presented. At least half the windows of fine old
painted glass, 'richly dight,' were broken; all the monuments
torn down; and the bones of the dead exposed to view, and
commingled with the ruins of their tombs, the names and
armorial devices being utterly defaced, and the coffins
taken away and converted into bullets. When the service
was finished, I went within the railing which incloses the
altar, to look at a large picture, representing the Ascension,
the figures of which are pierced through in more than
twenty places, by sabres and bayonets. An old man, who
was kneeling near the rails, observing my attention fixed on
the painting, told me, that in the vacant side-compartments
once stood two other pictures taken from holy writ: 'But,'
said he, 'they were so cut and hacked, that *we* were under
a necessity of taking them away.' A gentleman, who had
joined me in the church, informed me, that the altar and
confessionals which I saw had been brought hither from
another church; for that those belonging to this had been
either burnt, or broken into a thousand pieces: nay, that
the figures, with which the altar had been adorned, were
carefully separated from it, and triumphantly guillotined
in the middle of the great square of the town.

(2) A TEMPLE OF REASON

[April 4, 1795.] A building which would have excited
my curiosity more than the palaces of bishops and the
houses of nobility, I arrived here too late to see—a Temple of

Reason, built for the exercise of the new religion of France. It stood on the summit of a lofty hill, close to the town, and consisted only of a few posts, from which rafters met at the top in a point to support the roof, the sides being open. Within it was adorned with festoons of oak-leaves, and was backed by a tree of liberty. It was the favourite rendez-vous of the party of Robespierre, under whose auspicious reign it was erected. Here they swore eternal enmity to Kings, and extirpation to aristocrates, and here their dances and sports were held, and the laws were read. In July last (not above ten days before the fatal *neuf Thermidor*) all the unmarried young women, and even all the children of the town, down to seven years old, were compelled to march in procession up the hill, preceded by the mayor and a band of music, and to take an oath never to marry any but the republicans or *sans-culottes*. About three months ago this edifice was either blown down, or its foundation secretly undermined in the night; and only a few broken posts and a little thatch now proclaim '*Ilium fuit.*'

(3) A VIGILANCE COMMITTEE

[April 30, 1795.] Immediately after this disturbance was quelled, expresses communicative of the event were dispatched into all the districts. The carrier to this place arrived a little before noon on the 9th instant, and the drum was forthwith beat in every quarter of the town, inviting all '*good citizens*' to repair at two o'clock to the cathedral, to hear the account from Paris read, and to adopt measures in consequence of it. Being assured of not giving offence, I went at three to the place of appointment, and found the municipality, and about 150 people of the lower order, including a few officers, several soldiers, and many women, collected. They were listening to a man who was mounted into the pulpit, and reading to them a *bulletin*, stating the circumstances of the attempt which had been committed on the national representatives, and of its suppression; also the names of certain members whose arrest had been decreed; and lastly, that General Pichegru was called in, to preserve by an armed force the peace of Paris from the machinations of royalists and terrorists. Everybody wore their hats, and no insult was offered to us Englishmen, several of whom were present. When the reading was finished, an address to the convention was voted, on the patriotism and energy they had displayed; and several people got into the pulpit, and spoke in their turns. From these orators, a blacksmith was universally allowed to bear away the palm, haranguing with great fluency against the terrorists, and surprizing his auditors by the keenness of his sarcasms, and the justness of his observations. The speech of one who ascended the tribune was simply *'vive la republique!'* which was received with many plaudits. In conclusion they decreed, that the members of the ancient committee of *surveillance* of the town (which has long been suppressed) shall be deemed suspected persons, be disarmed, and obliged to appear every day before the municipality; and that henceforth they shall not be eligible to any office of trust or power in their commune.

The Committee of *surveillance* of Quimper consisted of twelve members, whose names and occupations were as follows:

Botibon, retail shop keeper	Rose, barber
Harier, butcher	Roland, merchant's clerk
Moreau, musician	Morivan, hog-butcher
Becam, taylor	Le Moine, gardener
Cariou, taylor	Montaigne, brazier
Keroch, barber	L'Hot, printer's devil

They were to a man the creatures of the creatures, ten gradations deep, of the committee of public safety. In such hands were the liberties and lives of Frenchmen deposited!

(4) REVOLUTIONARY RELIGION

[May 1, 1795.] In consequence of this decree on the back of the proclamation issued by Guesno and Gueurmeur, and of assurances from the constituted authorities that they shall not be molested, the moderate Catholics here assemble every Sabbath in the cathedral, the use of which (as an indulgence) is granted to them; but the more rigid, fearless of the law (which forbids it) hold little meetings in each other's houses, where the non-juring clergy officiate. This is known to the police; but the predilection of the country people, who flock in great numbers to these assemblies, renders it convenient to wink at them, and has hitherto restrained all attack upon them.

I went upon Easter Sunday to the cathedral, and found a numerous congregation there. The altar was lighted up by twelve large waxen tapers; the holy water was sprinkled upon the congregation; and the incense was burnt, with the accustomed ceremonies; but even here democratic spleen manifested itself in disturbing what it is no longer allowed to interdict. In the most solemn part of the service, the *Marseillois Hymn* was heard from the organ: that war-whoop, to whose sound the band of regicides who attacked their sovereign in his palace marched; and which, during the last three years, has been the watch-word of violence, rapine, and murder! How incongruous were its notes in the temple of the Prince of Peace! A blackguard-looking fellow close to me, whom I knew, by his uncombed hair, dirty linen, ragged attire, and contemptuous gestures, to be a *veritable sans-culotte*, joined his voice to the music, and echoed '*Aux armes, citoyens!*' Fear alone kept the people quiet; and of its influence in this country I have witnessed astonishing proofs, which demonstrate, beyond volumes of reasoning, the terror inspired by the revolutionary government.

As the observance of the Sabbath advances, the *Decadis* sink into contempt. I had heard much of civic feasts and other patriotic institutions celebrated upon them; but since I have been here, nothing of the sort has occurred. The national flag is displayed on the public offices, and if there is no pressure of business, the clerks have a holiday. A few zealous republicans also shut up their shops: but at present for one shop shut on the Decadi, there are six on a Sunday; for, however, the owners may differ on political questions, a sense of religion is not extinguished in the mass of the people, even of the town. I have, nevertheless, been assured, that six months ago, to have shewn this mark of respect for the Sabbath would have been a certain means of drawing down the resentment of the predominant faction. On every Decadi the laws are appointed to be read in the Cathedral, and the municipality attend. I had once the curiosity to go to this meeting, and found the number of auditors, which I counted, exclusive of the reader, and those who attended officially, to be twenty-seven persons, of whom, to my surprize, five were old women.

Major Trench [Quimper].

129. REVOLUTIONARY PLENTY

Theobald Wolfe Tone, implicated in a charge of treason against William Jackson in 1794, went to America in '95, and returned to France early in '96. Living in Paris, he helped to organize and took part in Hoche's abortive invasion of Ireland.

I HAVE now travelled one hundred and fifty miles in France, and I do not think I have seen one hundred and fifty acres uncultivated, the very orchards are under grain. All the mills I have seen were at work, and all the *châteaux* shut up without exception.

Paris.—Stop at the *Hôtel des Étrangers*, Rue Vivienne, a magnificent house, but, I foresee, as dear as the devil; my apartment in the third story very handsomely furnished, etc., for fifty francs per month, and so in proportion for a shorter time; much cheaper than the Adelphi and other hotels in London; but I will not stay here for all that— I must get into private lodgings. At six o'clock, dinner with d'Aucourt at the *Restaurateur's* in the *Maison Egalité*, formerly the Palais Royal, which is within fifty yards of our hotel. The bill of fare printed, as large as a play bill, with the price of everything marked. I am ashamed to say so much on the subject of eating, but I have been so often bored with the famine in France, that it is, in some degree, necessary to dwell upon it. Our dinner was a soup, roast fowl, fried carp, salads of two kinds, a bottle of Burgundy, coffee after dinner, and a glass of liqueur, with excellent bread—(I forgot, we had cauliflowers and sauce), and our bill for the whole, wine and all, was 1,500 livres, in assignats, which, at the present rate (the Louis being 6,500 livres) is exactly 4s. 7 ¹ d. sterling.

Theobald Wolf Tone [Feb. 12, 1796].

130   YOUNG SOLDIERS

This illustrates the national enthusiasm which created the revolutionary armies, and enabled the rise of Napoleon.

WENT to-day to the Church of St. Roch, to the *Fête de la Jeunesse*; all the youth of the district, who have attained the age of sixteen, were to present themselves before the municipality, and receive their arms, and those who were arrived at twenty-one were to be enrolled in the list of citizens, in order to ascertain their right of voting in the assemblies. The church was decorated with the national colours, and a statue of Liberty, with an altar blazing before her. At the foot of the statue the municipality were seated, and the sides of the church were filled with a crowd of spectators, the parents and friends of the young men, leaving a space vacant in the centre of [for?] the procession. It consisted of the État-Major of the sections composing the district, of the National Guards under arms, of the officers of the sections, and, finally, of the young men who were to be presented. The guard was mounted by veterans of the troops of the line, and there was a great pile of muskets and of sabres before the municipality. When the procession arrived, the names of the two classes were enrolled, and, in the meantime, the veterans distributed the arms amongst the parents and friends and mistresses of the young men. When the enrolment was finished, an officer pronounced a short address to the youths of sixteen, on the duty which they owed to their country, and the honour of bearing arms in her defence, to which they were about to be admitted. They then ran among the crowd of spectators, and received their firelocks and sabres, some from their fathers, some from their mothers, and many, I could observe, from their lovers. When they were armed, their parents and mistresses embraced them, and they returned to their station. It is impossible to conceive anything more interesting than the spectacle was at that moment; the pride and pleasure in the countenance of the parents; the fierté of the young soldiers; and, above all, the expression in the features of so many young females, many of them beautiful, and all interesting from the occasion. I was in an enthusiasm. I do not at all wonder at the miracles which the French army has wrought in the contest for their liberties.

Theobald Wolf Tone.

[March 30, 1794.]

131. FAREWELL TO PARIS

Henry Swinburne, husband of the Queen's friend (v. No. 20) had not been in Paris since before the Revolution. He was sent there in 1796 by the British Government to arrange for the exchange of prisoners of war.

I HAVE been running about Paris just as formerly. The beggars call me *milord*. How dull—how gloomy Paris is! All its hurry and crowds seem concentrated round the focus of this neighbourhood. The rest of the town is deserted. The Fauxbourg St. Germain can never recover. I had been told by English republicans and Americans, that wonderful things had been done, and magnificent works undertaken. I see many things pulled down, but except a repair in the roof of the Luxembourg, the alteration of the Palais Bourbon, and the finishing of the bridge, I have not seen one new stone put upon another. There are wood and plaster statues where brass and marble stood, dead poplar trees of liberty, and the words *'propriété nationale'* upon more than half the houses. These are the present ornaments of Paris. The Hôtel du Parc Royal is now a printing-house; the Hôtel de l'Université an office for the artillery. The Fauxbourg St. Germain is quite depopulated; its hotels almost all seized by government, and the streets near the Boulevard are choked with weeds. There is little bustle, except about the Palais de l'Egalité, which is a complete receptacle of filth. The buildings about it are ruinous. Poor Bablot, of the 'Parc Royal,' died of a broken heart. I have been at the site of the Bastille, now a timber-yard. As there have been fifty-seven new prisons instituted in Paris, I think I may say that the Parisians have uselessly destroyed an ornament of their town.

I am told there are weekly balls *par abonnement* of thirty-six francs, for the winter, where the ladies appear in fancy dresses, chiefly as nymphs with flesh-coloured clothing. The complexion of the women seems to me to be much improved, and there is not such a quantity of rouge used as formerly.

Henry Swinburne
[Nov. 17, 1796.]

INDEX OF PERSONS

Abancourt, Baron d', 170
Albitte, 253
Artois, Comte d', 9, 44, 57, 60
Auche, Comte d', 53

Bailly, 36, 40, 105, 115, 122, 140
Barentin, 29
Barère, 224, 255
Beaumarchais, 134
Beckford, William, 148
Bernis, Cardinal de, 116
Berri, Duc de, 10
Berry, Mary, 96
Biron, Duc de, 155
Blaikie, Thomas, 31
Bligh, Captain, 256
Bouillé, Marquis de, 91, 121, 131
Brézé, Marquis de, 40
Brienne, Cardinal de, 13, 18, 20, 149
Broglie, Maréchal de, 46, 57
Broussonet, 3
Brunswick, Duke of, 186
Burdett, Sir Francis, 26
Burges, Sir James Bland, 110, 231

Calas, 133
Calonne, Comte de, 2, 8
Campan, Mme., 33
Caraman, Comte de, 25
Carnot, 234, 242
Castries, Duc de, 98
Chartres, Duc de, 1
Châteauvieux, 91
Clermont-Tonnerre, Comte de, 60, 100, 170
Cloots, 128
Cobbett, William, 152
Colon, 247
Court, de, 107
Craufurd, Quintin, 125, 153
Crosne, de, 51
Curchod, Suzanne (Mme. Necker), 2

Dalrymple, Grace (Lady Elliott), 158
Daniel, F., 233
Danton, 206, 234, 255
David, 213
Dauphin, 18, 77, 83, 96, 102, 158, 159, 177
Dillon, Gen. Theobald, 155
Dorset, Duke of, 8, 49
Drouet, 124
Duchâtelet, 129
Dumouriez, 195, 204, 215, 235
Duplay, 253
Dupont, 103
Duquesnoy, 234

Eden, William (Baron Auckland), 65

Edgeworth, Abbé Henry, de Firmont, 228
Eldred, Thomas, 246
Elisabeth, Mme., 117, 229
Ephraim, 141
d'Eprémesnil, 18, 160

Fare, de la, 29
Ferrières, Marquis de, 26
Fersen, Count Axel, 125, 153
Fitzgerald, Lord Robert, 68
Flesselles, de, 50
Frampton, Mrs., 83
Freeman, Mrs. (v. Shepherd)

Garlike, B., 67
Gibbon, Edward, 131
Gobel, 109
Goelard, 18
Gower, Lord, 91
Grave, Marquis de, 155
Grétry, 93

Hailes, Daniel, 4
Hammond, George, 110
Hatsell, John, 36
Henriot, 27
Hérault de Séchelles, 243
Herman, 246
Hoche, 262
Holroyd, J. B. (Earl of Sheffield), 131
Hunter, William, 151

Ireland, Samuel, 64

Jean-Bon St. André, 246
Jerningham, Charles, 149
Jerningham, Edward, 149
Jones, Robert, 86
Juigné, Leclerc de, 53, 60

Keating, Lieut.-Col., 132
Knight, Lady, 231

La Fayette, Marquis de, 47, 62, 66, 80, 84, 98, 104, 108, 114, 115, 122, 139, 159
Lally-Tollendal, Marquis de, 47, 65
Lamballe, Princesse de, 189
Lambert, Sir John, 54
Launay, Marquis de, 50
Lauraguais, Baron de La Tour d'Amergne, 31
Lazowski, 9, 36
Legendre, 224
Levis, Duc de, 97
Liancourt, Duc de, 10, 11
Lindsay, William, 184, 190

De Lolme, 60
Louis XVI, 4, 10, 18, 43, 59, 71, 76, 83, 96, 99, 102, 105, 109, 112, 137, 145, 146, 158, 178, 185, 208, 221, 223, 229
Louvet, 210, 212
Luxembourg, Duc de Montmorency-, 44

Mackintosh, Sir James, 128
Malesherbes, 220
Mandat, Marquis de, 170
Mangin, 119
Manuel, 159
Marat, 205, 209
Marie Antoinette, 4, 5, 6, 10, 18, 32, 48, 71, 74, 77, 80, 90, 96, 102, 117, 148, 153, 158, 159, 164, 176
Massareene, Lord, 54
Maury, 95, 100
Mercier, 24, 150
Miles, Miss, 116
Miles, William Augustus, 89
Millingen, J. G., 62, 253
Mirabeau, Comte de, 24, 25, 95, 98, 112, 113
Monro, Colonel George, 190
Montmorency, Cardinal de, 114
Montmorin, Comte de, 42, 79
Moore, Francis, 137
Moore, Dr. John, 162, 190
Mounier, 60

Nares, Edward, 18
Necker, Germaine (Mme. de Stael), 2
Necker, Jacques, 2, 5, 21, 30, 34, 41, 42, 46, 65,
Noailles, Vicomte de, 143

Orléans, Duc d', 9, 18, 31, 42, 74, 88, 224, 226
O'Sullivan, J. B., 246
Oswald, John, 108
Owen, John, 118

Paine, Thomas, 128, 197, 202, 224, 236, 241
Palloy, 88
Palm, Etta (Baronne d'Aelders), 142
Patterson, N. S. J., 253
Perry, Sampson, 243
Pétion, 144, 159, 170, 190, 194, 224
Piozzi, Gabriel, 1
Piozzi, Hester Lynch (Mrs. Thrale), 1
Pius VI, Pope, 116
Priestly, Dr., 199
Prieur (de la Marne), 246
Provence, Comte de ('Monsieur'), 22, 104

Rabaut St. Etienne, 36
Réveillon, 26, 27

Rigby, Edward, 47
Robespierre, 106, 141, 142, 144, 150, 180, 206, 210, 224, 246, 249, 252, 253, 257
Rochambeau, 132
Rochefoucauld, Comte de la, 11
Roederer, Comte, 170
Rogers, Samuel, 100
Roland, 206, 210
Roland, Mme., 239
Rowan, Archibald Hamilton, 246

Sanson, 240
Santerre, 172
Ségur, Comte de, 116
De Sèze, 220
Shepherd, Mrs. Freeman, 150
Sieyès, 60, 129
Sinclair, Sir John, 2
Smith, Sir James Edward, 3
Stone, J. H., 243
Suffren, Bailli de, 9
Sullivan, Eleonora, 125
Swinburne, Henry, 32, 264
Swinburne, Mrs., 32, 72, 148

Talleyrand, 109
Tarente, Princesse de, 189
Target, 47, 81
Taylor, William, 78
Temple, Henry (Viscount Palmerston), 133
Théroigne de Méricourt, 105, 180
Thrale, Mrs., 1
Thouret, 143
Tone, Theobald Wolfe, 262
Tooke, Horne, 128
Tourzel, Mme. de, 189
Trench, Major, 256
Tronchet, 220
Twiss, Richard, 163

Villette, Marquis de, 133, 226
Villiers, J. C. (Earl of Clarendon), 19
Voltaire, 133, 138

Walpole, Mrs., 82
Wellesley-Pole, William (Earl of Mornington), 93
Weston, Stephen, 122
Whyte, J. F. X., 49, 53
Williams, David, 253
Williams, Helen Maria, 84, 243
Windham, William, 143
Withers, Thomas, 128
Wollaston, C. B., 83
Wordsworth, William, 86, 147, 212

Yorke, Henry Redhead, 108
Young, Arthur, 9